The Hidden and the Revealed

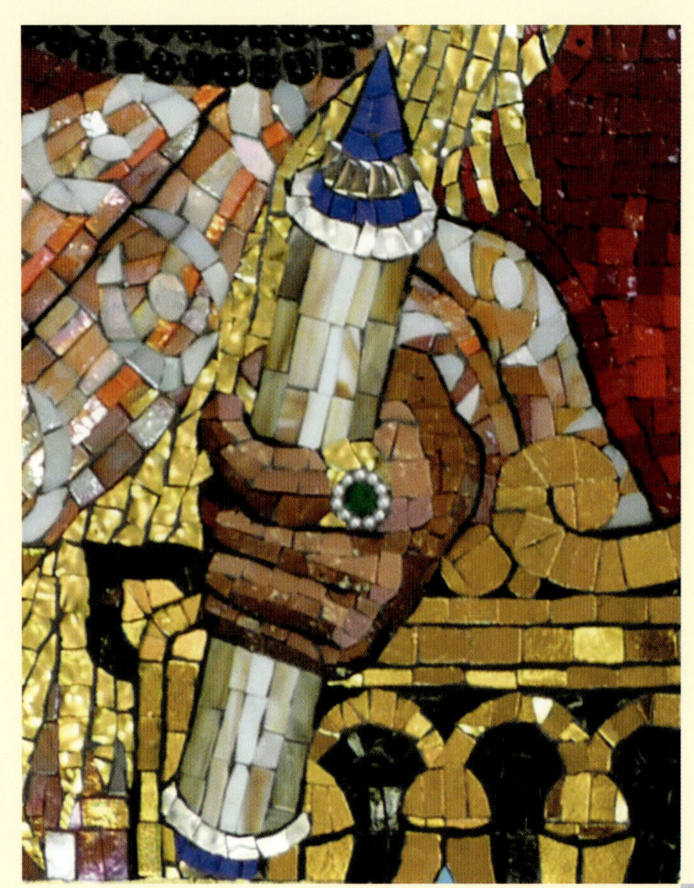

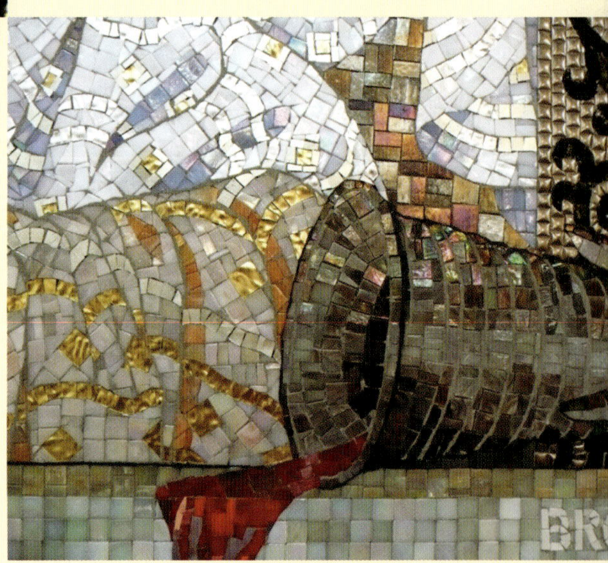

The Hidden and the Revealed

The Queen Esther Mosaics of Lilian Broca

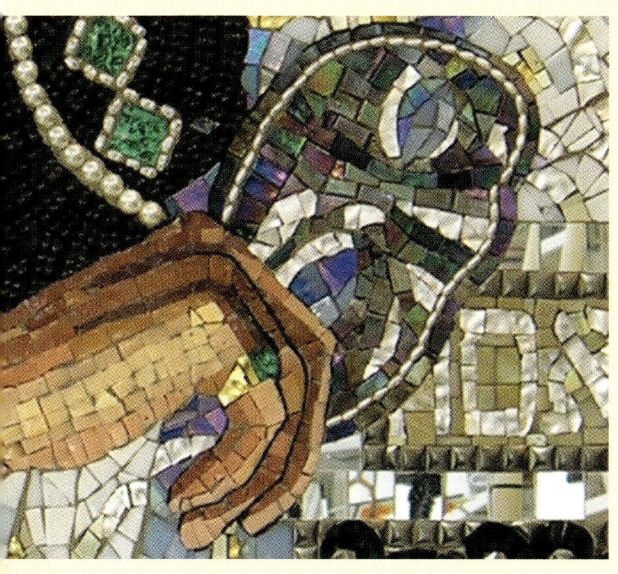

LILIAN BROCA
SHEILA CAMPBELL
YOSEF WOSK

With a Preface by
JUDY CHICAGO

Editor: Gareth Sirotnik
Designer: Linda Coe

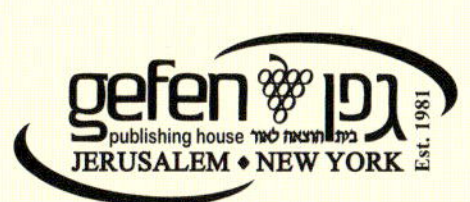

Gefen Books New York • Jerusalem

PHOTO CREDITS

Completed mosaics: Ted Clarke, image this photographics inc.

67, Copyright © Bayerische Staatsgemaeldesammlungen, Munich, Germany.

68, Copyright © The Metropolitan Museum of Art/Art Resource, NY.

74, Copyright © Museum het Rembrandthuis, Amsterdam (on long-term loan from Instituut Collectie Nederland).

75, Photo by John Parnell. Copyright © The Jewish Museum, New York, NY.

English translation of the Book of Esther reprinted from *Book of Esther: Tanakh, The Holy Scriptures,* Author/Editor: The Jewish Publication Society, © 1985 The Jewish Publication Society, with the permission of the publisher.

Jacket front
Detail from *Queen Esther Revealing Her True Identity.*

ii, iii, Details from *Surreptitious Dialogue* and *Queen Esther Revealing Her True Identity.*

vi, *Queen Esther with Mordechai,* work in progress.

Jacket and book design and typesetting Linda Coe Graphic Design Limited

Gefen Books
11 Edison Place 1-800-477-5257
Springfield, NJ 07081 USA
orders@gefenpublishing.com

Gefen Publishing House Ltd.
6 Hatzvi Street
Jerusalem 94386 Israel
orders@gefenpublishing.com

www.gefenpublishing.com
Send for our free catalogue

Printed in Israel
3 5 7 9 8 6 4 2

Library of Congress Cataloging-in-Publication Data
Broca, Lilian, 1946–
The hidden and the revealed: the Queen Esther mosaics of Lilian Broca / Lilian Broca, Sheila Campbell, Yosef Wosk; with a preface by Judy Chicago; editor, Gareth Sirotnik; designer, Linda Coe. – 1st ed.
p. cm
Includes bibliographical references.
ISBN 978-965-229-560-6 (alk. paper)
1. Broca, Lilian, 1946– Queen Esther mosaic series.
2. Bible. O.T. Esther–Illustrations. I. Campbell, Sheila D., 1938– II. Wosk, Yosef, 1949– III. Sirotnik, Gareth, 1947– IV. Bible. O.T. Esther. English. V. Title. VI. Title: Queen Esther mosaics of Lilian Broca.
NA3860.B76A73 2011
738.5'6092–dc22 2011012958

Contents

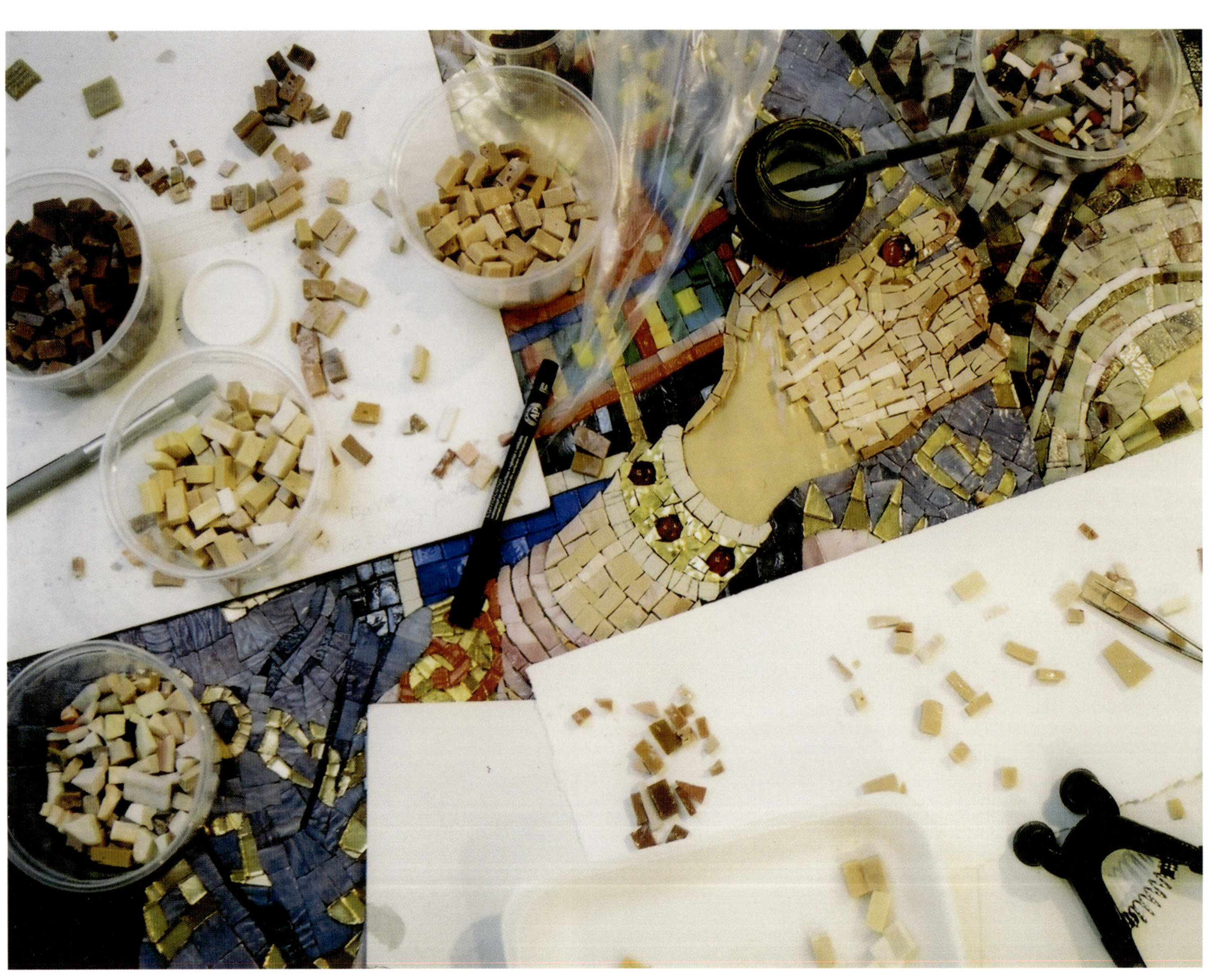

List of Illustrations

Foreword

In April 2004 the first four works in what would become a monumental achievement in the contemporary revival of mosaic art were unveiled at an opening at Vancouver's Zack Gallery. Those who saw the exhibit included scholar and rabbi Yosef Wosk and Sheila Campbell, an art historian specializing in ancient and Byzantine mosaics. Over the following three years, they waited in anticipation as each new panel in *The Queen Esther Mosaic Series* appeared. With the artist, Lilian Broca, they would join together to write this book. (Most of the mosaics were purchased in 2006 by a single Canadian art collector.)

Wosk, who was then Adjunct Professor of Humanities and Director of Simon Fraser University's Interdisciplinary Programs, spoke at the Zack Gallery opening about the religious and mythological figure of Esther. Deeply impressed by Broca's mosaics, he approached the artist and suggested they jointly produce a publication showcasing the series. Campbell was asked to contribute a chapter, and Linda Coe, a designer who had worked with Broca on a number of publications, readily agreed to design the book. Later, I joined the team to edit and coordinate the work.

Broca had only recently completed another expansive and much heralded series on the theme of Lilith, also a heroic female figure drawn from literature and lore. The works were executed, however, in the media the artist was already known and admired for – painting and drawing. In the opening chapter of this book, she explains what led her to Queen Esther as a subject and to mosaic as a medium. Mosaic had first captured her imagination back in her art school days, in Montreal and New York, but she also found in it a natural affinity with the Byzantine art that had dazzled her as a child growing up in the otherwise harsh world of Communist-ruled Romania.

In the last fifteen years, Broca has gravitated toward subjects of societal importance, particularly, she writes, "those involving women and their plight in historical times…[C]onsciously using these figures as metaphors and role models."

Esther fit perfectly. Accordingly, in the second half of her chapter – preceded first by a concise look at mosaic materials and techniques – Broca elucidates the richly meaningful narrative, symbolism, and composition in each work of the series.

For her chapter, Sheila Campbell, Professor Emerita at the Pontifical Institute of Mediaeval Studies, Toronto, concluded that, instead of focusing on the medium, namely Venetian glass mosaic, the more valuable contribution she could make was to situate Broca within the historical series of artists who had used the story of Queen Esther in oil, watercolor, drawing, and print. The story has inspired artists from at least the fourteenth century to the present, and to try to adequately cover all these representations would itself require a large volume. So Campbell selected instead a representative sample of past artists, highlighting by comparison the originality of Broca's panels, keeping in mind the artist's original statement of what she was saying in each work.

The final contributor to this book, Yosef Wosk, initially set out to expand the academic analysis he had introduced at the opening exhibition back in 2004, examining Esther "through multiple lenses," including the biblical text, comparative mythological and religious reference, and rabbinical commentaries. Finding, however, that much had already been published on these aspects, he allowed instead for his imagination to burst forth into "a combination of essay, poem, and narrative conversation" in which he speaks in the voice of, as he calls her, Estr: "not the voice of the young or middle-aged Estr," he writes, "but rather of Estr as elder, woman as sage." The richly nuanced picture that emerges complements the feminist intention of Broca to show Esther as a woman who was at first fearful, then gradually gained the courage, wisdom, and maturity to accomplish her monumental task of saving the Jewish people.

For ready reference, the full Scroll of Esther in Hebrew is included as an appendix, accompanied by an English translation.

From the inception of this book to its completion, all involved have been united and inspired by the magnificence of Broca's masterful mosaics. As Broca herself observes (and as is manifestly demonstrated in the art that shines throughout this book), mosaic is very much "an art for today."

Gareth Sirotnik, 2011

Preface

Envisioning (S)heroism
Judy Chicago

One of the challenges of the Bible for women is that, as Suzannah Heschel states in *On Being a Jewish Feminist* (New York: Schocken Books, 1983):

> ...our most basic understandings of human nature are drawn primarily from men's experiences. A patriarchal outlook begins by making men's experiences normative, equating the human with the male. Not only are women excluded from the process of shaping the outlook, but women's experiences are projected as something external, "other" to that norm.

So how does a woman artist approach, understand, and depict stories like Esther's that definitely embody a "patriarchal outlook"? Lilian Broca's mosaics represent one woman's efforts to depict the biblical story in a way that celebrates Esther's (s)heroic status. Perhaps one could view the mosaic series as a visual midrash, a term that means to seek, to examine, and to investigate. Traditionally, midrash refers to interpretations of biblical verses and has long been considered a sacred activity because study and interpretation of the Bible is seen as leading to the redemption of the world by bringing God into it.

There is considerable debate as to whether contemporary explications of biblical verses or narratives should rightly be called midrash an activity from which, for centuries, women were excluded. At the same time, midrash was the rabbinic method of coping with social, political, and theological change and of integrating that change into Jewish tradition. Certainly, the Jewish people have been struggling with how to best integrate the many issues feminists have raised about the position of women: for example, the question of ordaining women – which has also vexed many Christians – has been answered affirmatively by the Reconstructionist, Reform, and Conservative wings of Judaism and negatively by the Orthodox.

However, if women are to be successfully integrated into the mainstream, they must be able to be not only rabbis and leaders but also, most of all, respected interpreters of Jewish traditions. Thus, it would seem appropriate for Jewish women artists to look at female biblical figures for inspiration and to reinterpret their stories in a contemporary context, as Lilian Broca has done with Esther and, before her, the more controversial figure of Lilith.

At the same time, it is interesting to note that for Esther, Broca has chosen the ancient technique of mosaics to create a modern-day visual midrash. It also seems important to point out the incredible mosaic at the Basilica of San Vitale in Ravenna, which features Theodora, the most influential and powerful woman in Byzantine history, and which might be said to be an antecedent for Broca's work. I can still remember visiting the Theodora mosaic, which stands opposite a comparable panorama honoring her husband, Justinian, and is a testament to their historic partnership.

In fact, I included a place setting honoring Theodora in *The Dinner Party* (my monumental symbolic history of women in Western Civilization now permanently housed at the Elizabeth A. Sackler Center for Feminist Art at the Brooklyn Museum) because she is considered a pioneer of feminism due to the many laws she passed benefiting women's rights. Moreover, the design for her plate and runner are based on the mosaic technique.

Like Theodora and so many other women in the historic narratives compiled primarily by men, the meaning of the Megillat Esther (which puts forth Esther's story and is used as the basis for the celebration of Purim) has been contested. Recently, some feminist scholars have critiqued it for underscoring patriarchal ideology, arguing that the biblical narrative rewards obedience and submissiveness in a woman and portrays women getting their way only when they are sly and deceptive.

In contrast, scholars like Alice Ogden Bellis, Professor of Hebrew Bible at Howard University School of Divinity and an ordained Presbyterian minister, view the Esther story as one of the most liberating messages for women of any of the stories in the Bible, a view with which I would imagine Broca would agree. Certainly, her depiction of Esther is entirely sympathetic – from the first mural depicting her in the harem of the Persian King Ahashvayrosh to the last mosaic showing Esther revealing her true identity as a Jew. Having grown up Jewish in Communist Romania, Broca must surely have related to the danger such a revelation might prove to be.

Broca's stated intention was to show Esther as a woman who was at first fearful, then gradually gains the courage, wisdom, and maturity to accomplish the daunting task of saving the Jewish people. The story that Broca illustrates is well known. King Ahashvayrosh was married to Vashti, who defied his command to present herself to a gathering of men so that he could show off her beauty. Alarmed that other women might take it upon themselves to defy their husbands, Vashti is banished and the king holds a beauty pageant to find a new queen.

Esther wins the contest and marries the king without divulging her faith. Her cousin and guardian Mordechai alienates Haman, counselor to the king, who convinces the king to issue an edict condemning all the Jews of Persia to death. The only false note in the series of mosaics is Mordechai's visit to Esther in the harem, for surely, other than the eunuchs, men were not allowed to enter the women's quarters. In the biblical story, Mordechai sends a message to Esther beseeching her to intercede, which she does though she risks her life by approaching the king without being summoned. Haman is put to death, the Jewish people are saved, and Mordechai becomes an honored adviser to the king.

Seven years in the making, the Esther mosaics by Lilian Broca contribute to the vital historic task of what the biblical scholar Naomi Graetz called for in *S/He Created Them: Feminist Retellings of Biblical Tales* (Chapel Hill, NC: Professional Press, 1993): "...to put woman's voice back where it should have been in the first place." The glittering mosaic panels in *The Queen Esther Mosaics* were executed with Venetian glass using classic mosaic techniques, an historic method to honor an important woman in history.

Acknowledgments

This book is a result of Rabbi Dr. Yosef Wosk's initiative and support when my Queen Esther mosaic series was only partially completed. Since then, with his vast theological knowledge, he has proved a reliable source of information and has provided thought-provoking perspectives. I consider myself fortunate and honored to have him as a friend and a collaborator.

I would also like to thank Dr. Sheila Campbell for her recognition of my work years ago when mosaic was a new medium for me. Our friendship developed in conjunction with her deep insight and strong encouragement during the making of *The Queen Esther Mosaic Series*. Sheila's learned expertise in Byzantine art and ancient mosaics has proven invaluable.

The publication of this book is greatly enhanced by the talents and hard work of the rest of our team, including Linda Coe, a gifted book designer with whom I have successfully joined forces in the past, and master of words Gareth Sirotnik, our general editor who successfully united three varied artistic fields (poetry, prose, and art) and combined their distinct voices in a coherent and eloquent manner.

I also wish to acknowledge my studio helper, Riki Triantafillou, and art collectors Horatio and Jackie Kemeny, the owners of *The Queen Esther Mosaics,* who have made the works readily accessible whenever called upon.

I am dedicating the mosaic series and this book to my beloved husband and life partner, David Goodman, my principal muse in life.

Lilian Broca, 2011

Mosaic art for Lilian Broca is a way of recapturing a triple ascendance and giving shape to a profound identity, simultaneously artistic and human. Her themes are Judaic, drawn from the Old Testament, but her technique, while Byzantine in manner, reflects the post-Byzantine and Orthodox Romanian milieu in which she grew up. As well, in her work the figurative code of the image, the powerful articulation of its corporality, and the illusion of three-dimensional space all point straight to classic Western European Renaissance forms.

Consequently, for an artist of such complex sensitivity as Lilian Broca, mosaic represents more than just its materials and techniques; it serves as a magic mirror in which, through contemplation, the artist regains her past, preserves her present and foresees her future. The medium also acts as a receptacle in which the Middle East and European hypostases – from East to West and all the way in its extension to North America – co-exist and express themselves as an indestructible entity of astounding inner coherence.

— Pavel Susara, February 2011.

Pavel Susara is a researcher at the Institute of Art History at the Academy of Romania, Bucharest. Specializing in contemporary art history, Susara also writes art criticism on various subjects. Since 1992 Pavel Susara has written a permanent column on art criticism for the prestigious weekly newspaper The Literary Romania, *and is involved with the international anti-establishment radio program* L'Europe Libre.

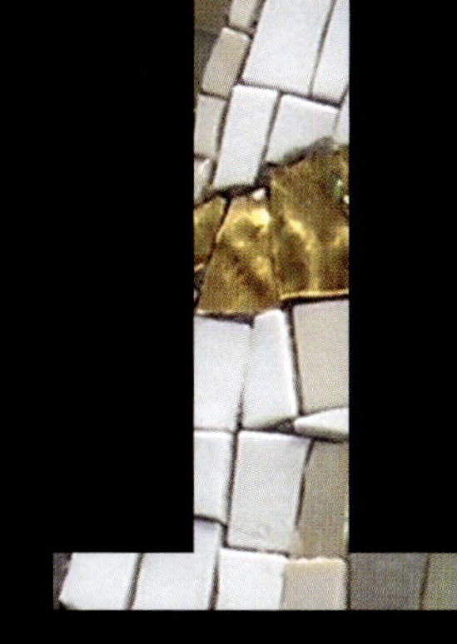

Bringing Esther to Light

The Queen Esther Mosaics

LILIAN BROCA

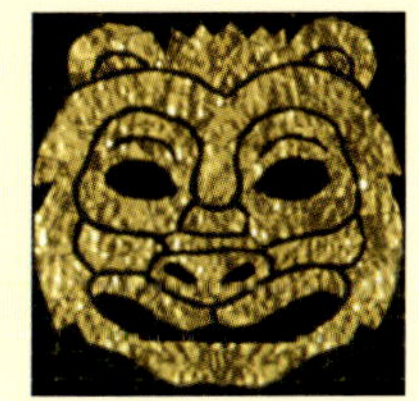

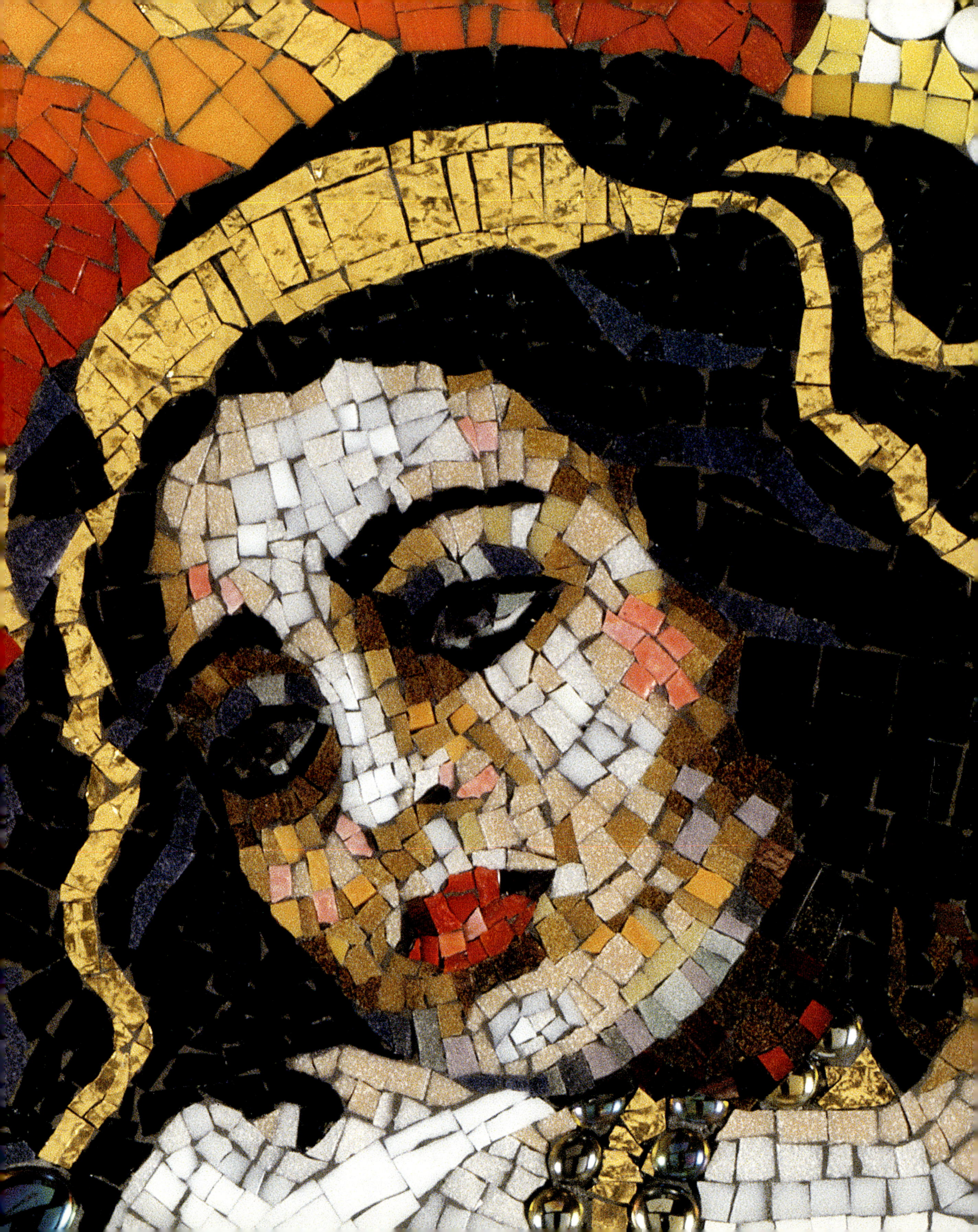

Bringing Esther to Light

Lilian Broca

Inspired by classical Byzantine style but imbued with contemporary meaning, *The Queen Esther Mosaic Series* arose organically from my earliest aesthetic instincts. Indeed, my fascination with art itself and, in particular, with mosaic art of the Byzantine style originates from my childhood. This artistic affinity matched my attraction in later life to the story of Esther and its symbolism.

I was born shortly after the end of the Second World War and spent my early years in Bucharest, Romania's capital. As a school girl, I was steeped in Romanian history and art. Due to its geography, that part of the Balkan Peninsula had fallen under the influence of the old Eastern Byzantine Empire, centered in the capital city of Constantinople, today's Istanbul. Byzantine icons, ample remnants of which remained in Bucharest, left an indelible impression on my young mind. Glowing in candlelight, the bright colors, glittering gold, and graceful and refined outlines of the icons brought some light into an otherwise dreary period.

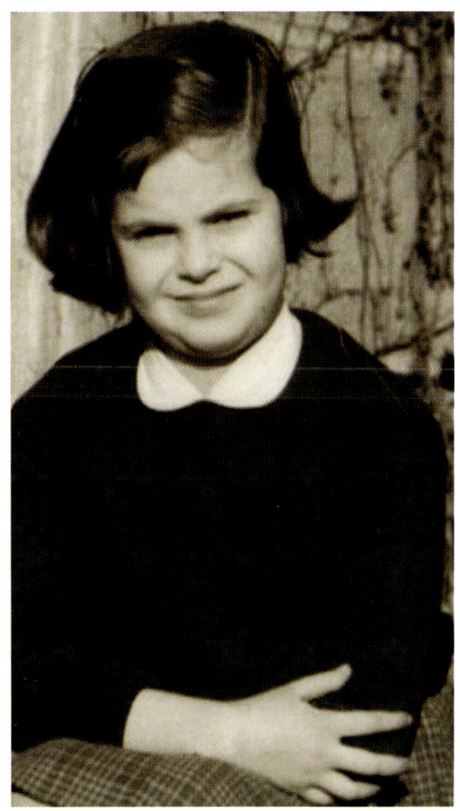

The artist at seven

During those dark, lean years, when the population endured unspeakable shortages of essential goods and personal fear on a daily basis, little else other than art shone in my life. Certainly, stories from the Hebrew Bible played no part in a time when one's Jewish identity, not unlike Esther's in the Persian court, was better left hidden. A welcome respite from this bleak world, art engraved itself on my mind both then and during the ensuing years of upheaval and change. In 1958 my family immigrated to Israel, leaving behind Romania's cruel Communist regime. Four years later we left for Canada.

Earlier, as a five-year old, I had already demonstrated an aptitude for drawing, and with considerable sacrifice my parents enrolled me in an art school in Bucharest, which generally catered to aspiring adults. It was in Canada, however,

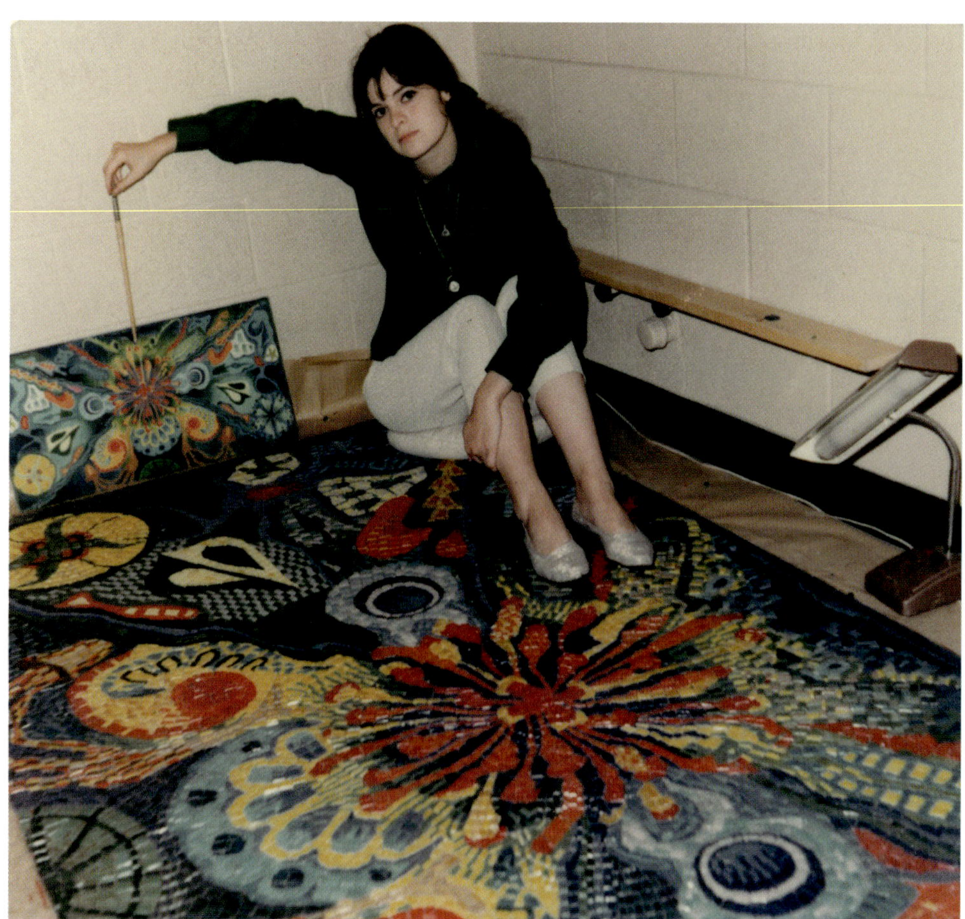

First mosaic work, Concordia University, 1967

where I eventually pursued my dreams of becoming a visual artist, graduating first from the fine arts program at Montreal's Sir George Williams (now Concordia) University.

In my second year at university, one of my painting professors invited the class to see his mural in progress. To my amazement, it was a glass mosaic. I immediately asked him for help; I, too, wanted to make mosaics. The unique interplay between light and the material essence of glass mosaic, which literally brings luminescent life to a subject, captivated me then as it does still. Fortunately, my professor allowed me to create a mosaic mural during the last semester of that year, albeit without any instruction. Still, having managed to learn the basics through trial and error, I was able to complete the work. Ultimately, the mural became part of the university's permanent collection.

I continued my art studies at the Pratt Institute, in New York City, where in 1971 I received a master's degree in Fine Arts. Although I majored in painting and art history, while there I completed a second mosaic, my only other opportunity to work in that medium before becoming a professional artist.

Facing page
Lilith, 1993
Acrylic, spackle on panel
78 X 36 in. (198.12 x 91.44 cm)
Collection: Ms. Letia Richardson

After graduation I married and moved to Vancouver, British Columbia. For many years, I taught painting and drawing while I worked in my studio and exhibited regularly. Each time our family changed residence, I carefully protected and carried with me my precious collection of the glass pieces left over from my first two mosaic murals. I always knew that one day I would return to this medium.

What leads an artist to gravitate to a particular image and use a particular medium remains a mysterious, subtle, and ongoing revelation to me.

Inspired by Human Relationships

Throughout my artistic career, I have explored human relationships and the nature of the human condition. In past works, I used the symbolism of fairy tales, marriage, and everyday objects such as purses to propose questions about the relevance of allegorical role models for today's youth. I raised issues respecting the exalted position of brides on their wedding day. And I offered new and original contexts for the personal belongings in women's handbags.

What leads an artist to gravitate to a particular image and use a particular medium remains a mysterious, subtle, and ongoing revelation to me. In the past fifteen years, I have turned my attention to societal issues, especially those involving women and their plight in historical times. I have looked to mythological and biblical stories of courageous females who, despite overwhelming odds, have prevailed through sheer courage and wise resolve. Consciously using these figures as metaphors and role models, I find them relevant to contemporary society and employ them to shed light on today's concerns.

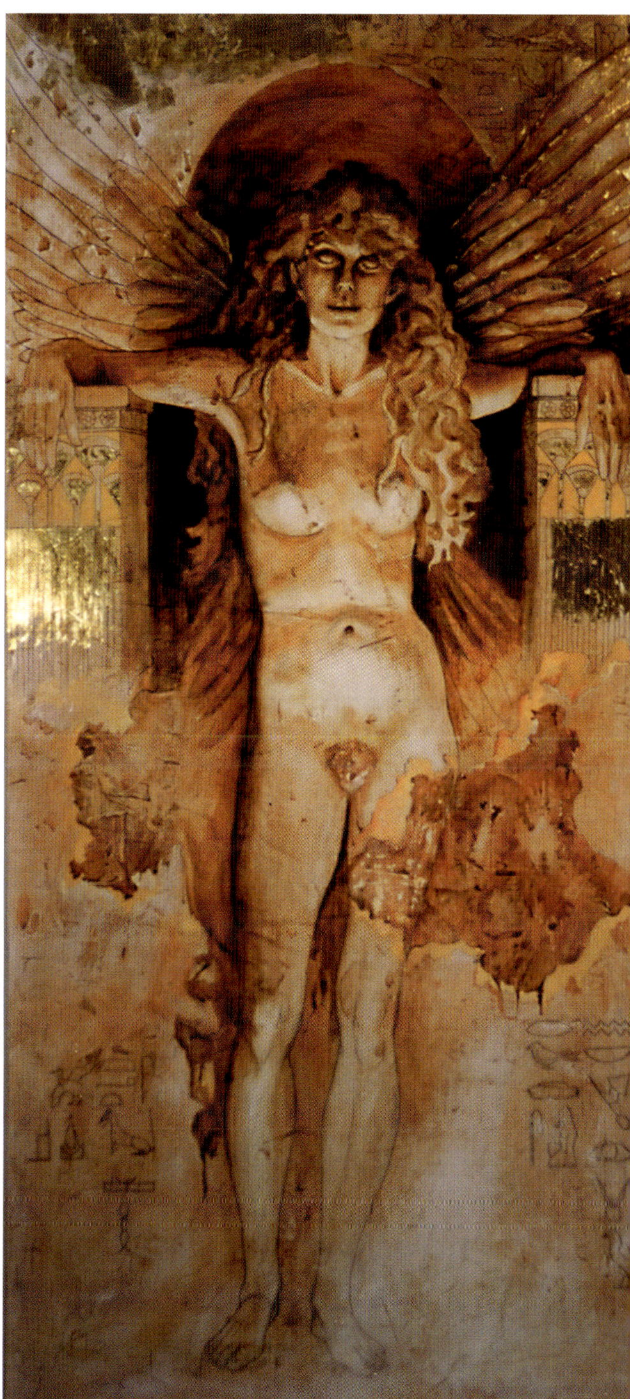

Two series based on biblical stories have emerged during this time: Lilith, a legendary figure who was created before Eve, and Esther, a young Jewish girl living in Susa (in today's Iran) who became queen of Persia.

Drawing from the rich symbolism of fifth-century midrashic legends and fifteenth-century Zohar texts, I first explored the Lilith character. I interpreted her as the messenger of and hope for human courage and egalitarianism, not only for women but for all humanity. Through the body of work that became *The Lilith Series,* I demonstrated the need to reassess this legendary figure, advocating that both Lilith and Eve's attributes be included in our notion of a successful, fulfilled twenty-first-century woman.

A Great Leader and Hero

After seven years of working on *The Lilith Series,* I turned my attention to Queen Esther, the biblical hero who became a great leader of her people. According to ancient Persian folk tales, as well as the Bible, this event transpired in the fifth century BCE in ancient Persia, today's Iran.

The story of Queen Esther, filled with drama and intrigue, has long captivated writers as well as visual artists and inspired them to create works based on its powerful narrative. The story made many appearances, for example, in seventeenth-century Holland:

> Theatres in Amsterdam presented several dramas, both Dutch and French, based on The Book of Esther. Nicolaes Vonteyn's play *Esther,* also known as *The Picture of Obedience,* was popular. The nation's favorite poet, van den Vondel, wrote two poems based on the Esther story. And in France, playwright Jean Racine also wrote a dramatic play called *Esther* in 1689, quickly performed in Holland.[1]

In the visual arts, Rembrandt was one of the most important and famous artists to paint scenes from the Book of Esther, such as *Haman Begging Esther for Mercy, Esther Preparing to Intercede with Ahasuerus, The Triumph of Mordechai,* and *Esther Fainting Before Ahasuerus.* Rembrandt's colleagues and students soon followed his example, including Jan Victors, Aert de Gelder, Jan Steen, and Jan Lievens. Other artists who drew on the Esther story include Tintoretto, Rubens, Artemisia Gentileschi, Luca Signorelli, Nicholas Poussin, and even Michelangelo in the ceiling of the Sistine Chapel.

The biblical Book of Esther addresses the themes of sacrifice and female empowerment, two subjects that particularly intrigue me.

The biblical Book of Esther addresses the themes of sacrifice and female empowerment, two subjects that particularly intrigue me. The story thus naturally led me to portray the biblical queen as a prototype for the courageous, selfless heroine who wins against all odds and whose previously hidden true nature rises to the surface and powerfully reveals itself. As an article on Esther from the Jewish Agency website suggests, after a sudden and dramatic transformation in character, at a time of crisis, Esther fulfilled her destiny to become a leader with intelligence, persistence, and dedication.[2] Today, we can view her as a role model and, as such, she contributes to the status of women in all societies.

For me Esther especially personifies the theme of sacrifice. She was completely disinterested in competing in the beauty pageant that determined which maiden would be crowned Persia's new queen. As the Bible text emphasizes, she went to the palace grudgingly. Like all obedient women of antiquity, Esther behaved compliantly and obeyed her cousin Mordechai's instructions. (Mordechai was also Esther's foster father and guardian. Reflecting this special relationship, some sources refer to him as her uncle.) Even after being crowned, she continued doing Mordechai's bidding. "As Queen of Persia, Esther was as inferior in status as any other woman," says the article from the Jewish Agency website. Certainly, she enjoyed a luxurious life at court, but since she was completely isolated in the king's harem among women of a different culture and custom, she must have felt miserable and lonely, unable to share stories about her Jewish family and upbringing. Mordechai had insisted that she keep her background a secret from everyone at court.

Soon after sacrificing her maidenhood, Esther was obliged to put her very life at risk when her cousin ordered her to go before King Ahashvayrosh (aka Ahasuerus, Khashayarshah, Xerxes) and reveal the treacherous plans the evil Haman had designed against the Jews without the king's knowledge. She knew she faced grave and imminent danger: anyone who approached the king uninvited was liable to be condemned to death. Nevertheless, once she agreed to Mordechai's demand that she seek the king's mercy on the Jewish people, her previously hidden adventurous spirit rose to the surface. With deft cunning, she conceived a plan in which she played Haman and King Ahashvayrosh against each other. Within this context, I consciously set out to bring light to Esther's character, portraying her as a figure who transforms herself into a glorious winner despite all the demands and sacrifices the patriarchal culture required of her.

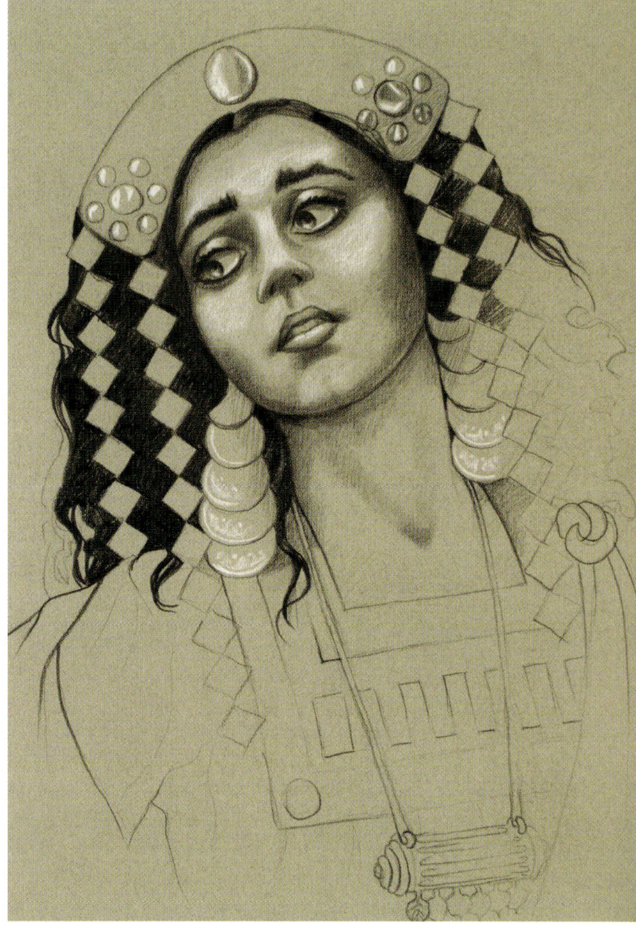

Sketch for *Queen Esther Holding Evidence of Haman's Guilt*, graphite and pastel on paper, 20 x 17 in. (50.8 x 43.18 cm)

Interpreting the Esther Narrative

In the Byzantine manner, the Queen Esther series naturally takes a narrative direction, featuring scenes pivotal to the story and immediately recognizable to anyone familiar with the biblical book. Similar also to Byzantine icons and religious scenes, the mosaics include numerous symbols that emphasize the story's continuity. For example, wrought iron appears in each work, altered to convey varying meaning depending on the scene.

Similar also to Byzantine icons and religious scenes, the mosaics include numerous symbols that emphasize the story's continuity.

One common element emerges in all accounts of Esther, including the Bible's – her dramatic transformation of character. At the beginning of the story, the young Esther is a beautiful, passive, and obedient maiden, as all young women of antiquity were trained to be. Her loyalties fell to the closest adult male in her family. In the absence of parents, Mordechai, the domineering head of the family, gives her strict directions on how to behave at the royal court and tells her that she must keep her religious identity secret at all times.

Then, suddenly, after she learns of Haman's diabolical plan to destroy the Jewish people in Persia and is told by Mordechai to seek King Ahashvayrosh's mercy, a new Esther appears. Out of character, radically different from her former subservient nature, she refuses Mordechai's request and declares her unwillingness to appear before her husband, the king, without an invitation – an action that would have risked being executed.

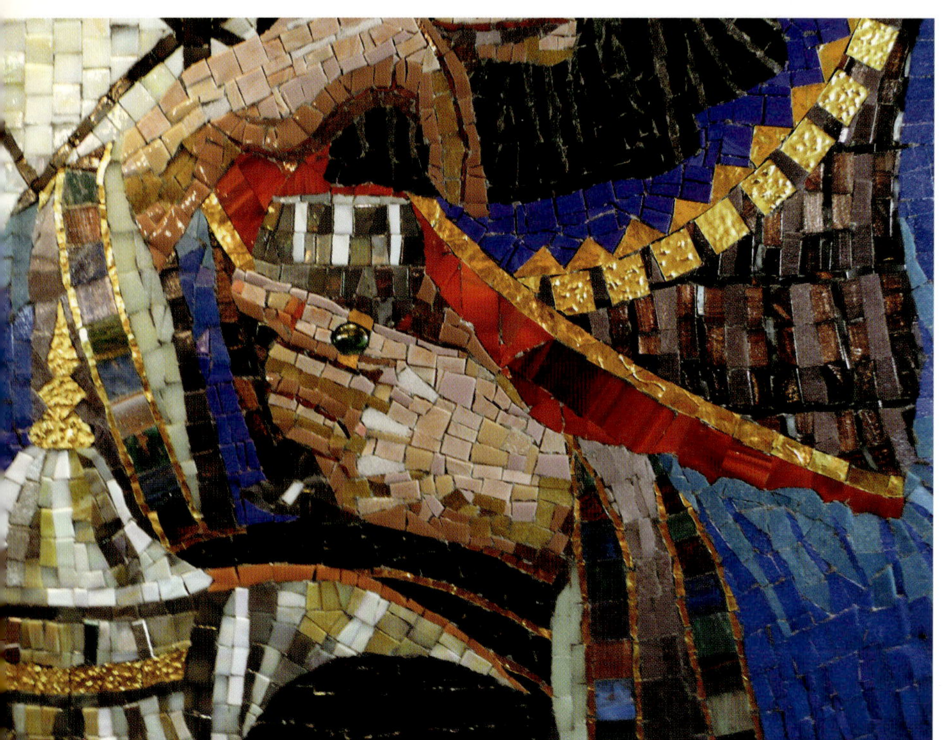

Detail from *Queen Esther's Banquet*

Much surprised, Mordechai lectures the new, rebellious Esther, warning her of her own ultimate fate: once all her people are massacred, no matter how elevated her role within the king's court, she, too, he says, will be slaughtered. He tells her that saving her people from genocide could well be her destiny and the now-revealed hidden reason she had risen to become queen.

Mordechai's words bring about a further, dramatic metamorphosis in Esther's personality, prompting a "second" Esther to surface – assertive, courageous, and, eventually, masterful. As their roles reverse, it is now *she* who designates tasks for Mordechai to do, as well as for the rest of the Jewish population. Mordechai accepts her leadership, following her directions to the letter.

As the Israeli educator and essayist Dr. Gili Zivan writes in her article "Transformation in the Personality of Queen Esther," the story of Esther tells of both sacrifice and female empowerment.[3] It encourages women to believe in their own strength, even in a patriarchal society where women are usually submissive and dominated by men. All women possess the potential to be the "assertive Esther" – one hidden inside a shy, reserved, and obedient girl. As a wise woman and heroine, she remains a role model for all contemporary humankind. In my opinion, Queen Esther's story also exemplifies a successful intermarriage of two people from different cultures, namely Jewish and Persian.

With my attention now focused on Queen Esther, the bright, seductive, shining colors of Venetian glass and smalti that I had used in creating mosaics many years earlier suddenly beckoned to me again. Here was an opportunity to literally bring light to the story of Esther.

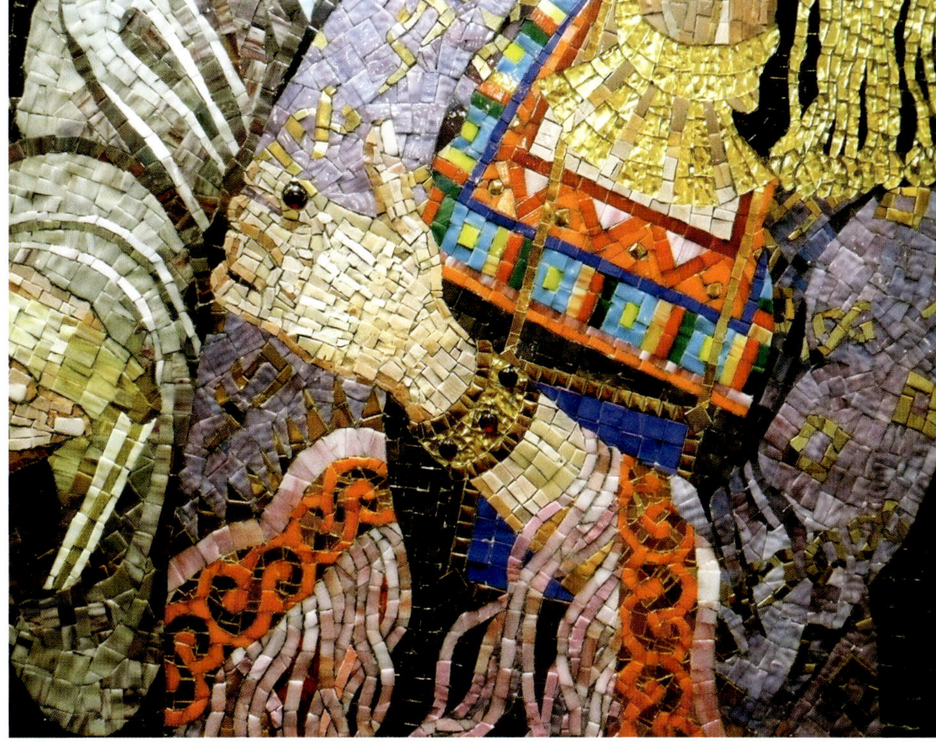

Detail from *Queen Esther with Mordechai*

Thwarting the evil Haman's conspiracy to commit genocide against the Jewish people is often seen as the story's focus. But a number of biblical commentaries on the Book of Esther, properly called the Scroll of Esther or Megillat Esther, also describe the story as having a theatrical aspect of distinctly comedic proportion. Taking advantage of this interpretation, I chose for my series to use a perspective no deeper than that of a theatrical stage. For hundreds of years, the best mosaics used little if any perspective. The medium is naturally suited to creating flatter and less three-dimensional images. As mosaic expert and author Peter Fisher explains in his book *Mosaic: History and Technique*, the conflict between flatness and depth pervades the history of glass as a medium; however, the two can be reconciled by breaking down the painted cartoon's shapes and colors in a more stylized manner, achieving a striking balance between depth and flatness.[4]

My unexpected discovery that one of the earliest if not the earliest written reference to mosaics occurs in the biblical Book of Esther, in the passage describing King Ahashvayrosh's palace, further contributed to my decision to return to this powerful, singular art form. My supplementary research suggested that the luxurious palace in which she and the king resided had floors inset with precious rubies and porphyry arranged in a pleasing design. It was a good omen: I had my sign that it was the right time to return to mosaics and, hence, Byzantium. And so my childhood attraction to Byzantine art was reborn with a passion – a passion that has taken hold of my life for the last seven years.

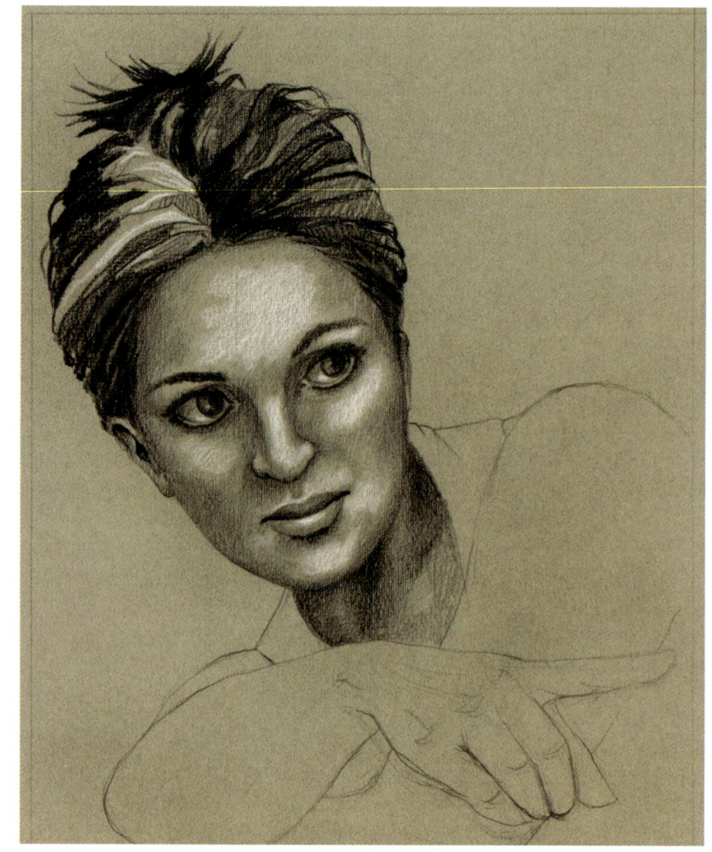

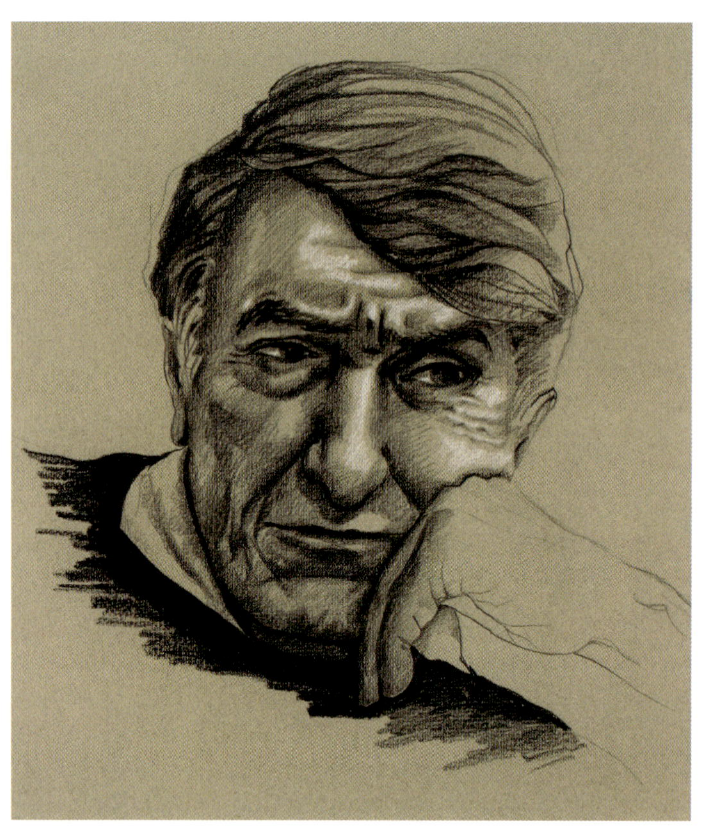

Clockwise left to right
For *Queen Esther's Banquet,* sketch of king's head, graphite and pastel on paper, 20 x 17 in. (50.80 x 43.18 cm); sketch of queen's head, graphite and pastel on paper, 21 x 17 in. (53.34 x 43.18 cm); compositional sketch, graphite on tracing paper, 19.5 x 40.25 in. (49.53 x 102.24 cm)

Facing page
Painted sketch for *Queen Esther's Banquet,* acrylic on illustration board, 19.5 x 37 in. (49.53 x 93.98 cm)

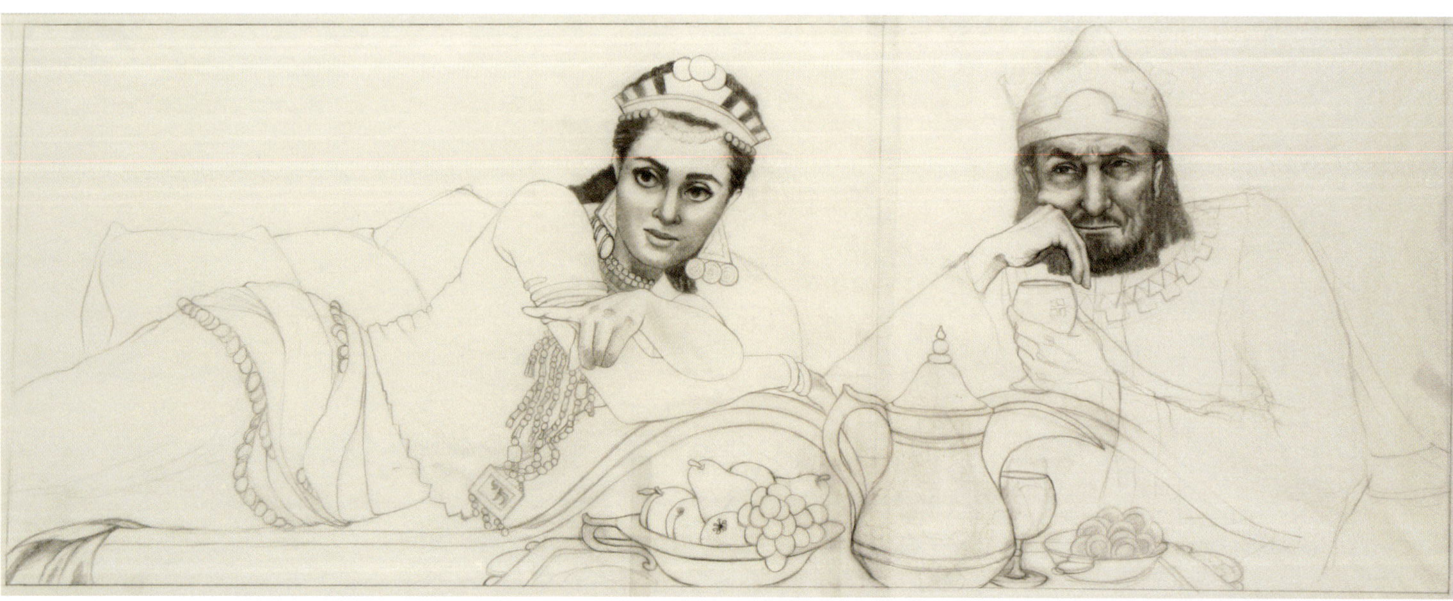

The Reverse Method in Mosaic

In *The Queen Esther Mosaic Series,* I have used two traditional working methods for creating mosaics – what are known as the *direct* and the *indirect* methods. The common element in both is that I begin by sketching numerous ideas for the finished work, and only then do I paint my final choice as a reference guide.

All but one of the Esther mosaics were executed in the *indirect* or *reverse* method. Before laying out a mosaic work with this technique, I use my final sketch to create a reverse cartoon enlarged on a strong sheet of paper to the size of the finished mosaic. This paper is then stretched out on a panel that supports the mosaic while it's assembled.

The *tesserae* (small cubes of marble, stone, glass, or other material used to make a mosaic) are then cut with wheeled glass cutters or nippers. Using water-soluble glue, these small pieces are glued face down on the paper sheet that bears the inverted design. The pieces in the Esther series comprise mostly vitreous and *smalto* glass, plus 24-carat gold sandwiched between two thin layers of transparent glass.

A classic mosaic material, smalto glass is characterized by its dazzling range of brilliant opaque colors. Four or five shades of each color are employed to enhance the visual effects. In this manner, the surface becomes more forcefully integrated, thereby creating an overall unity, figure, and ground merging into one another. Except for the first work in the series and the first one I executed, smalti was used to enrich all the Esther mosaics with this genuine – and costly – traditional material. I was convinced that the purity of color of smalto glass makes it worth its high cost.

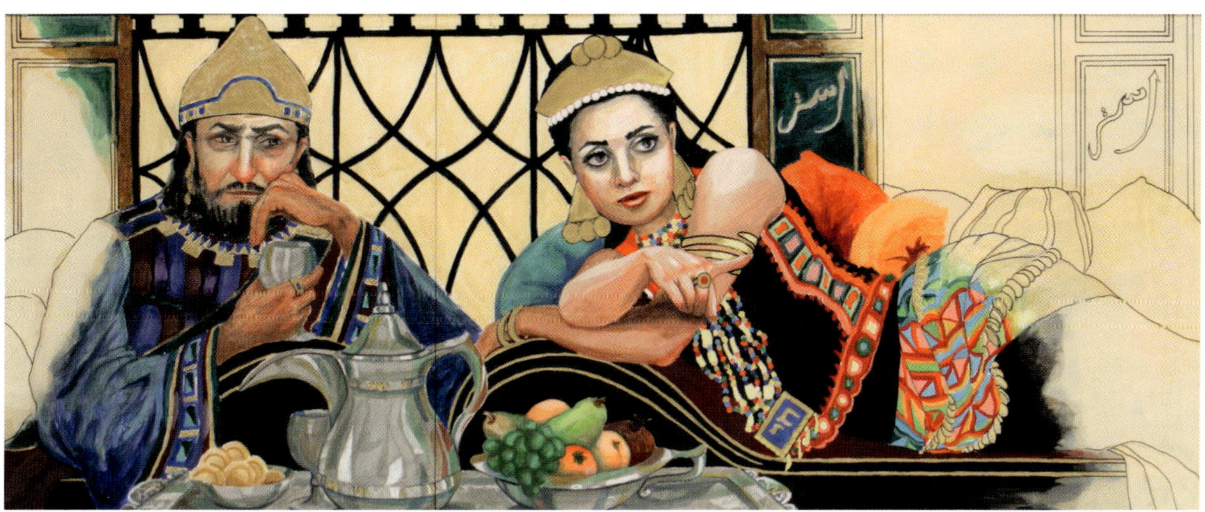

Buying smalti at the Orsoni factory in Venice is quite an experience. Upon entering this charmed workspace, a mosaic artist grows giddy with a desire to own as many shades of colors as are produced, an impossible dream.

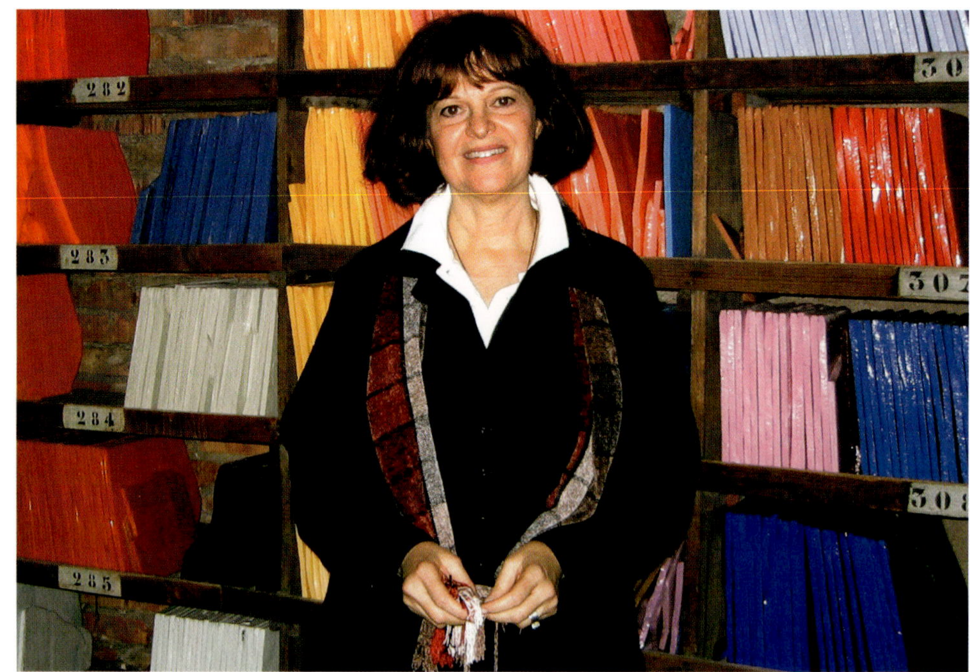

Buying smalti at the Orsoni factory in Venice is quite an experience. Upon entering this charmed workspace, a mosaic artist grows giddy with a desire to own as many shades of colors as are produced, an impossible dream. The glass tesserae look like candies sparkling enticingly in a multitude of bins. As in a fairytale, the artist proceeds from room to room, witnessing where the glass-making ingredients for various colors are mixed and fired at extremely high temperatures; where a dozen or so workers hand cut the glass "pizzas," the traditionally round (but now square) full glass sheets poured on slabs of stone or metal; where several stock rooms hold the entire collection of hundreds of available color tones. "Shop till you drop" is an apt description of the delirious buyer's experience – literally so, since a good collection of smalti feels as if it weighs a ton.

When the design is completely covered with glass tesserae and any changes have been made, the exposed rear face is "buttered" with a permanent binder (in my work, thinset cement) and "flipped" onto the permanent substrate or panel, which has also been buttered with thinset. Once this "sandwich" has set, the temporary panel is separated from the reverse paper image of the mosaic, and then the paper itself, now facing up, is dampened with hot water and slowly and carefully removed as well. Once revealed, the front surface of the mosaic receives a good scrubbing to remove any excess cement and glue. The cleaning revives the colors and the mosaic shines.

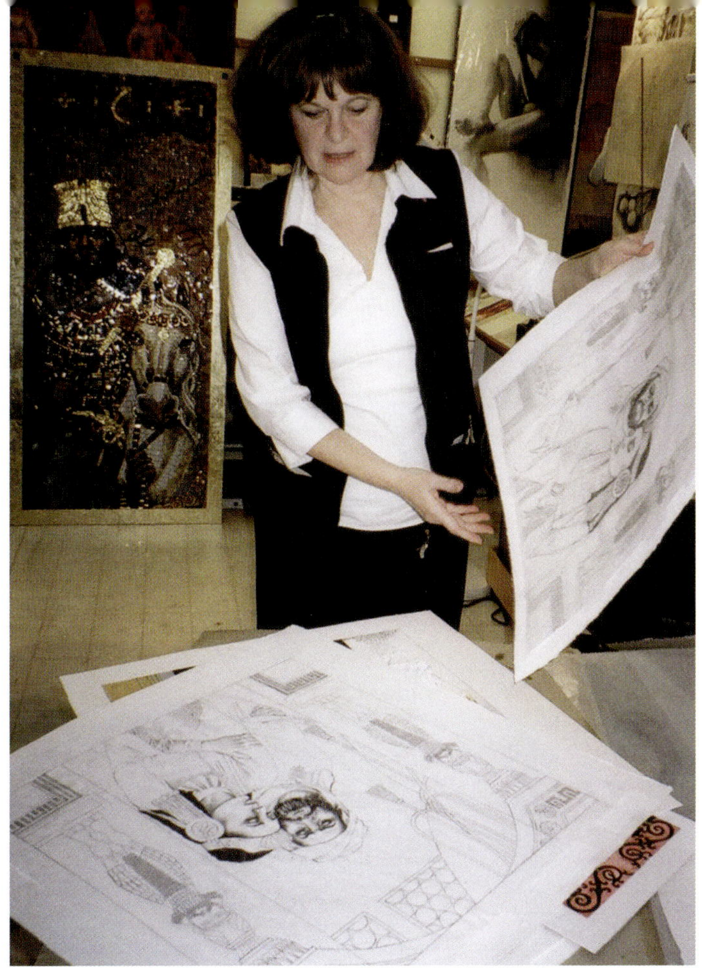

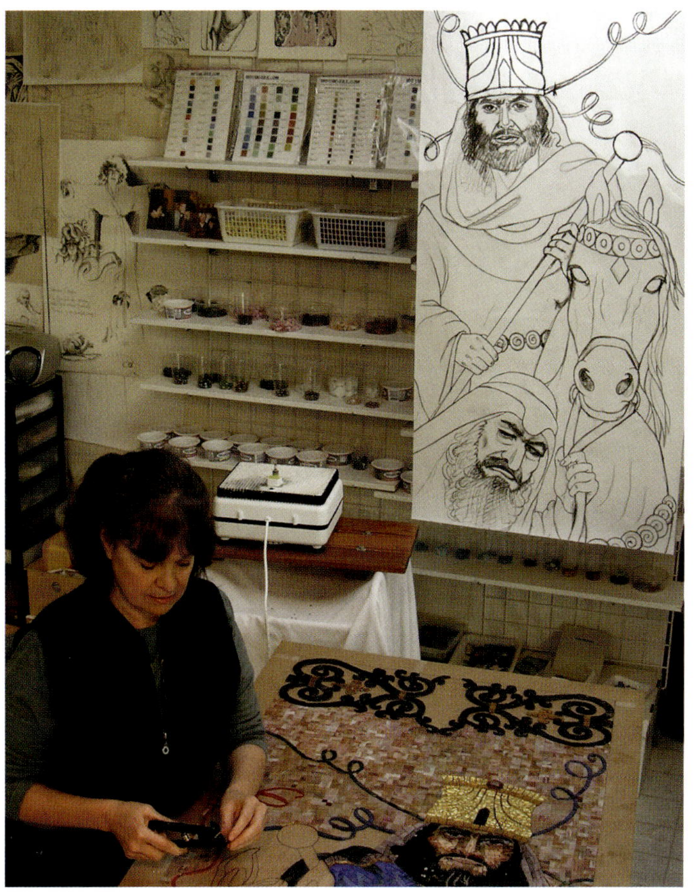

Selecting sketches, mosaic work in progress, the artist's studio, Vancouver, 2006

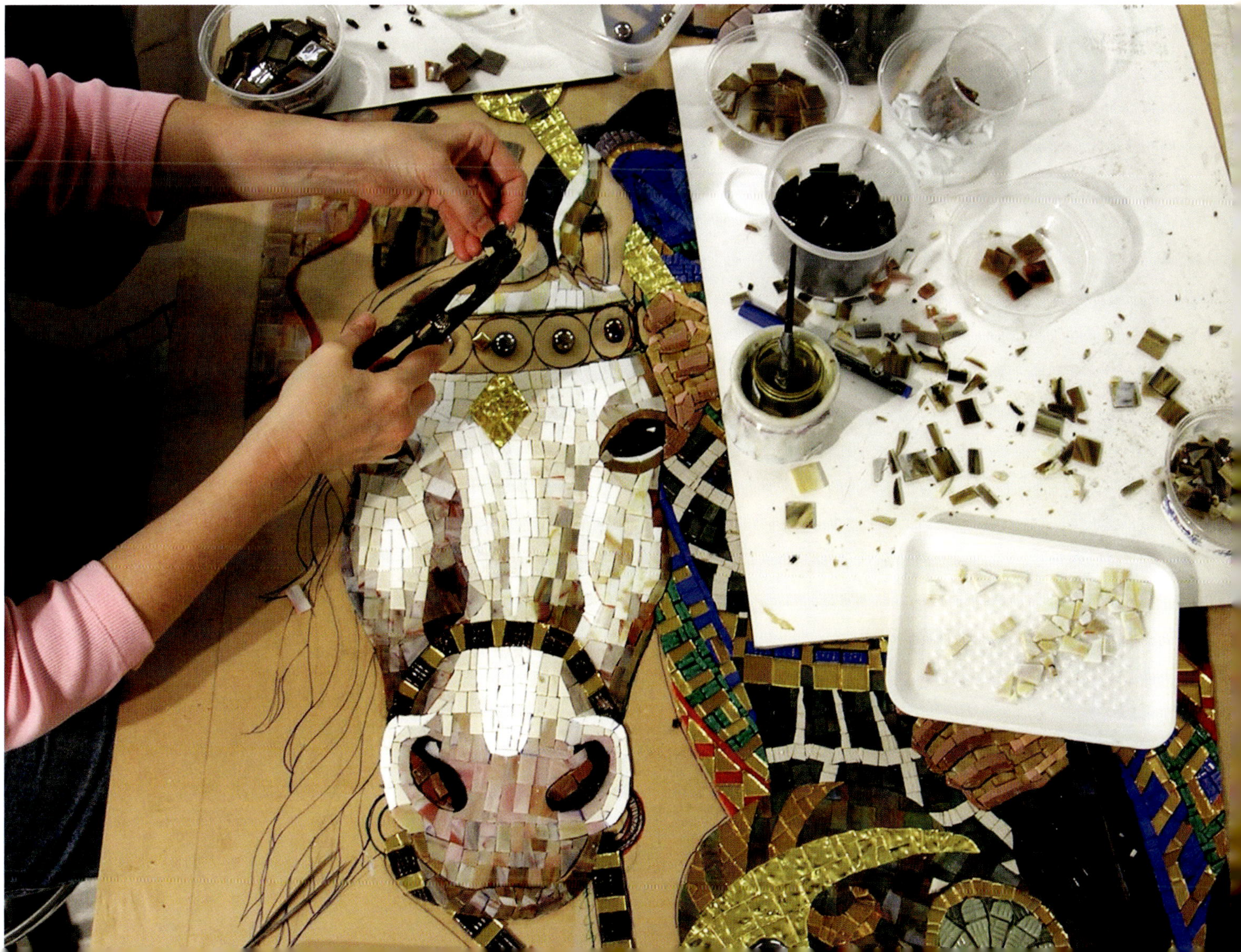

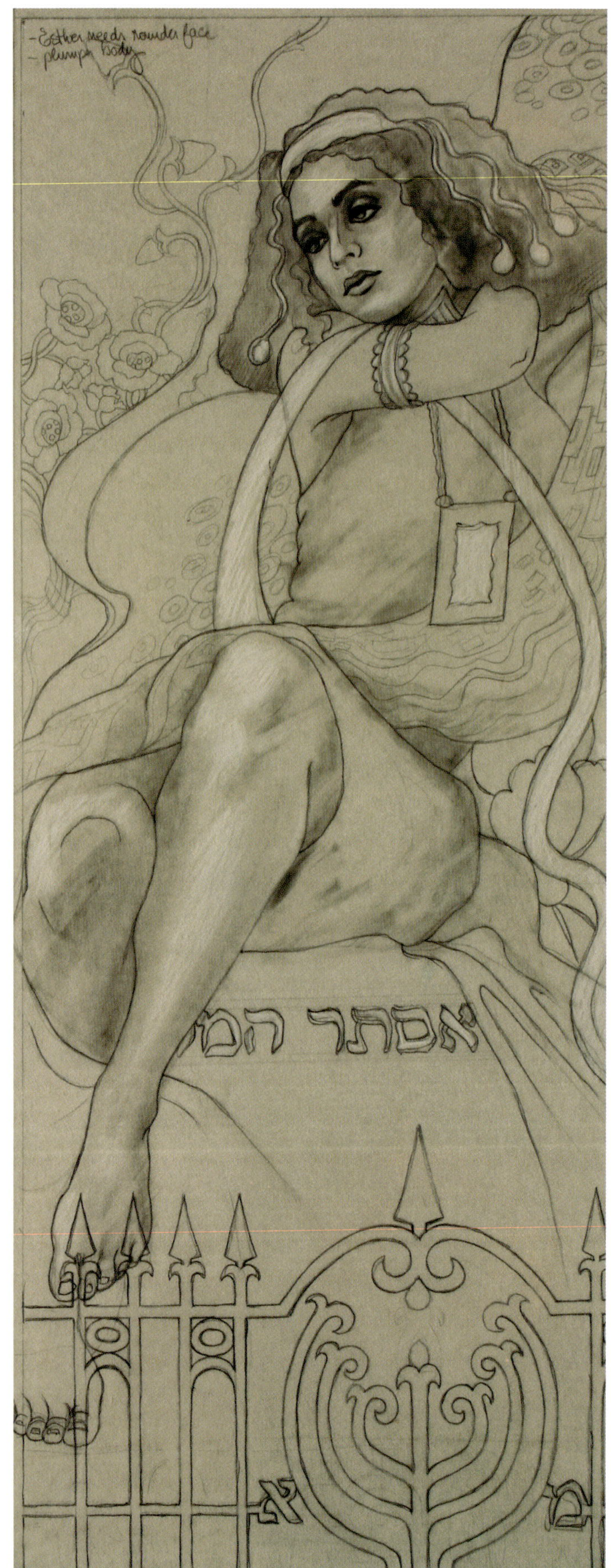

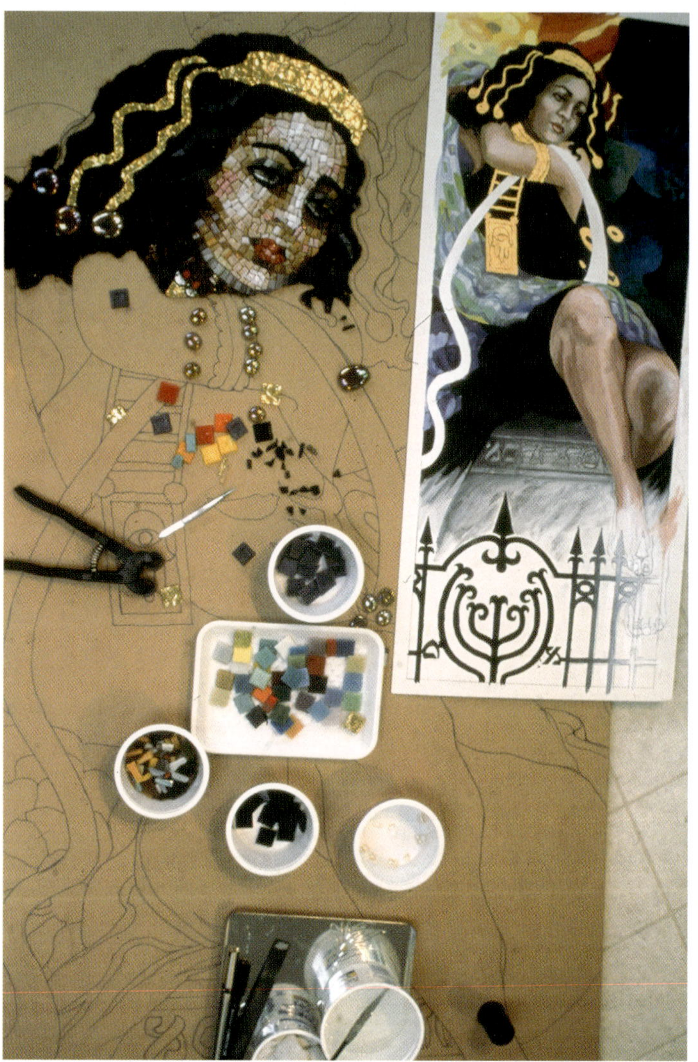

Left

Sketch for *Queen Esther,* graphite on paper,

36 x 18.5 in. (91.44 x 46.99 cm)

Above

Queen Esther, work in progress, with painted sketch

This reverse method of creating mosaics is especially well suited to floors and tabletops where flat surfaces are a must. For a wall mosaic or a hanging mosaic, however, where the surface need not be even, the angles of the individual tesserae can be manipulated by hand, which must be done while the cement is still wet and flexible. This enables light rays to hit the tesserae from different directions, creating reflections of glittering spots of moving light that bring the mosaic to life.

The greatest advantage of the indirect or reverse method is that it allows for changes to be made with minimum fuss at any time while the mosaic is being assembled. By wetting the paper with water, the temporarily glued tesserae are easily removed and replaced or repositioned. This method, however, also has its drawbacks. The tiles may shift in the process of flipping the work onto its final surface. As well, the artist must envision the mirror image of the design since only the backs of the tiles are seen, the colors of which are not always the same as on the front. Having a good memory is a great plus. I also find it helpful to use a mirror during the execution of a mosaic to make sure, at least partially, that the human features in reverse, as they will be seen from the other (the eventual front) side, are anatomically balanced.

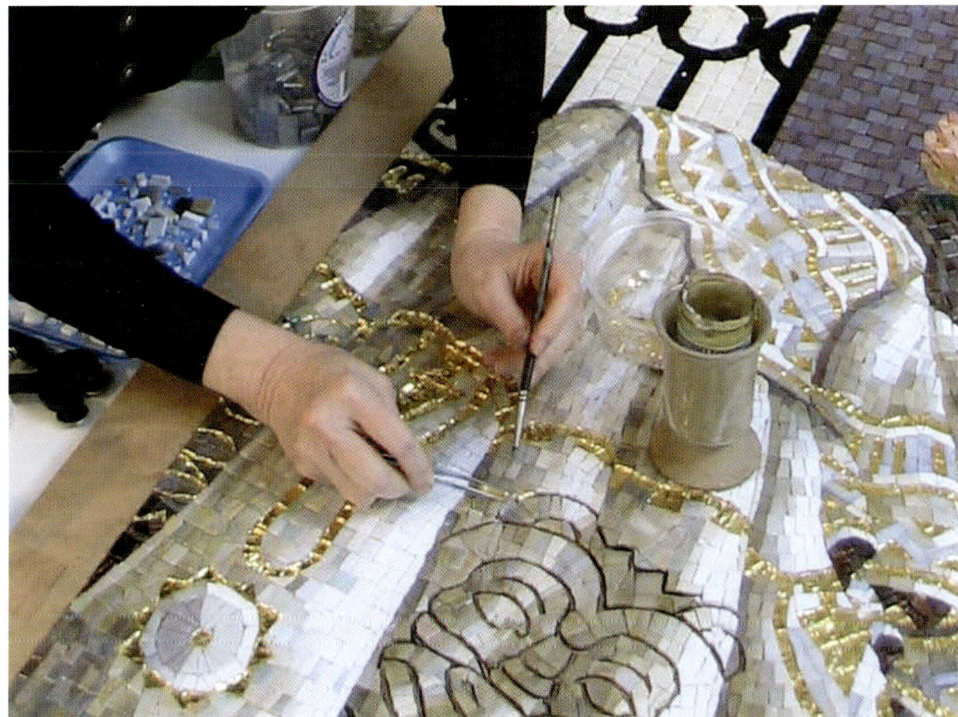

The greatest advantage of the indirect or reverse method is that it allows for changes to be made with minimum fuss at any time while the mosaic is being assembled.

The big advantage is that an irregular surface can be created, ideal for reflecting light since the tesserae are applied at different angles from the start.

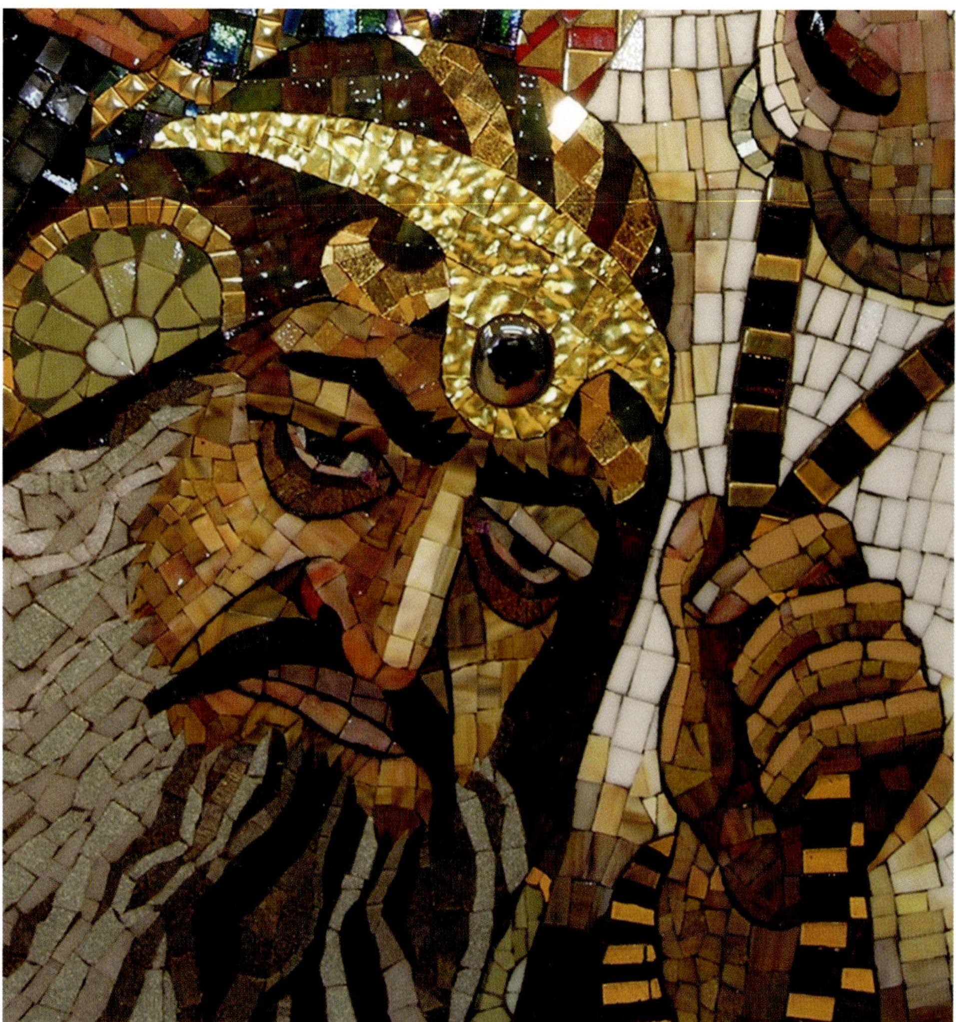

Detail from *Haman Leading Mordechai on the Royal Horse*

The Direct Method in Mosaic

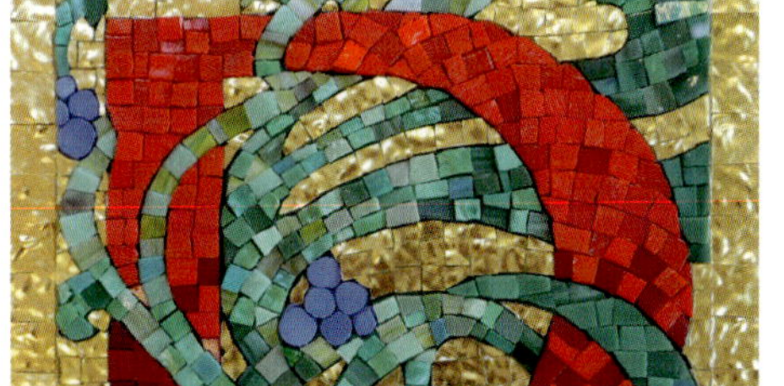

In contrast to the indirect method, the *direct* method of constructing mosaics is just that: the artist places and glues each individual tessera directly onto the final surface or substrate, which has already been buttered with cement. This method suits smaller mosaics that are easily transported, as well as three-dimensional objects such as clay pots, glass vases, and stone containers.

Here again, the big advantage is that an irregular surface can be created, which is ideal for reflecting light since the tesserae are applied at different angles from the start. The main disadvantage of the direct method, particularly for my style of work, is that making corrections is limited to a short window in time, right after application, as the cement dries in only a few hours. Also, with the direct method, the artist must work for extended periods of time directly on location, which can be grueling with large projects.

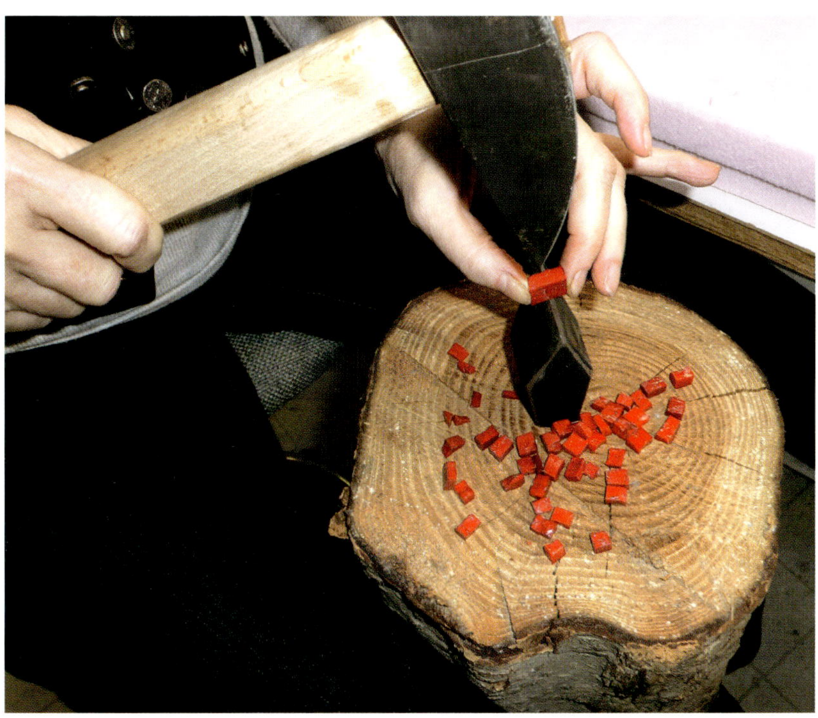

Cutting smalti with hammer and hardie

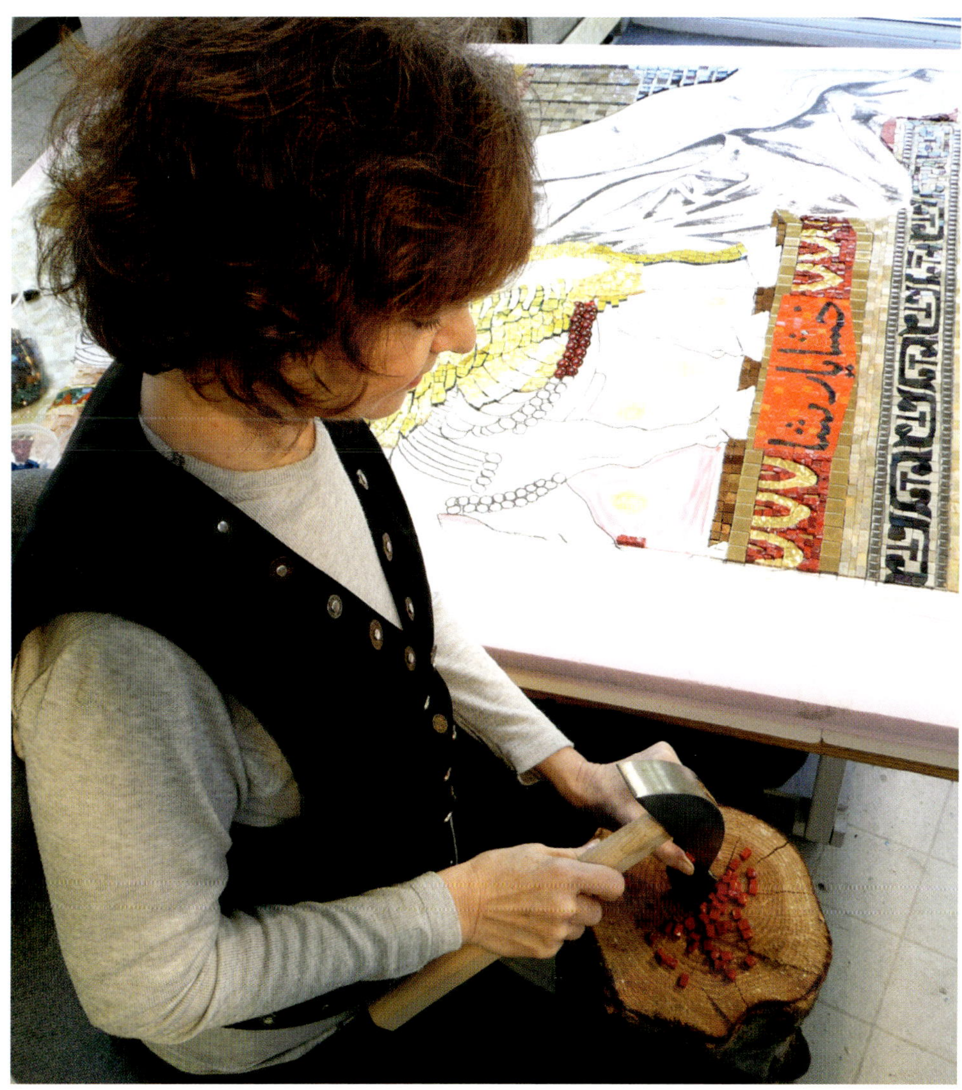

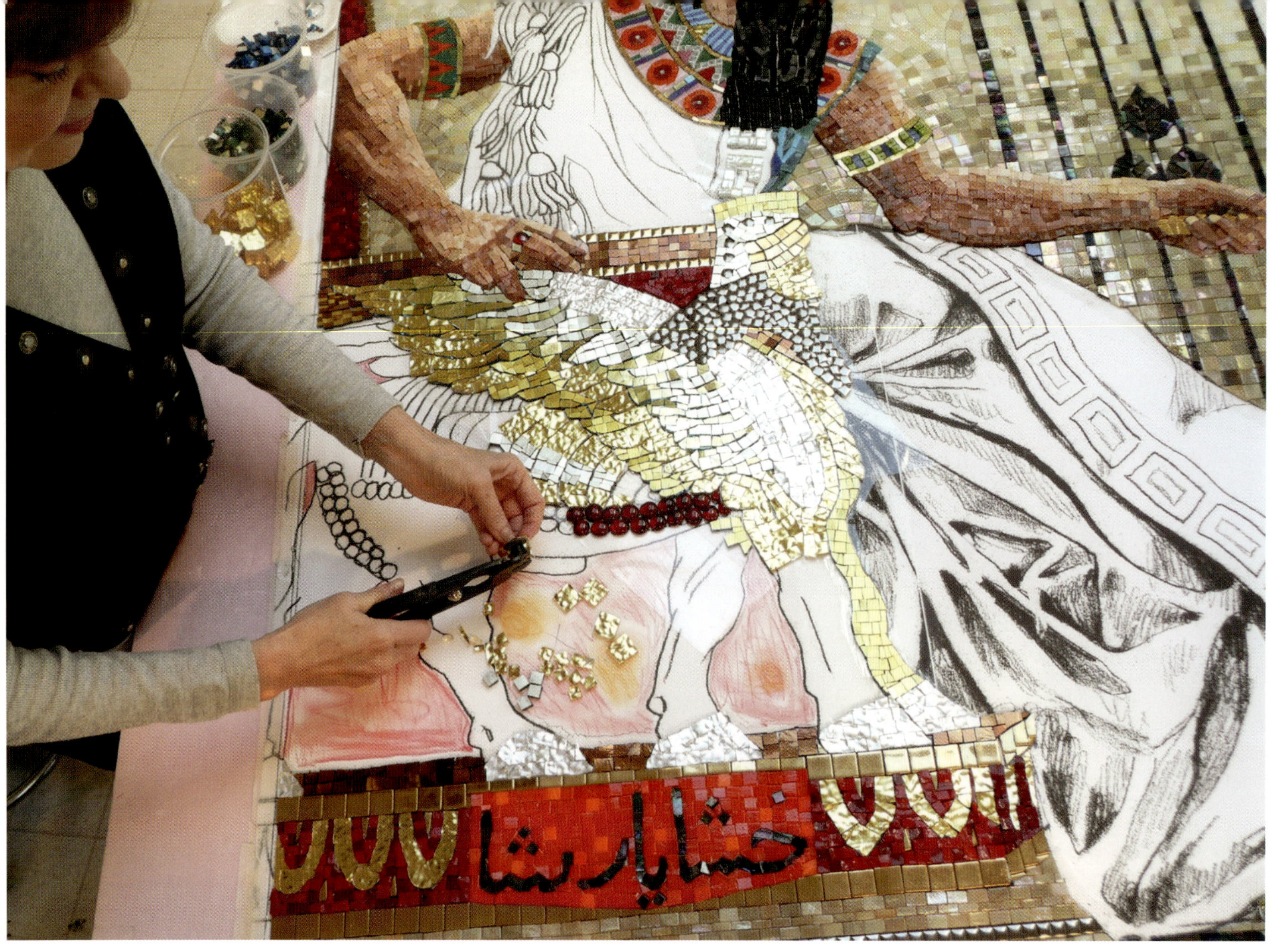

Queen Esther Seeking Permission to Speak, left panel, work in progress

Another method used extensively is sometimes called *double indirect.* The tesserae are placed face-up on adhesive-backed paper or sticky film, the work appearing exactly as it will when installed. When the mosaic is complete, thin sheets of cheesecloth are glued onto the surface of the mosaic with rabbit skin glue, and the work is allowed to dry until stiff. This "sandwich" is then turned over, the original sticky underlying surface is carefully peeled off, and the piece is installed as in the indirect method described above. Although supposedly an easier method, since the artist can see the final colors and design from the start, I find the sticky film difficult to work with. Nevertheless, I employed this method in the left panel of the large diptych *Queen Esther Seeking Permission to Speak.*

In a modern version of the direct method, the tesserae are cut and then glued onto a fiberglass mesh. The mosaic can thus be constructed with the design visible on the surface and transported to its final location. This method is well suited to large works since, with the finished mosaic glued to the mesh, sections can be cut up into smaller units and then be reassembled during installation.

Facing page
Queen Esther Seeking Permission to Speak, right panel, work in progress, direct method on mesh

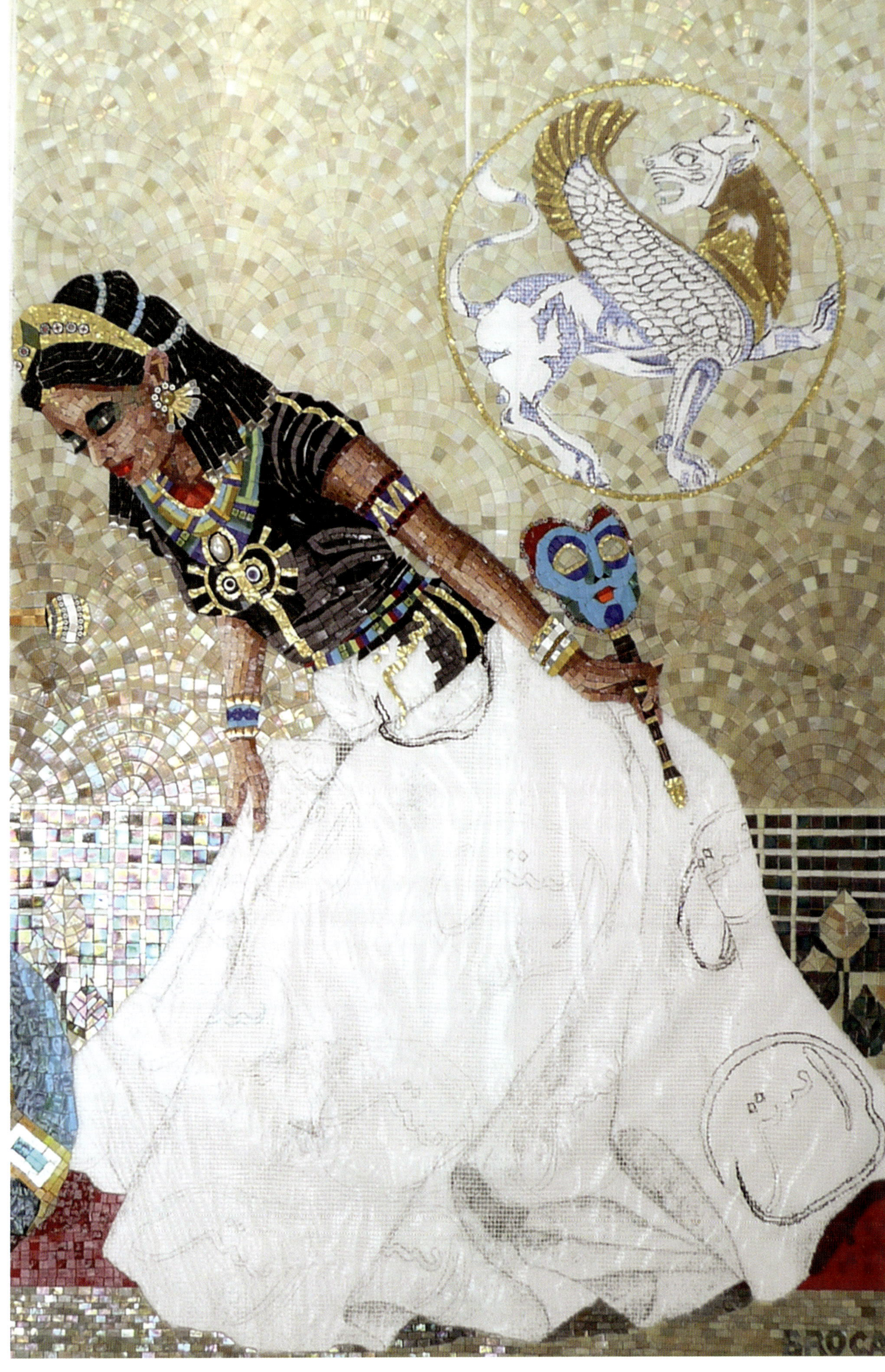
BROCA

The direct method, which I successfully used in the right panel of *Queen Esther Seeking Permission to Speak*, allows the artist to work in the comfort of a studio rather than at the installation site.

In Byzantine times, a similar method was used to execute small, easy-to-transport mosaic medallions, formerly called *emblemata* in Hellenistic Greece. A lime mortar bed served as a temporary backing. When dry, the medallion was lifted out of the bed, its back side was cleaned, and, after heavy wrapping, the work was carefully transported to the installation site, where it was inserted into a mosaic floor. These relatively small works, fine examples of a naturalistic mosaic style, were executed by individual artists. In contrast, the huge floor mosaics were assembled by teams of stone workers who cut and embedded the tesserae directly into simple, geometric floor designs, in situ.

Wall mosaics in churches are also thought to have been executed in Byzantine times using the direct method. The artist designed the image, enlarged it directly on the wall, and then painted it in the chosen colors. Once finished, workers who specialized in cutting and gluing the glass or marble tesserae would take over and fill in the colored areas, much like our contemporary "paint-by-number" kits. A hammer and hardie (a specialized kind of anvil) were used – and still are today – to cut the stone or glass. Years of practice were required to master this method. As a result, many contemporary mosaicists use instruments that are easier to cut with, such as the Leponitt two-wheeled glass cutter.

Revisiting Byzantine Technique

In the fall of 2010 I traveled to Ravenna, Italy, to experience firsthand the true Byzantine mosaic technique. There I spent an intense but fulfilling and illuminating week studying with Luciana Notturni, mosaicist, teacher of mosaic art at the prestigious Academy of Fine Art of Ravenna, and head of Scuola Nazionale del Restauro di Ravenna, probably the most important mosaic restoration school in the world. Notturni is also the founder of the renowned Scuola Arte del Mosaico di Ravenna.

By recreating the same likeness in the authentic Byzantine manner, the striking differences between the two techniques are readily apparent.

During my time with Maestra Notturni, I created a small mosaic of Queen Esther's head utilizing the classic Byzantine technique. I had already depicted the identical image in 2002 as part of a large mosaic entitled *Queen Esther,* but using the indirect method. By recreating the same likeness in the authentic

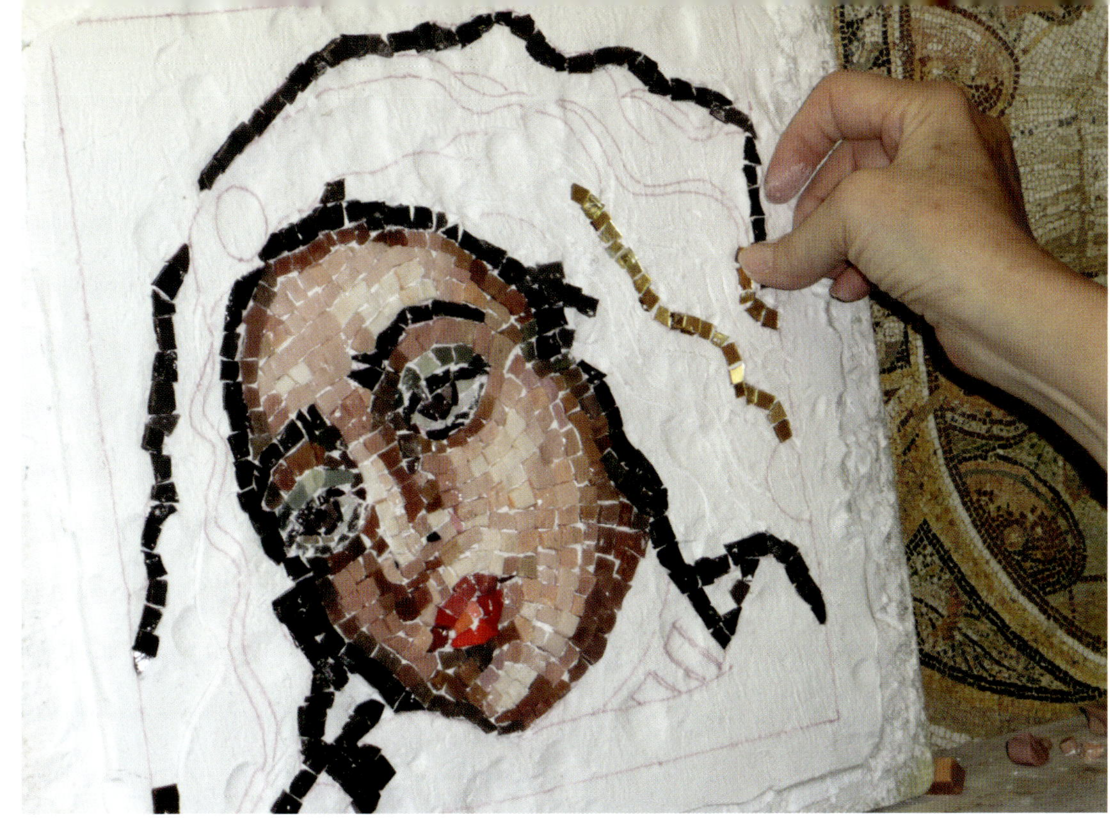

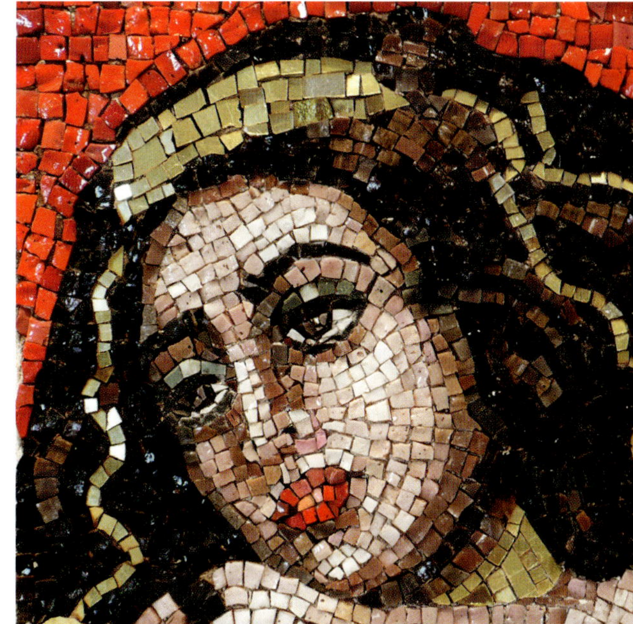

Byzantine manner, the striking differences between the two techniques are readily apparent. (Both images are reproduced on this page.) This difference is particularly evident in regard to *andamento* – the technical term for the manner of laying tesserae to create spatial movement or flow. In the Byzantine face, the andamento is more methodical and the components are more cohesively arranged. As well, the nature of the procedure (the tesserae being directly inserted at various angles in a bed of wet lime mortar) produces a more uneven texture, with deep, visible interstices. By contrast, my earlier version has less texture but more varied andamento, which from my twenty-first-century point of view results in a more dynamic image of Esther. As well, it articulates the expression of Esther's feelings in a more coherent visual form.

In Ravenna I adhered to the ancient traditional rules according to which the tesserae must always be inserted in rows that coil around facial features and lead the viewer's eye smoothly from one area to another. Working this way, I had to anticipate space requirements and, hence, future steps in the process, much like in chess where a player plans each move well in advance. Each time a space became wider, the last tessera in the working row had to be cut bigger in order to accommodate a split of that line into two new rows; and then these two rows, in turn, would each split into two rows, and so on, until the larger space was filled. I was amazed how quickly the eye stopped seeing the splits and simply glided over the smooth direction of the andamento. The end result looks and feels almost medieval without my having tried to make it so.

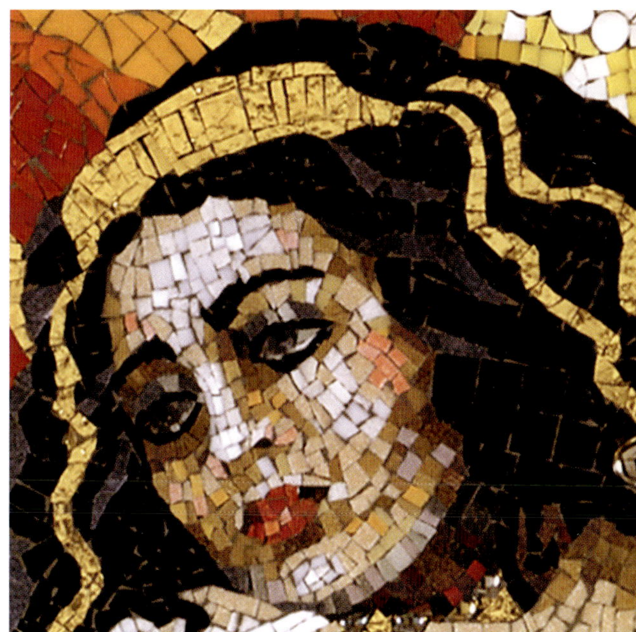

Top left and right
The Ravenna Head, created in the classic Byzantine method

Above
Detail from *Queen Esther*, created in the contemporary method

An Art for Today

The material itself possesses an integrity that can never be subdued; whereas oil paints, acrylic paints, pencils, charcoal, and conte all obey the will of the artist.

Unlike most other artistic disciplines, the making of glass mosaics is governed by the will of the medium. The material itself possesses an integrity that can never be subdued; whereas oil paints, acrylic paints, pencils, charcoal, and conte all obey the will of the artist: the artist need only think and instruct the hand to achieve the expected result. Not so with glass and mosaic: the material dictates the outcome and must be obeyed. Even with this limitation, artists can still express themselves in glass or stone and in abstract or figurative form, and create works of contemporary meaning and impact. One learns how to "think mosaic" very quickly.

People sometimes wonder if a large mosaic is worth all the painstaking work entailed. I must admit that there are moments when I myself have pondered this question: when agonizing over the pace of building a mosaic piece by piece; or realizing sometimes midway that a color scheme is flawed and requires a change in course; or enduring the terrifying "mosaic flip" (when one tiny wrong move can destroy six months' work); or scrubbing excess cement off for hours on end. Nevertheless, once the bright, freshly cleaned mosaic comes to life in its full glory, sparkling and shining brightly and lighting the whole studio with its awesome impact, at that moment all the labors are utterly worthwhile. And so deeply satisfying.

To create art in mosaic successfully, the intended image and the andamento must function interdependently: each small piece of glass retains its individual identity, yet the eye assimilates the pieces into a whole image. It is this characteristic of mosaic art – the dramatic portrayal of a subject using vibrant colors that are emotive though laid out in an orderly and rational fashion – which most reflects the present stage in my own artistic development. I still draw, but for now mosaic is my chosen medium.

Coincidentally, the art of mosaics and decorative mosaics is undergoing a strong revival. Mosaic images frequently appear in architectural magazines as well as in furniture and interior design magazines. Unfortunately, however, not enough museums and galleries have broadened their narrow conception that mosaics belong strictly to the decorative arts, and regrettably mosaic is not yet recognized as a serious art form in its own right.

Interestingly, a new international movement called TE21 (Tessellated Expression 21) was launched in 2008 solely to counteract mosaic's marginalized position and promote it as a bona fide discipline of fine arts. Its prominent founders are Elaine Goodwin (England), Toyoharu Kii (Japan), Lucio Orsoni (Italy), and Dugald MacInnes (Scotland). According to a 2010 article about the group's founding,[5] Elaine Goodwin had repeatedly appealed to Sir Nicholas Serota, a curator at the Tate Gallery, London, but his response had always been the same: mosaic works belong solely in the applied and decorative arts institutions, such as the Victoria and Albert Museum, London.

TE21 was founded specifically with the purpose of reversing such attitudes and giving established professional artists who work with mosaic, including myself, a distinct voice and an opportunity to exhibit together. United, I believe we will have a better opportunity to obtain a deserved platform within the often elitist fine arts intelligentsia. I anticipate that in the coming years less biased and more enlightened museums and art galleries will support the re-emergence of this ancient and spectacular artistic discipline, and give weight to exhibitions of contemporary mosaic art.

The revival of mosaic is also evident in the growing membership in such mosaic associations as the International Association of Contemporary Mosaicist (AIMC), the British Association for Modern Mosaic (BAMM), the Society of American Mosaic Artists (SAMA), the Mosaic Association of Australia (MAANZ), and the Mosaic Association of Japan (MAAJ).

In many countries, mosaic studios and schools are opening up due to a growing demand to learn this specific skill. At the same time, some of the oldest Italian mosaic schools continue to teach both ancient and modern techniques. They include the Scuola Mosaicisti del Friuli, Italy, the previously mentioned Scuola Arte del Mosaico di Ravenna founded by Luciana Notturni, and the Orsoni Master Classes in Venice founded by Lucio Orsoni.

In many countries, mosaic studios and schools are opening up due to a growing demand to learn this specific skill.

In describing Maestra Notturni's opinion of the contemporary mosaic approach, mosaic specialist and author Dr. Patricia Witts writes: "[Notturni] argues that mosaicists who choose to avoid studying ancient techniques for fear that this will inhibit their creativity will end up missing a trick and that it is better to have an 'age-old knowledge' and only then consider breaking the rules."[6]

This view coincides with my own. Just as drawing skills are necessary before attempting courses in painting, carving, printmaking, and so forth, for mosaics one should first study the ancient methods by examining or even copying them. Once equipped with a complete understanding of why mosaics were executed in their traditional manner, the artist can then express himself or herself in the chosen personal style.

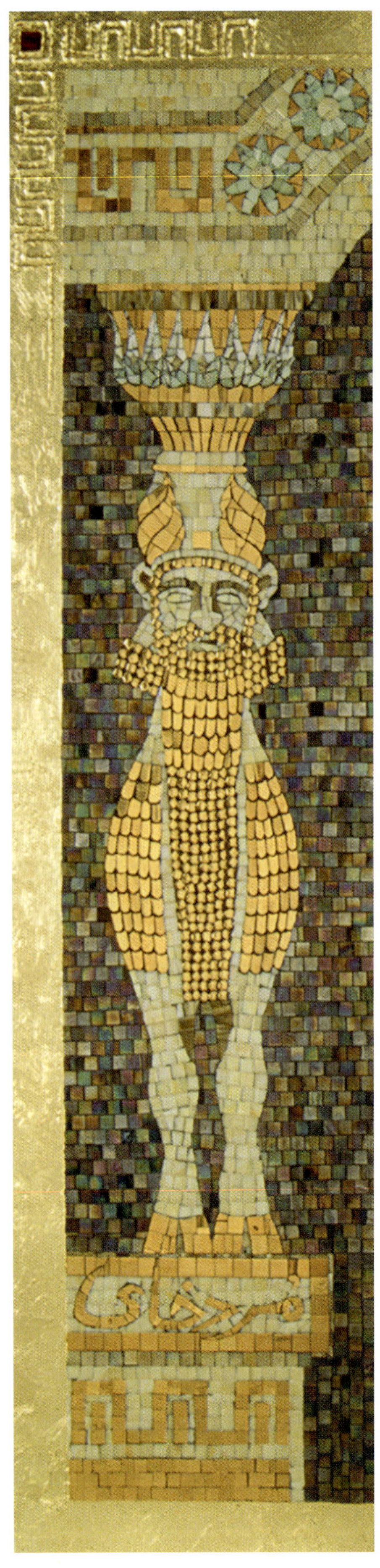

Expressing Symbolic Meaning

Throughout my career, I have considered myself a symbolist no matter what medium or subject matter I have chosen to work in: and no less so in approaching *The Queen Esther Mosaic Series* with a Byzantine treatment, where I found no obstacle to freely expressing my personal symbolism. That being said, like most visual artists, I feel reluctant to discuss any finished artworks, preferring instead to allow the viewer the pleasurable and creative act of personal interpretation. By revealing all, I remove the mystery of my works and affect the viewer's judgment. Nevertheless, due to the narrative nature of this particular series and for the sake of this book, I make an exception in the remainder of this chapter and discuss the research I conducted, the symbolism I used, and why I selected specific compositions and scenes from the story.

Researching the times, costumes, architecture, and jewelry of Queen Esther was not enough; I had to brush up on art history as well, namely the Byzantine period. As with all of my art series, I researched the entire subject thoroughly, striving for authenticity in covering ancient subject matter and empowering it with contemporary meaning.

In creating a mosaic, I begin by making dozens of sketches using still life or live models, depending on the particular work. Choosing the best sketches and deciding on the composition are dictated by how I visualize the finished work as it appeared in my mind's eye, well before I begin to assemble the actual mosaic. During the ever-evolving work in progress, however, I inevitably deviate from the original cartoon and color selection. The material has a life of its own, and despite meticulous advance planning, the spontaneity in actually executing each work gives me great pleasure.

Left and facing page
Details from *Queen Esther with Mordechai*

Queen Esther

In *Queen Esther*, the first of the series, I incorporate both her background and her status in the king's harem during the months of preparations when all the chosen contestants for the position of queen receive elaborate beauty treatments. I found no need to portray Esther as a young girl at home before the beauty contest.

The mosaic depicts an unhappy, albeit rich, young Esther whose hands are tied and her options limited, a reference also to her vulnerability later when, as the king's wife, she will approach him with the extraordinary request to save her people. Despite all the riches available to her in her new life at the court of King Ahashvayrosh, Esther remains a tragic figure living in a harem of predominantly Persian women where, having sworn to keep her Jewish identity secret, she cannot share or display anything about her culture. Day after day Esther must hide her identity. The songs, dances, music, and stories that fill the concubines' daily lives must sadly remind her of the culture she has left behind.

A young, attractive woman served as my model when I began work on *Queen Esther* in the winter of 2001. As usual, I started by doing a portrait in black graphite on grey paper, which allows me to create highlights in white chalk, giving the head a distinct three-dimensional appearance. To express the sorrow and impotency of Esther's predicament, I asked the model to hide her arms and hands behind her, as in the adage "my hands are tied."

Since the scene needs to suggest the wealth and riches of the harem in the famous Ahashvayrosh Palace, Esther is shown wearing precious jewelry; colorful fabrics, pillows, and scarves appear in the background. Despite all the luxury, her face conveys the melancholic mood of a poor little rich girl who never wished in the first place to live in the king's court. In the outline of the whole body and surrounding objects, I introduce aspects that allude to her background and religion. Around Esther's neck hangs the *hamsa*, a stylized hand with five fingers, a symbol used in amulets, charms, and jewelry to protect against the "evil eye." Jews do not consider the hamsa to have any Islamic connection other than the shared name, which means five in both Arabic and Hebrew.

From the knees down, the young Esther's figure slowly dissolves into a black and white line drawing of bare legs and feet. This symbolizes Esther's poor origins. Her toes are intertwined with wrought iron bars, which customarily were used in the ancient architecture of window coverings for the women's quarters. The iron bars symbolize a woman's status as a rich man's "assets" that must be

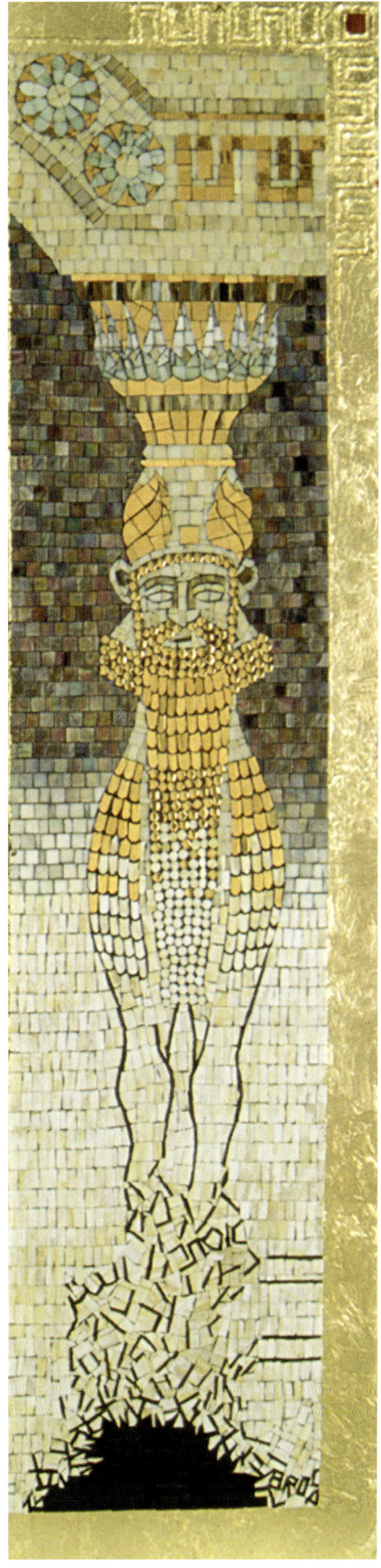

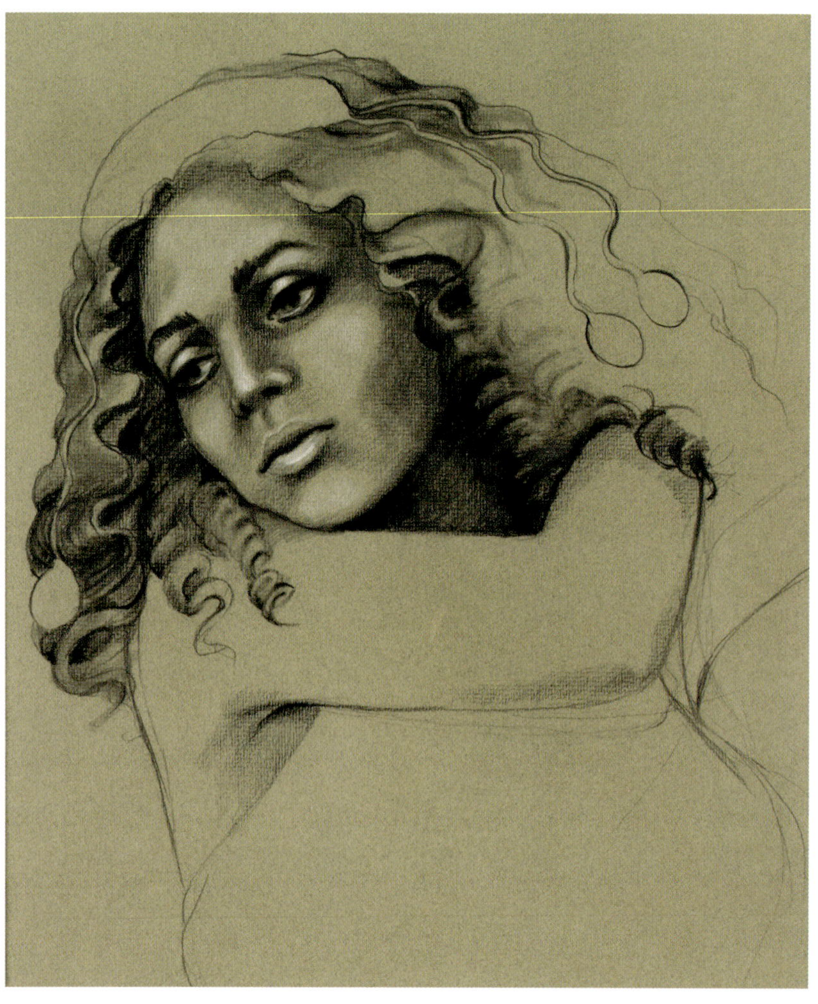

Sketch for *Queen Esther*, graphite and pastel on paper, 20 x 17 in. (50.80 x 43.18 cm)

protected from assault or kidnapping. My interpretation of Esther here proposes a question: as the design of the iron bars also suggests a stylized menorah, could this Hebrew symbol represent a further aspect of her "imprisonment"– that being Jewish has possibly put her into this predicament in the first place?

When the line drawing was completed, I painted the image on regular illustration board. This small painted sketch served as my guide throughout the time I assembled the larger mosaic. Since I used the indirect method to create this work, the graphite drawing also had to be recreated as a reverse cartoon in an appropriately proportioned larger size. The cartoon was produced on brown kraft paper that was then stretched on plywood. Now I had a gigantic drawing and a small painted version to refer to.

Starting with the face and facial expression, I next cut and glued the tesserae using water soluble white glue – a mixture of boiled flour and water paste. For this first mosaic I had only vitreous glass in my studio, smalti being too expensive. However, besides other materials I wanted ideally to use, I needed gold if I were to give the work a truly Byzantine treatment.

While working on the face, my wedding anniversary also happened to be approaching. When my husband, David, suggested I mark the occasion by modernizing my engagement ring, I thought immediately that, instead of this expensive indulgence, for the same amount of money he could buy me Italian gold tesserae for the mosaic. David agreed. Later, the dream of featuring Byzantine gold areas in the entire series also became a reality.

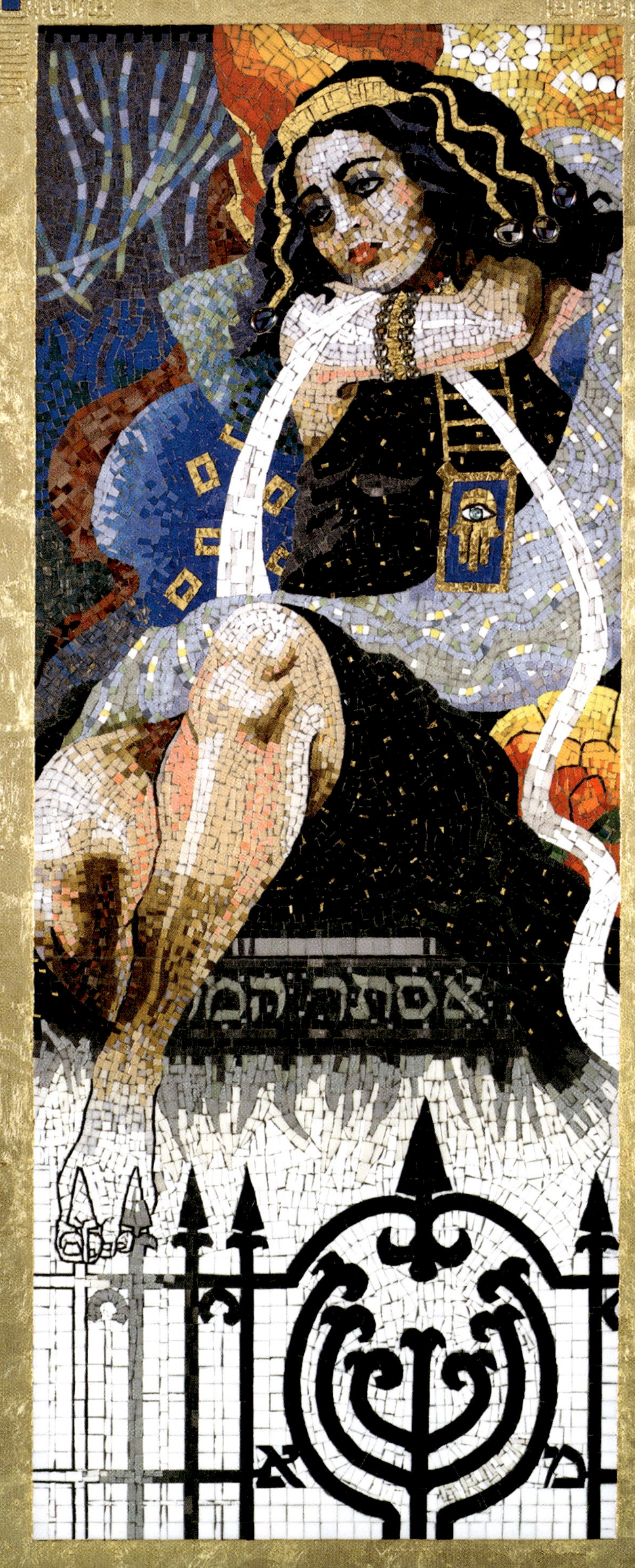

Queen Esther, 2002
Venetian gold glass and smalti on panel
75 x 33 in. (190.50 x 83.82 cm)

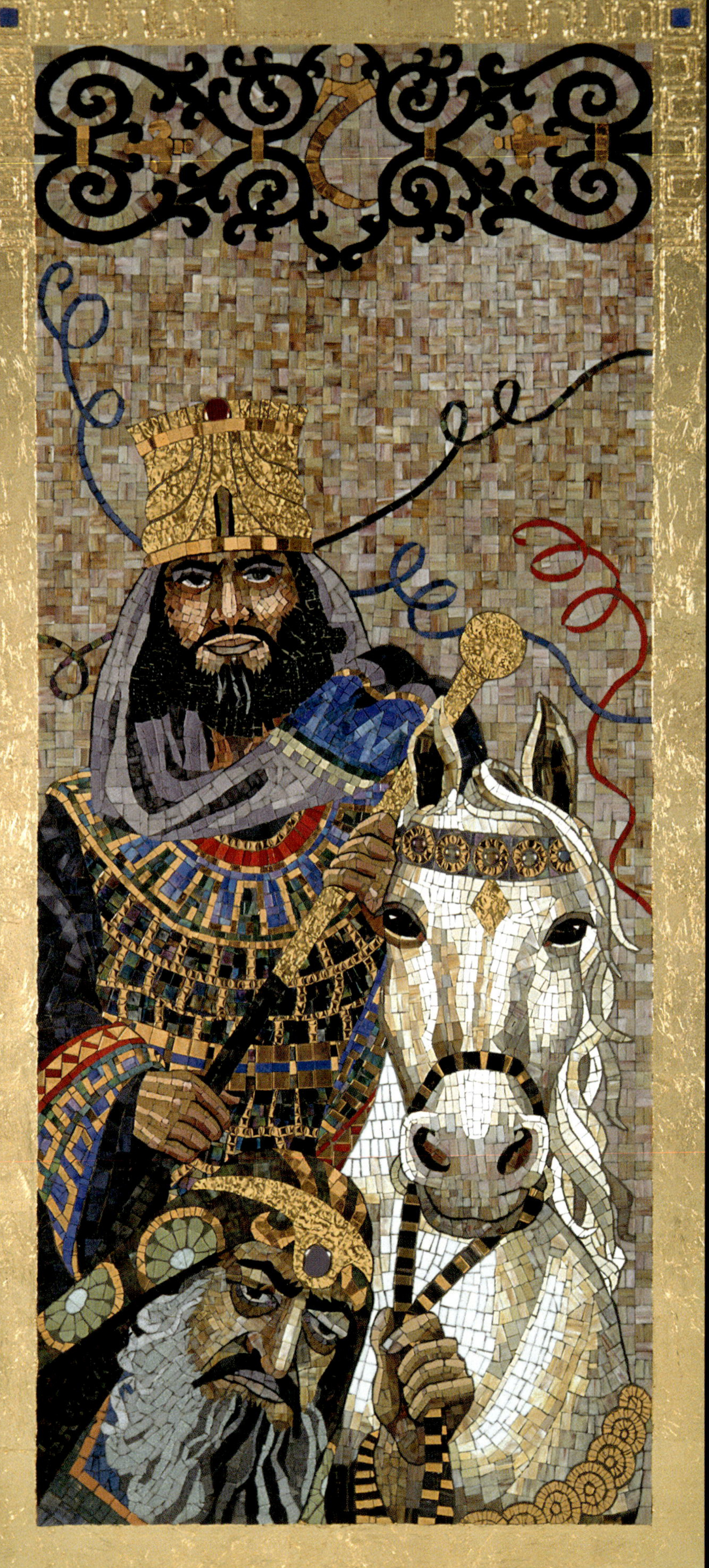

Haman Leading Mordechai on the Royal Horse, 2006
Venetian gold glass and smalti on panel
70 x 33 in. (177.80 x 83.82 cm)

Haman Leading Mordechai on the Royal Horse

The idea of using wrought iron bars as a common motif running through each work in the series came to me while executing the *Queen Esther* mosaic. On the odd occasion when Esther herself does not appear in one of the mosaics, the iron bars become an architectural motif, as in the case of *Haman Leading Mordechai on the Royal Horse.*

Importantly, this scene introduces the story's antagonist, Haman, as well as one of the two key protagonists, Esther's cousin, Mordechai.

Importantly, this scene introduces the story's antagonist, Haman, as well as one of the two key protagonists, Esther's cousin, Mordechai. The sequence of mosaics establishes by now that Esther is the story's central hero. This work establishes Mordechai as the other hero and as, in effect, her co-conspirator in the plan to counter Haman's evildoing. Here, the wrought iron motif – which elsewhere symbolizes the oppression and segregation of women in an ancient patriarchal society – takes on a different meaning, becoming part of the opulent palace gate, with the royal initial appearing in its center.

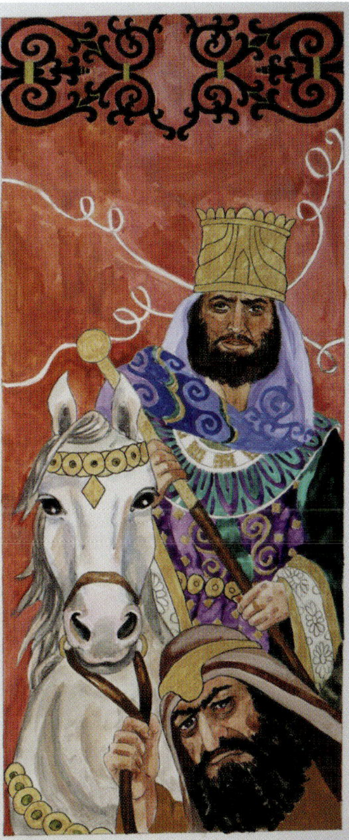

Since heavy mosaics are very difficult to hang on an unreinforced wall, I devised a composition that includes two figures and a horse in one small space – hence, the vertical triangular composition. The streamers behind Mordechai represent the public celebration given in his honor. A sour-faced Haman, dark with anger and displeasure, is seen pulling the royal white horse whose rider is none other than Mordechai. The latter, whom Haman had plotted to kill but who now receives the king's highest honor, is dressed in the king's attire and wears his crown. The idea for such an honor came from Haman himself, who believed that the king, in asking him to suggest how to properly reward a loyal servant, was about to give the honor to him. Haman's hatred for Mordechai, who had earlier repeatedly refused to bow to him with respect, drove the evil minister so mad that he "resolved to revenge himself on the whole of Mordechai's race…"[7] To this end, he craftily secured the king's permission by written decree to carry out his genocidal intentions.

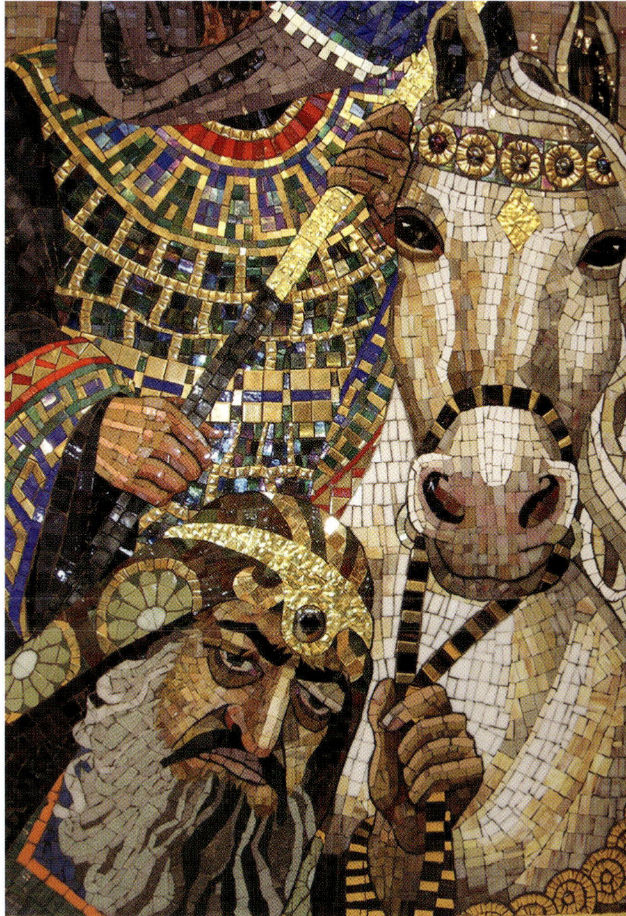

Above left
Painted sketch for *Haman Leading Mordechai on the Royal Horse,* acrylic on illustration board, 18.5 x 8 in. (46.99 x 20.32 cm)

Above right
Detail from *Haman Leading Mordechai on the Royal Horse*

Esther's Offering

There being no wedding ceremony in the Book of Esther but plenty of banquets, *Esther's Offering* follows Byzantine narrative style by combining multiple story elements in one image: the announcement of her winning the beauty contest and her marriage. To represent this, she is seen in bridal attire. I also chose to show her dressed in this fashion when my research led me to discover that bleached white fabrics and pearl jewelry were commonly worn in Persia in the fifth century BCE.

This work in the mosaic series connects the two cultures, Hebrew and Persian, presenting Esther in her struggle to combine her attachment to Judaism with an added loyalty to the king. The piece focuses on the young Esther as the bride-to-be (and queen) just at the fateful moment when her name is called as the winner. However, there is more to be read in this artwork.

The royal appointment took the form of a competition among many young virgins carefully selected from throughout the realm, all beautiful, all deemed worthy of the king's attention. But only one would become queen of Persia. Suddenly, Esther, who reluctantly participated in this competition under the firm pressure of her cousin Mordechai, in one pivotal moment now sees her future completely altered. A huge challenge awaits her and she's determined to succeed. In my image Esther appears frightened but determined, dressed in an elegant white dress symbolizing purity of heart and soul. Curtseying to the king, she raises her handkerchief, embroidered with her name in Farsi, the language of the Persians, thus signifying in one gesture both her identity and her submission to the king's will.

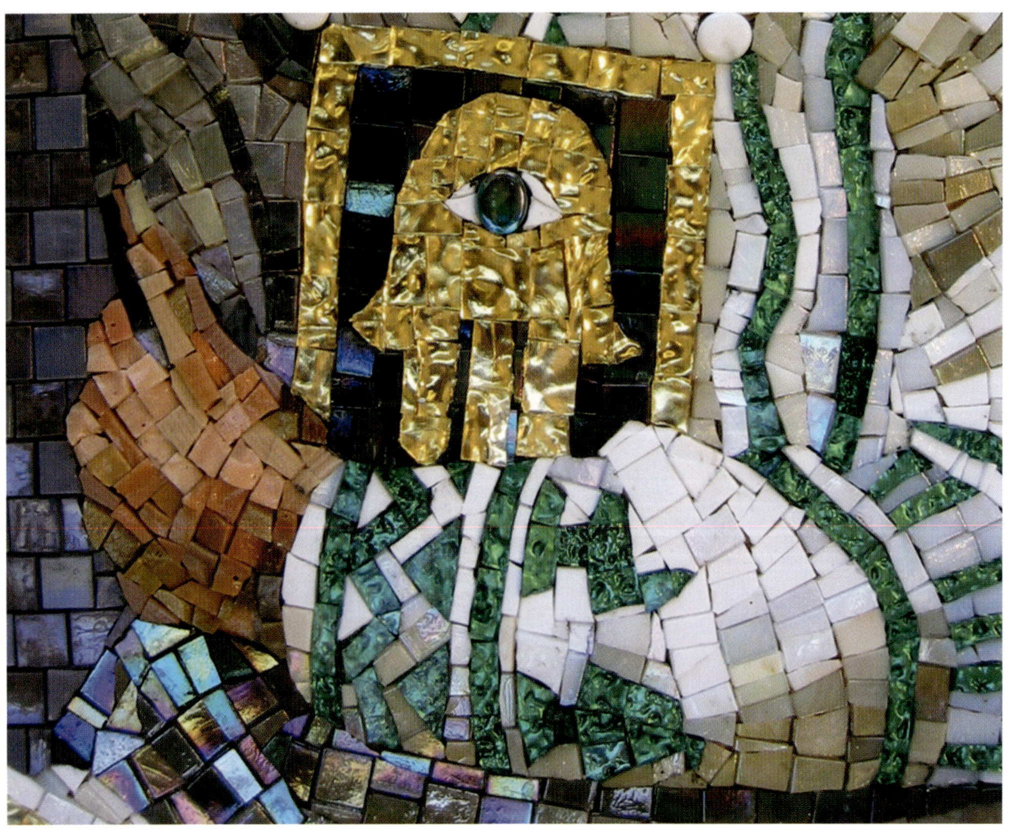

Detail from *Esther's Offering*, work in progress

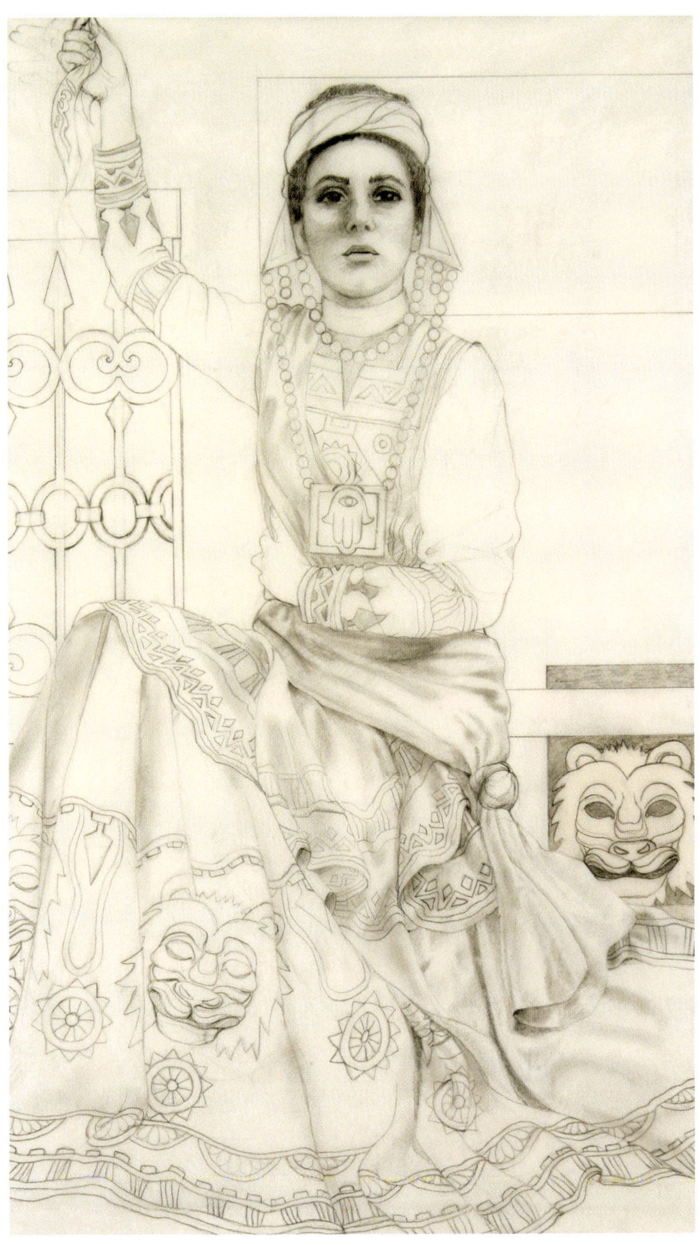

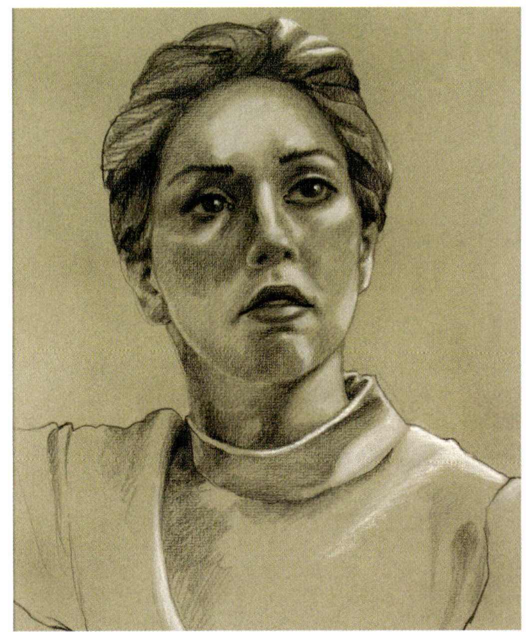

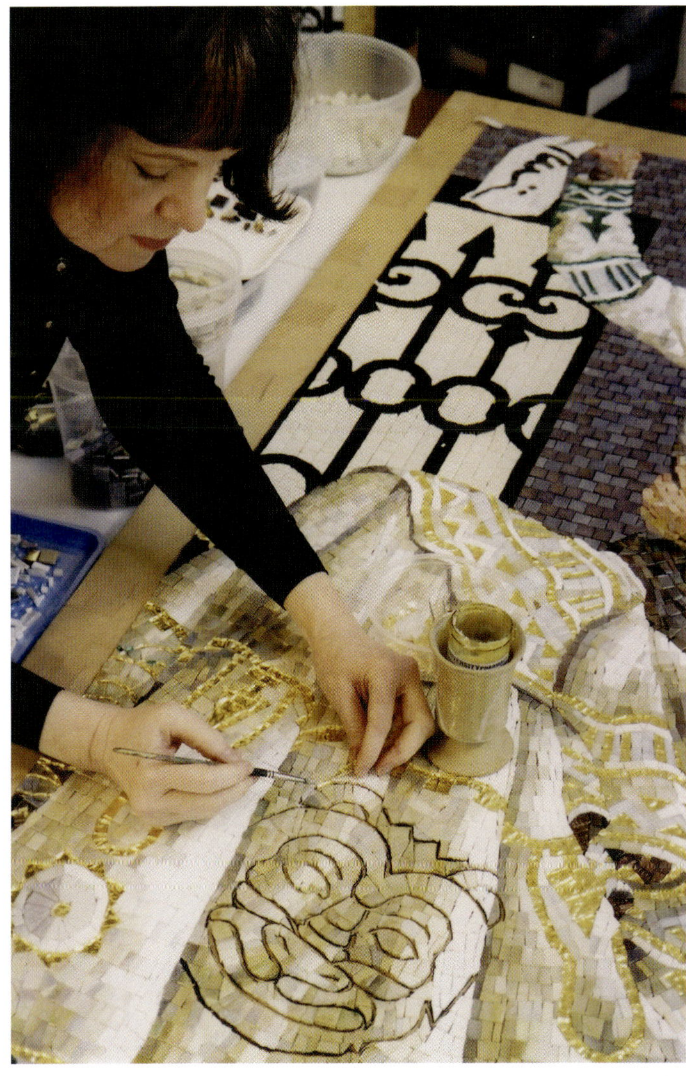

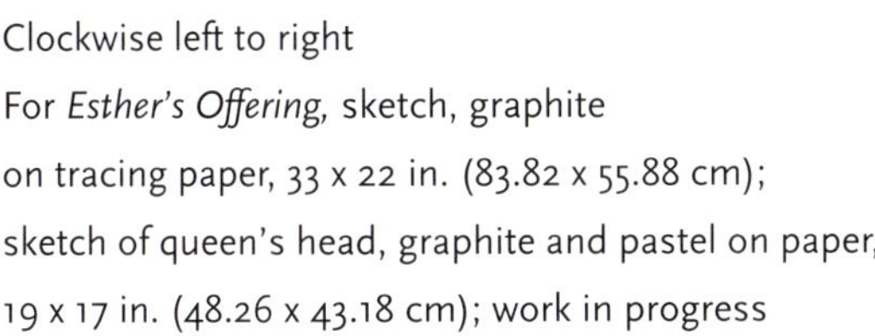

Clockwise left to right
For *Esther's Offering,* sketch, graphite on tracing paper, 33 x 22 in. (83.82 x 55.88 cm); sketch of queen's head, graphite and pastel on paper, 19 x 17 in. (48.26 x 43.18 cm); work in progress

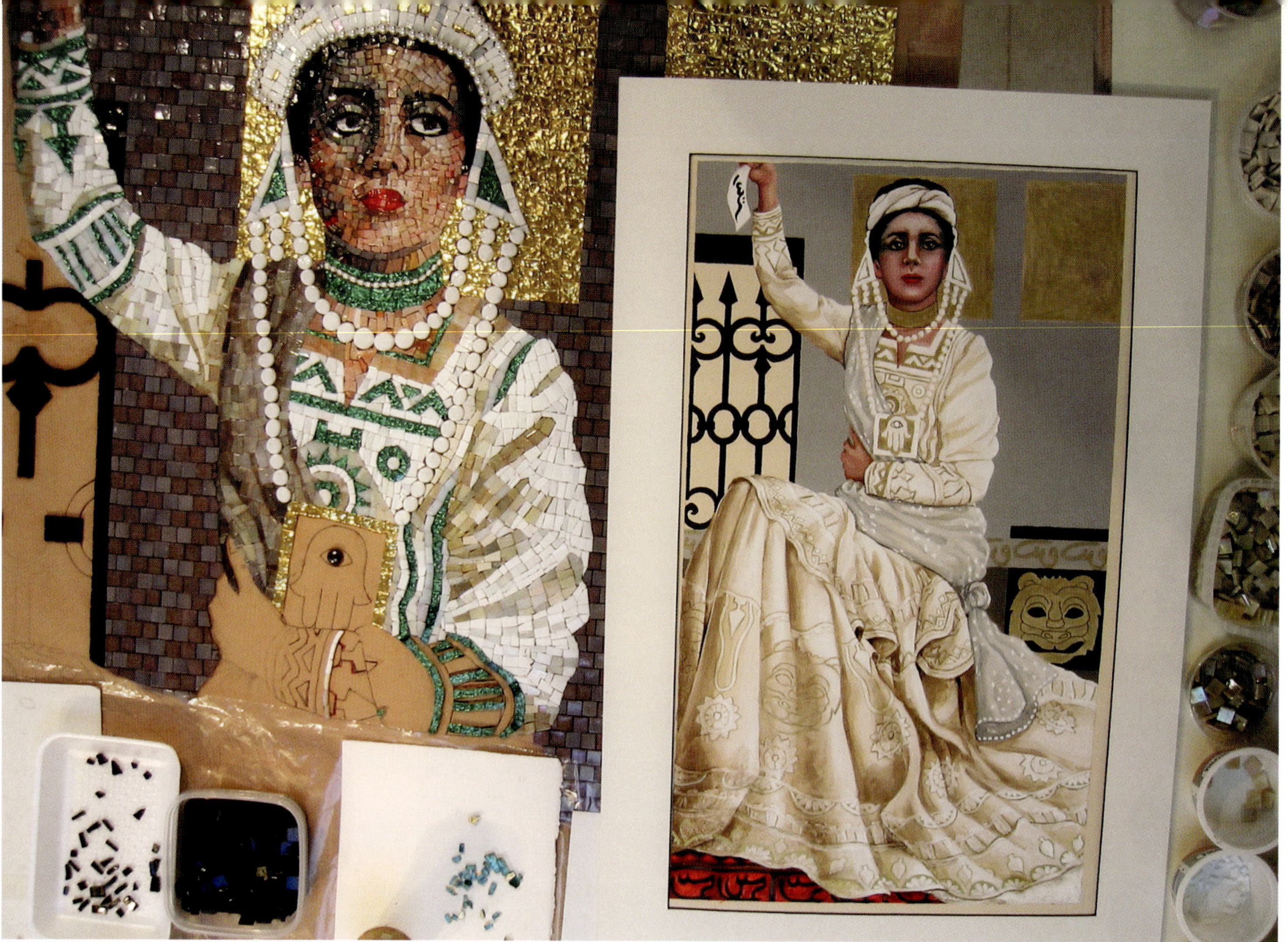

Esther's Offering, work in progress, with painting guide, acrylic on illustration board, 34 x 23 in. (86.36 x 58.42 cm)

Alongside Esther appears a mask of a lion, the symbol most associated with Persia, with its astrological reference to the constellation of Leo. The lion also refers to ancient symbols of royal lineage and divinity, power, and braveness. Lion imagery is commonly found, for example, on royal thrones, where it was traditionally thought to offer protection to the occupant. Signifying both protector and sovereignty, it also symbolized royalty and courage in the tribe of Judah – in Israelite lore, the "Lion of Judah" – the lion ruling over the animal kingdom as the king rules over mankind. Given this Judaic as well as Persian reference, in the mosaic the lion becomes the newlyweds' unifying symbol.

The divine color of gold is used for the Persian lion mask in the background and the lion decorations on Queen Esther's dress. Both images derive from the stylized lionesses found in wall decorations of Persepolis. With the repetition of the lion motif, the two cultures are represented as connected even though the king is ignorant of Esther's background. The theme of hiding and revealing, an essential characteristic of the story, is further amplified by the word *secret* written several times in Middle Farsi (the language of the period) on the black area above the lion mask.

Facing page
Esther's Offering, 2004
Pearls, gems, and smalti on panel
70 x 43 in. (177.80 x 109.22 cm)

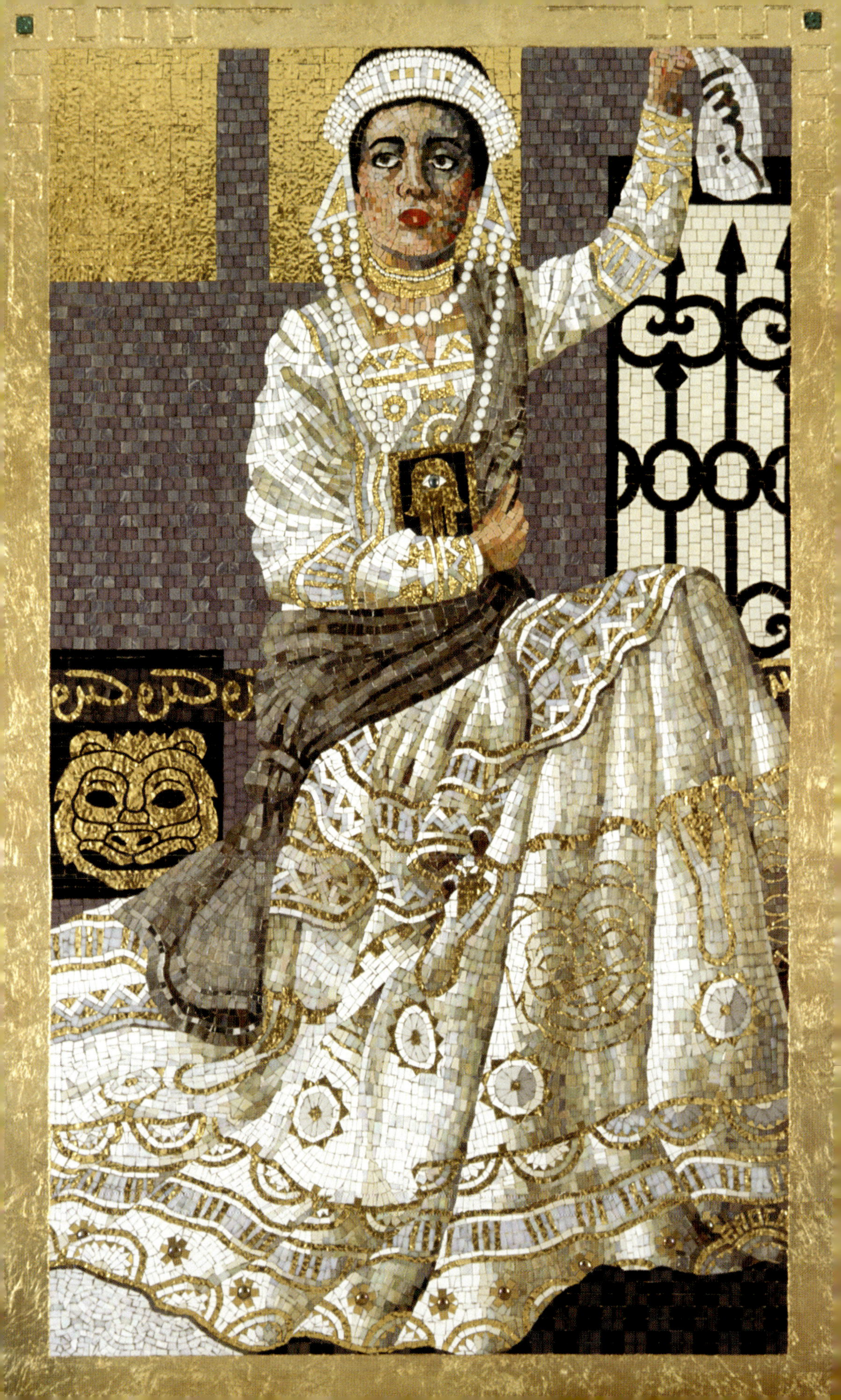

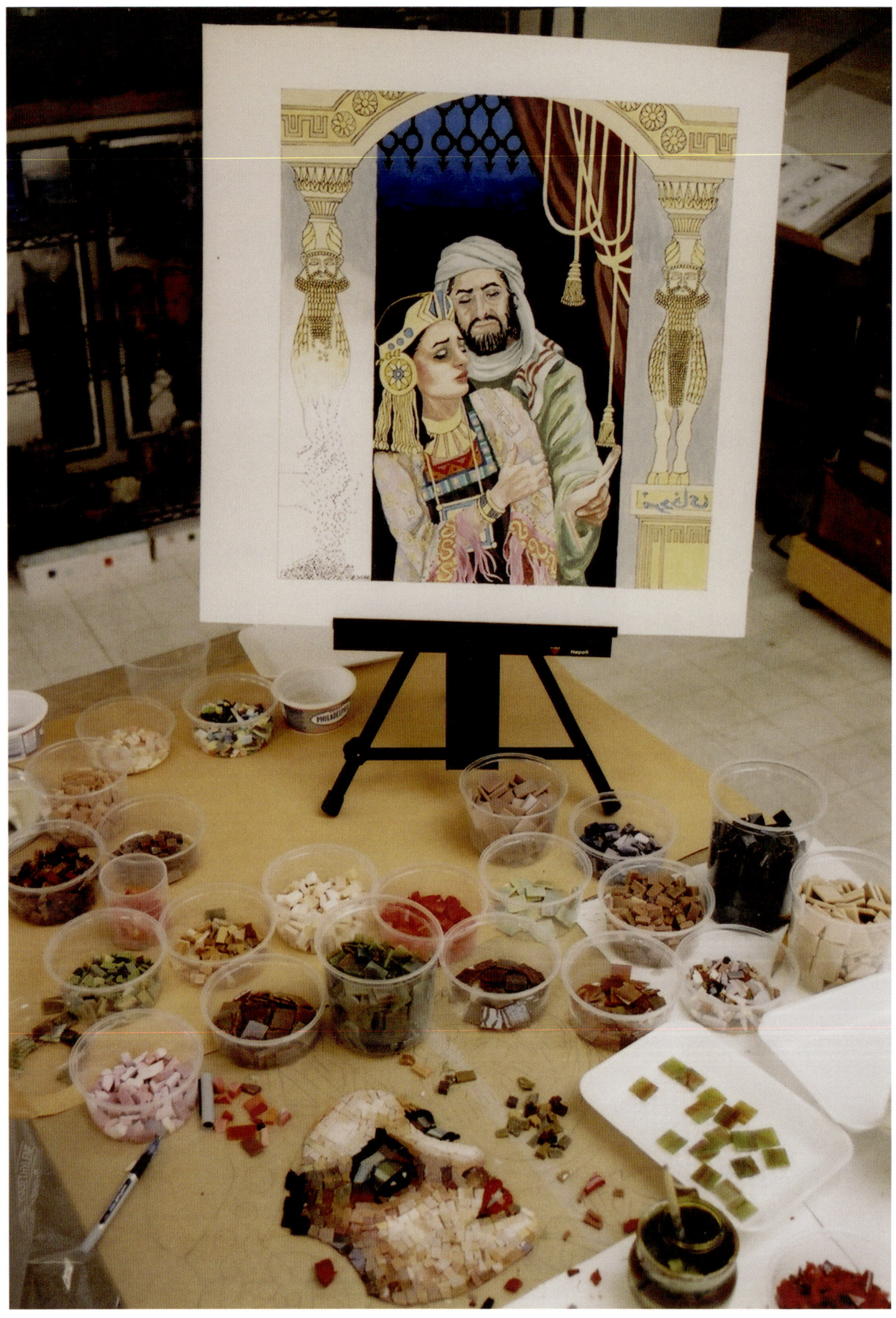

Queen Esther with Mordechai, work in progress, with painted sketch, acrylic on illustration board, 18.75 x 17.5 in. (47.63 x 44.45 cm)

Queen Esther with Mordechai

Similar to many stories set in royal courts, full of intrigues, secrets, and spies, the next event of importance in Esther's story happens after an unspecified length of time, when Haman conspires to obliterate the Jewish minority living in the Persian kingdom, for which he obtains the king's approval through shrewd and devious conniving. I have chosen to represent this dire threat with only one scene – the moment that Mordechai reveals to the queen this shocking turn of events.

A triptych, *Queen Esther with Mordechai,* depicts the two in the king's harem at his palace in Susa. Mordechai has just brought Haman's decree announcing the planned genocide of Esther's people in Persia. She reels in horror as she reads the scroll. Although the Bible describes this verbal exchange as having been conveyed back and forth by palace eunuchs (since outsiders, particularly males, were prohibited from entering a harem), I show them together to create a more visceral scene. As portrayed, Mordechai commands his cousin to beg the king, her husband, for forgiveness and leniency toward her people. After first refusing, Esther is convinced by Mordechai's words and logic. She realizes at this moment that her role as the king's submissive wife is about to change, and she prepares to sacrifice her own life in order to reveal Haman's secret plans to the king and seek justice. For this leadership role she will need all the wisdom and courage she can muster.

She realizes at this moment that her role as the king's submissive wife is about to change, and she prepares to sacrifice her own life in order to reveal Haman's secret plans to the king and seek justice.

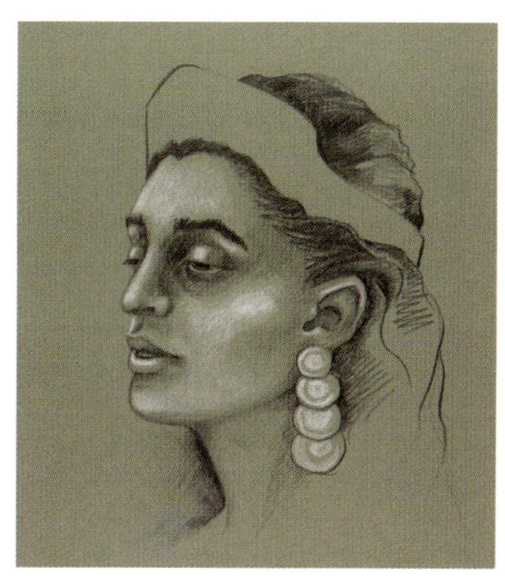

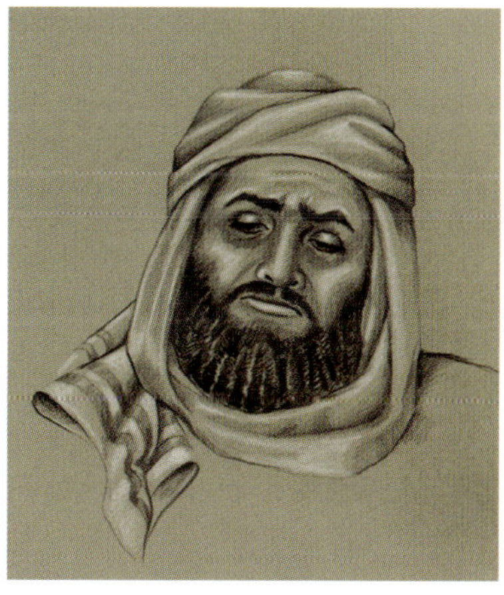

Left, top, above
For *Queen Esther with Mordechai,* sketch, graphite on tracing paper, 19.5 x 18.5 in. (49.53 x 46.99 cm); sketch of queen, graphite and pastel on paper, 20 x 17 in. (50.80 x 43.18 cm); sketch of Mordechai, graphite and pastel on paper, 20 x 17 in. (50.80 x 43.18 cm)

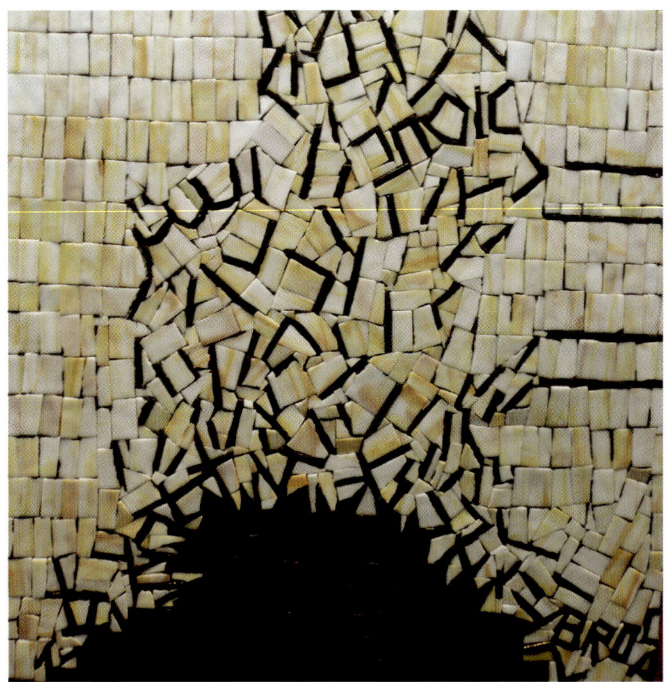

Detail from *Queen Esther with Mordechai*

The middle panel of the triptych shows Queen Esther with Mordechai, while the side panels represent the palace's ornate architecture and vast riches. In this work and throughout the series, I aim for an authentic look consisting of architectural details, furniture and household items, body and facial features, and clothing styles. This mosaic features images of the capitals of the well-known Persian columns from the Persepolis ruins, the often-seen winged bulls with human heads called *lamassu,* which also appear at Persepolis (at the Gate of Xerxes), and other Persian references such as the twelve-petal flower, a common motif in the architecture of the period.

In the right panel of the triptych, the image of the column melts down at the bottom, first becoming two dimensional and monochromatic, next a line drawing, and finally the line pixelating into small colored fragments that form a shapeless mound of tesserae. This visual degeneration symbolizes the defeat and destruction of the Persian empire soon after the reign of King Ahashvayrosh and Queen Esther, representing as well the basics of mosaic construction where the technology of tesserae and modern pixelization intriguingly coincide. The falling pixels or tesserae also form Esther's name in both Hebrew and Farsi.

In the left panel the Farsi says "Mordechai." Esther's name appears embroidered in Hebrew on her clothing. The wrought iron motif makes a showing again, here in a window at the background of the central panel, taking the form of a lattice and representing how keenly protected harems were.

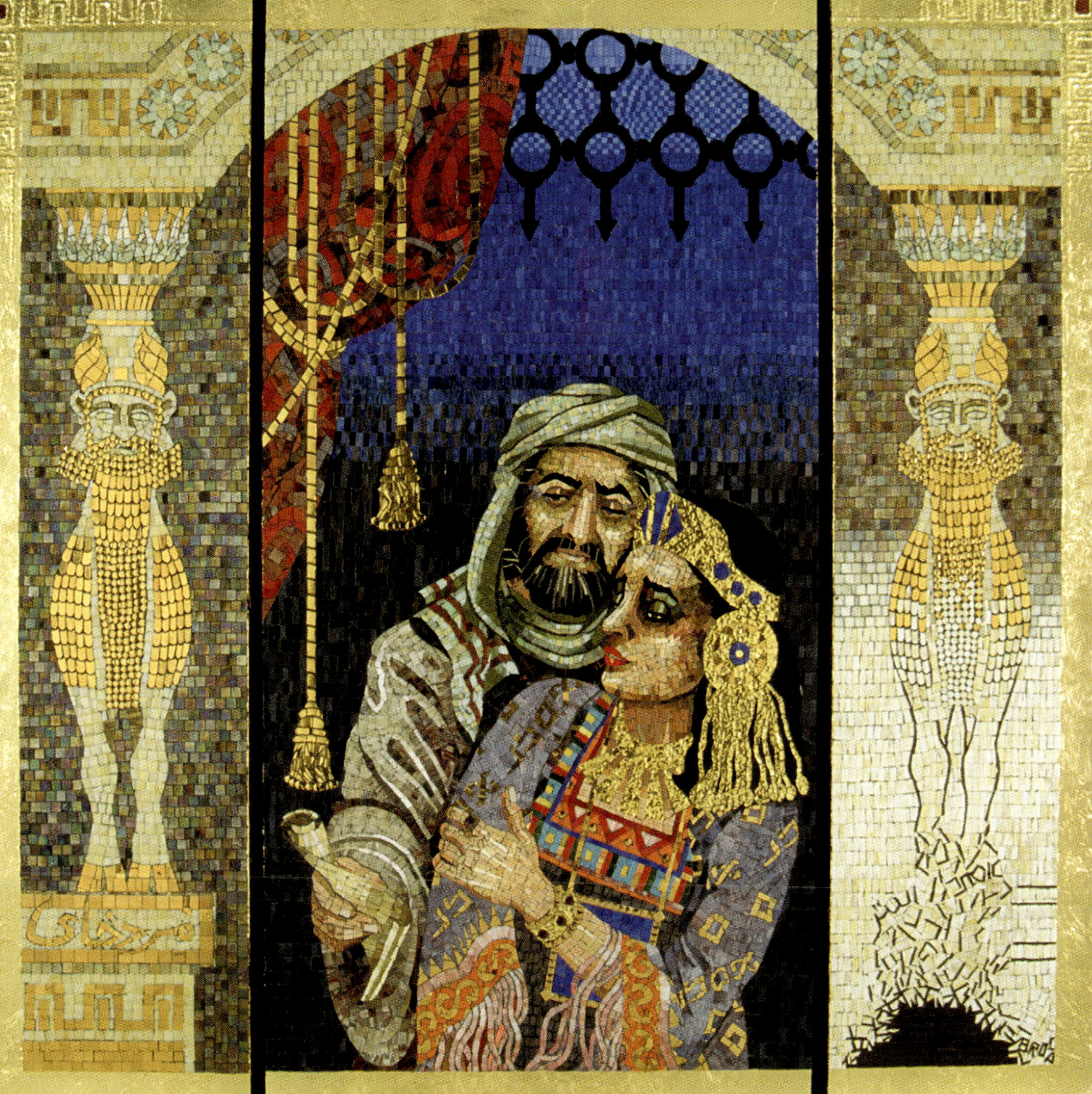
مردخای

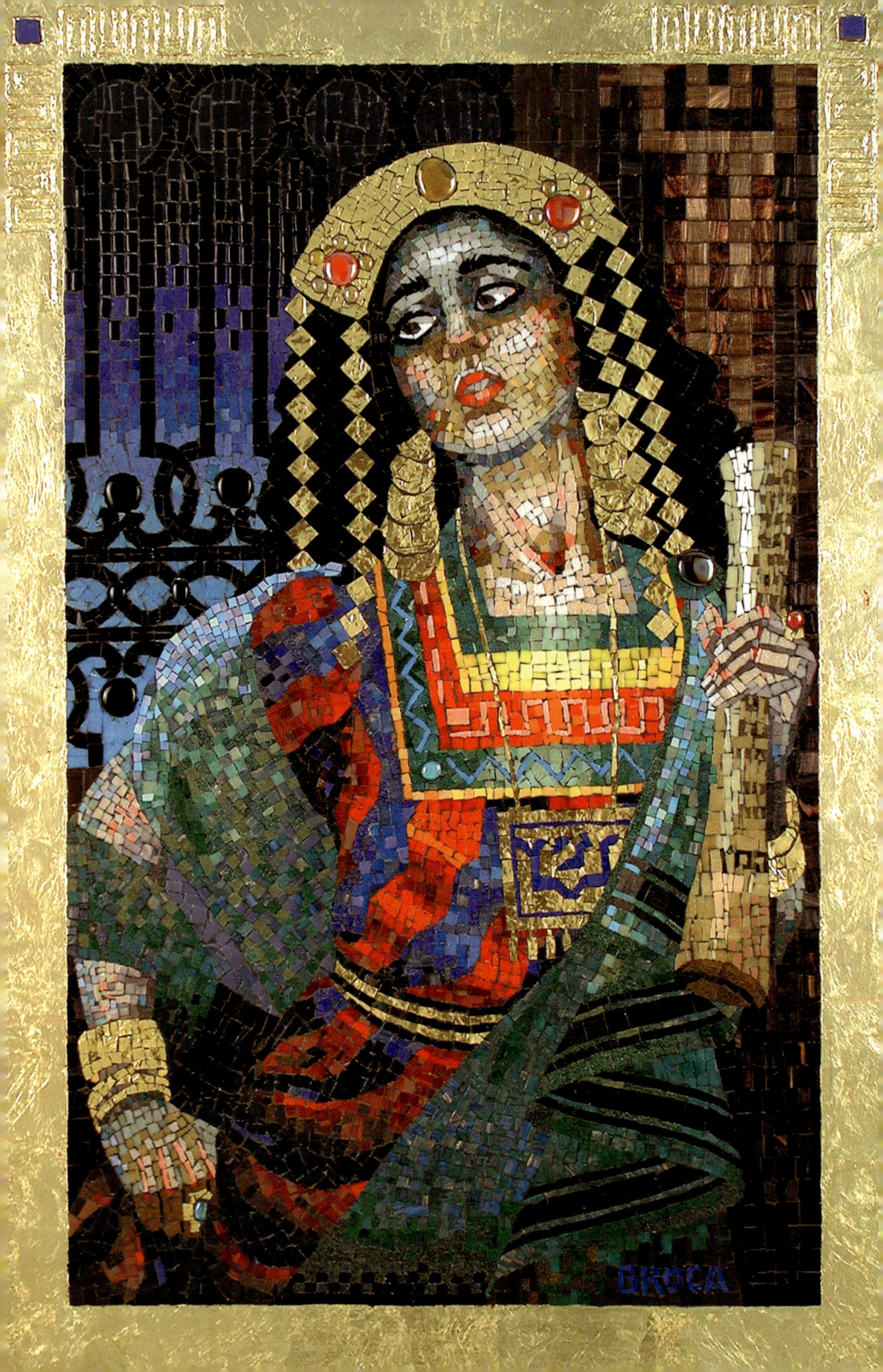

BROCA

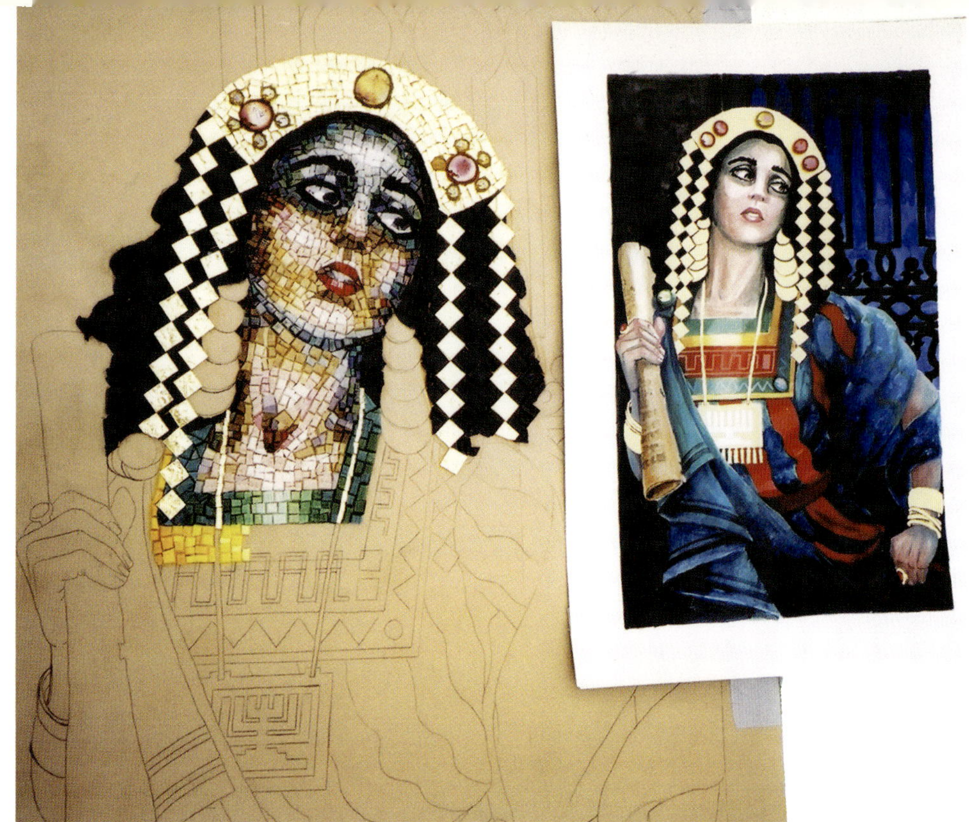

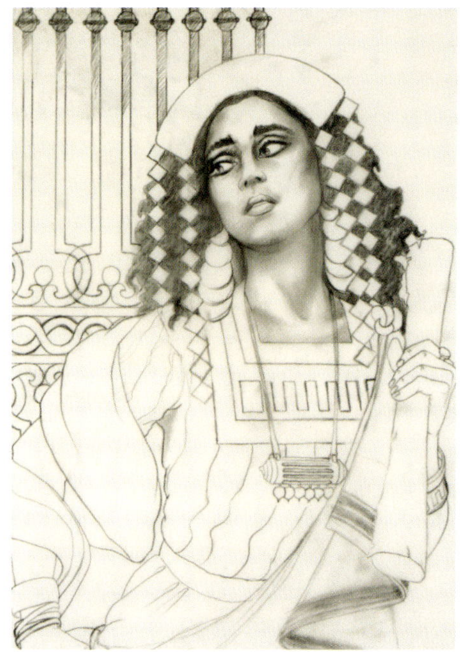

Queen Esther Holding Evidence of Haman's Guilt

Queen Esther Holding Evidence of Haman's Guilt follows the lines of the plot. The queen is seen sneaking close to the walls of the dark corridor leading to her chamber, terrified of being followed by the palace spies, holding in her hand Haman's decree that Mordechai gave her only minutes before. Her facial expression shows her fear of what may follow. Exaggerated chiaroscuro is used to emphasize the drama of the moment.

In her hands, she holds the scroll with Haman's order for all Israelites to be executed on a certain day. This massacre would all but totally obliterate the Hebrew lineage from the face of the earth – hence eliminating Christianity in the future as well – since the Israelites sent by King Cyrus back to Jerusalem to rebuild the Temple were too few in number to preserve the Jewish lineage. Thus, Queen Esther's task to stop the genocide has monumental, historic consequence. She must devise a strategy that guarantees a successful outcome. Her timing and appearance must be impeccable.

The stylized Hebrew word *Zion* on Esther's necklace pendant is purposely written in reverse, just as Leonardo da Vinci did in his notebook in trying to hide his thoughts lest they lead to otherwise certain arrest and trial by the Inquisition. Remember, Queen Esther is bound by Mordechai to secrecy; her background must remain hidden from everyone at King Ahashvayrosh's court. Only a member of her tribe could understand the message on the pendant written in reverse.

Queen Esther's task to stop the genocide has monumental, historic consequence. She must devise a strategy that guarantees a successful outcome. Her timing and appearance must be impeccable.

Facing page
Queen Esther Holding Evidence of Haman's Guilt, 2002
Venetian gold glass and smalti on panel
48 x 32 in. (121.92 x 81.28 cm)

Above left and right
Queen Esther Holding Evidence of Haman's Guilt, work in progress, with painted sketch, acrylic on illustration board, 29 x 21 in. (73.66 x 53.34 cm); sketch, graphite on tracing paper, 25 x 18.5 in. (63.50 x 46.99 cm)

Queen Esther with Scroll

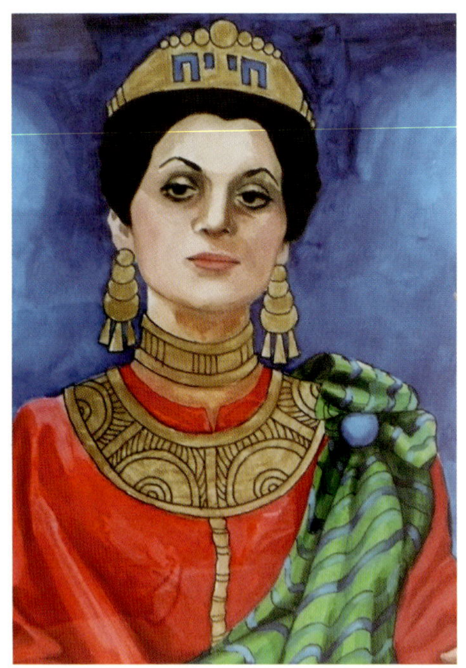

Queen Esther with Scroll shows a private moment in the drama as Esther contemplates the gravity of the decree perpetrated by Haman. This is the second of the two mosaics that portray Esther's state of mind, at the moment of highest crisis, as she is about to embark on the ensuing, life-threatening task of thwarting the proclamation. Here, I portray her as a thoughtful figure, with eyes full of unspoken misfortunes. Concealing her identity requires that she remain calm and collected, despite the ominous threat, and to prepare for the task ahead she conceives the idea that the Jews hold a three-day fast. Her preoccupied gaze indicates her inner struggle as she devises a plan that assures both her people and she will survive. The head ornament has the letters *het* and *yod,* which form the word *hy,* meaning "life," signifying that she must protect the gift of life for those condemned to die. The plan forms in her mind as she stares blankly out to space but full of thought.

Her preoccupied gaze indicates her inner struggle as she devises a plan that assures both her people and she will survive.

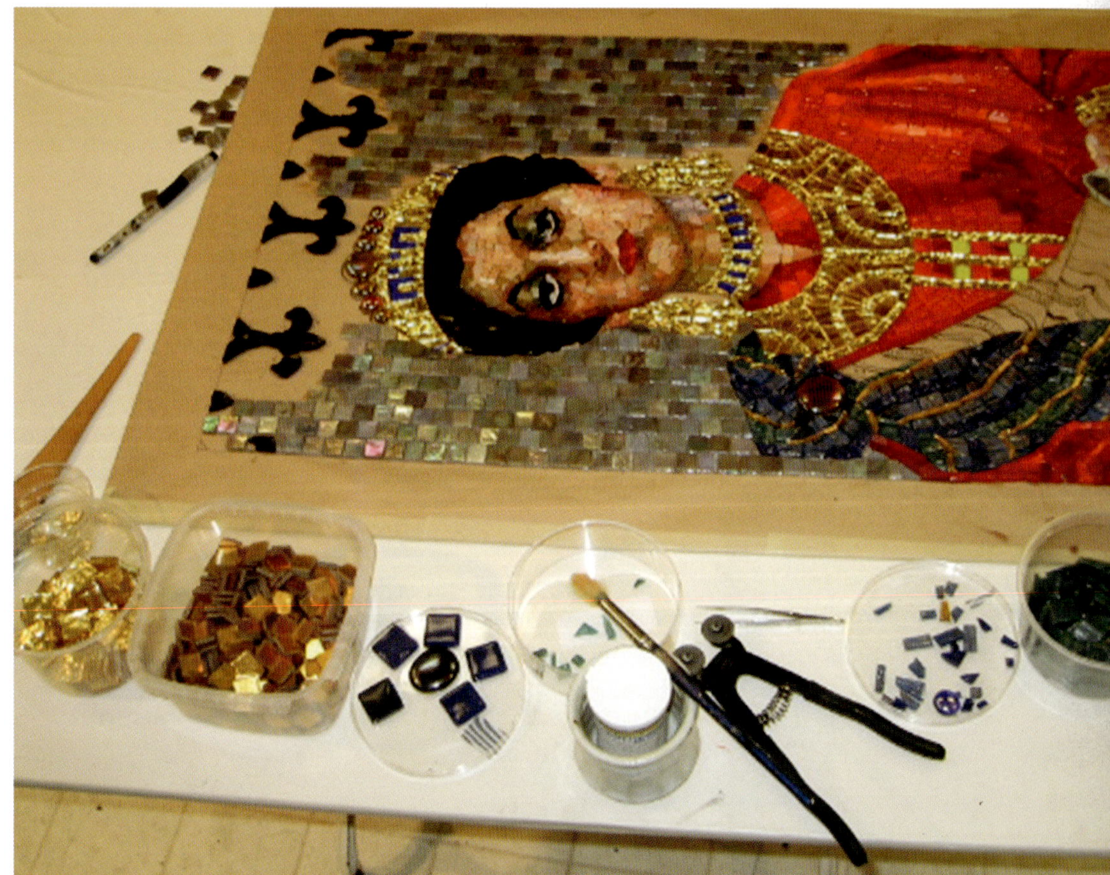

Above
Cropped painted sketch for *Queen Esther with Scroll,* acrylic on illustration board

Right
Queen Esther with Scroll, work in progress

Facing page
Queen Esther with Scroll, 2005
Venetian gold glass and smalti on panel
26 x 35 in. (66.04 x 88.90 cm)

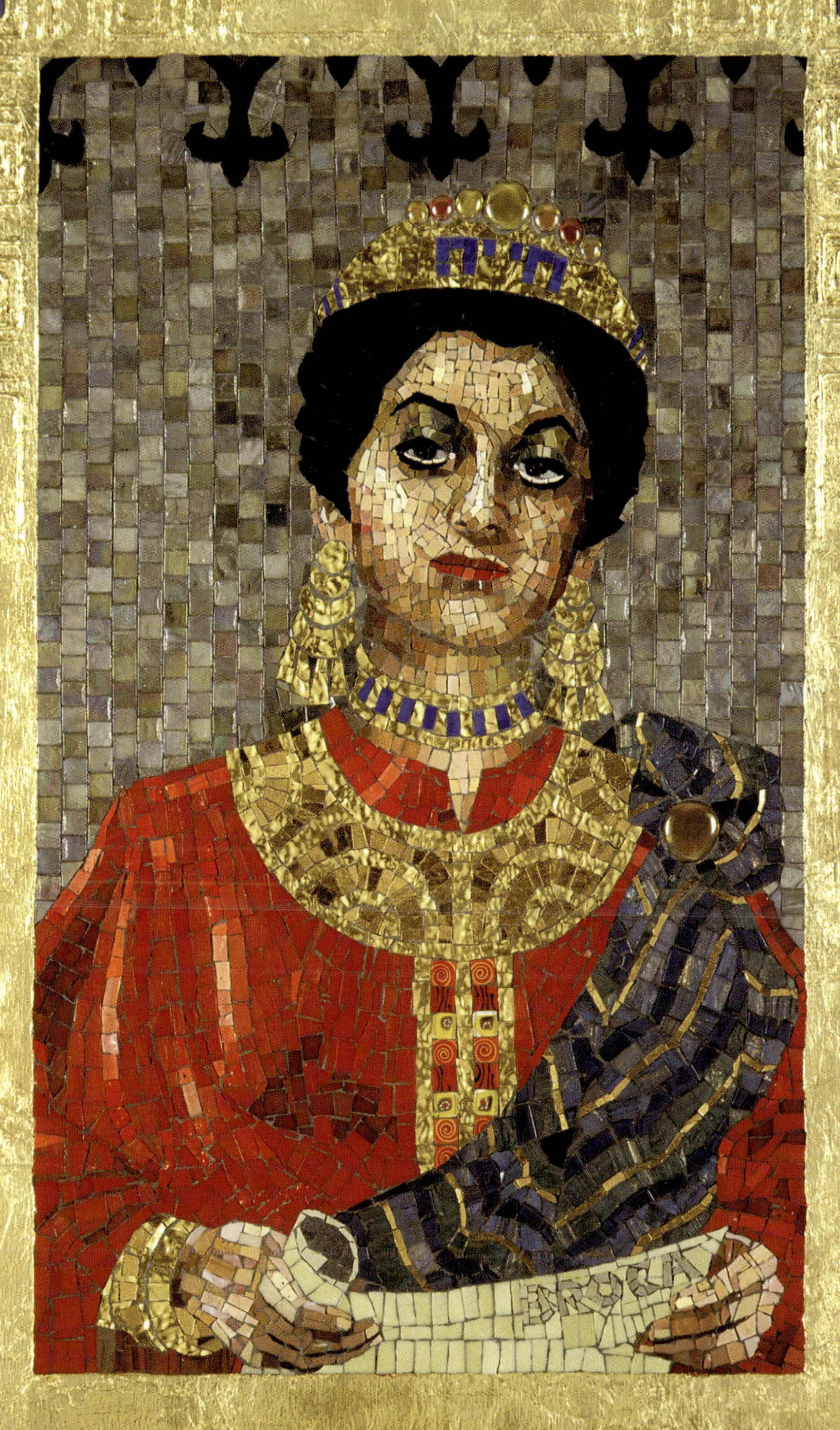

Queen Esther Seeking Permission to Speak

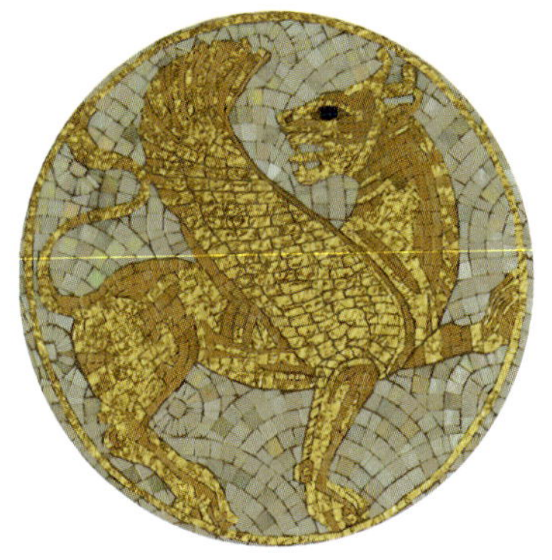

Queen Esther Seeking Permission to Speak shows the queen as she confronts her daunting mission and determinedly sets out to strike ahead. A diptych, this mosaic portrays the first part of Esther's secret plan, as she appears in the great hall before the throne, precariously uninvited but beautifully dressed and bejeweled.

> She was trembling from the audacity of her action; but at the same time she also probably looked charming, for Xerxes, instead of displaying anger at such an infraction of a rule imposed to spare him from the tumultuous importunities of harem intrigue, turned his golden scepter towards her to show her she was forgiven.[8]

For the left panel of the diptych, my husband posed for the figure of the king, wearing a taffeta fabric I bought specially for the occasion. As in all the other mosaics, I changed my model's facial features to match those of a typical Persian in the fifth century BCE, plenty examples of which can be seen in the magnificent carvings on Persepolis palace's outer walls.

In the right panel, Queen Esther bows to her husband, Ahashvayrosh. The king appears completely taken back by Esther's beauty and gladly makes the lifesaving gesture of extending the royal scepter, signifying his approval for her to approach and speak. In one hand she holds a mask away from the king's eyes, symbolizing the facade she must present to the world. In the other hand she holds a corner of her rich skirt, embroidered with her name. The wrought iron motif in this work acts as a decorative divider between queen and king. The throne is pure gold and silver, with precious stones embedded in the lamassu carvings that act as arm rests. Once more, the lavish extravagance of the king's surroundings speak loud and clear of the power he holds over his subjects.

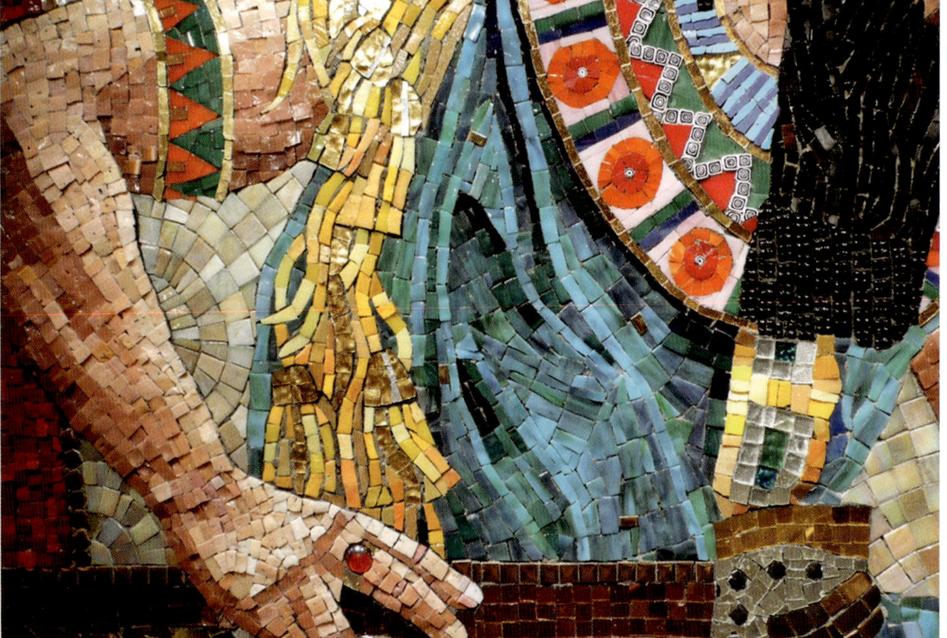

Detail from *Queen Esther Seeking Permission to Speak*

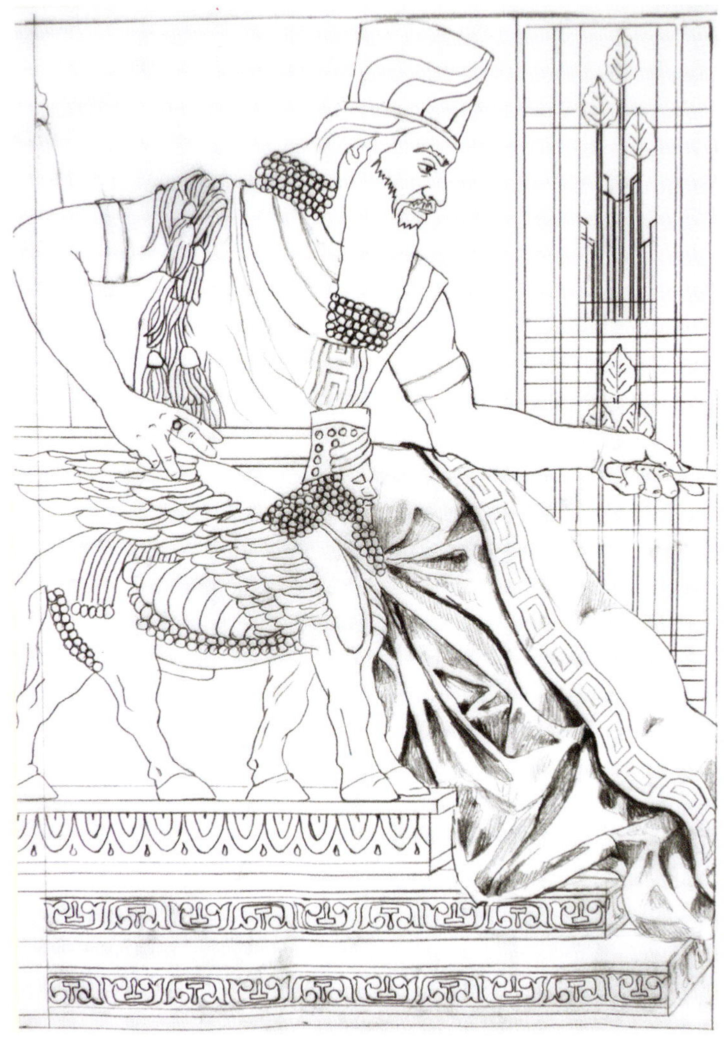

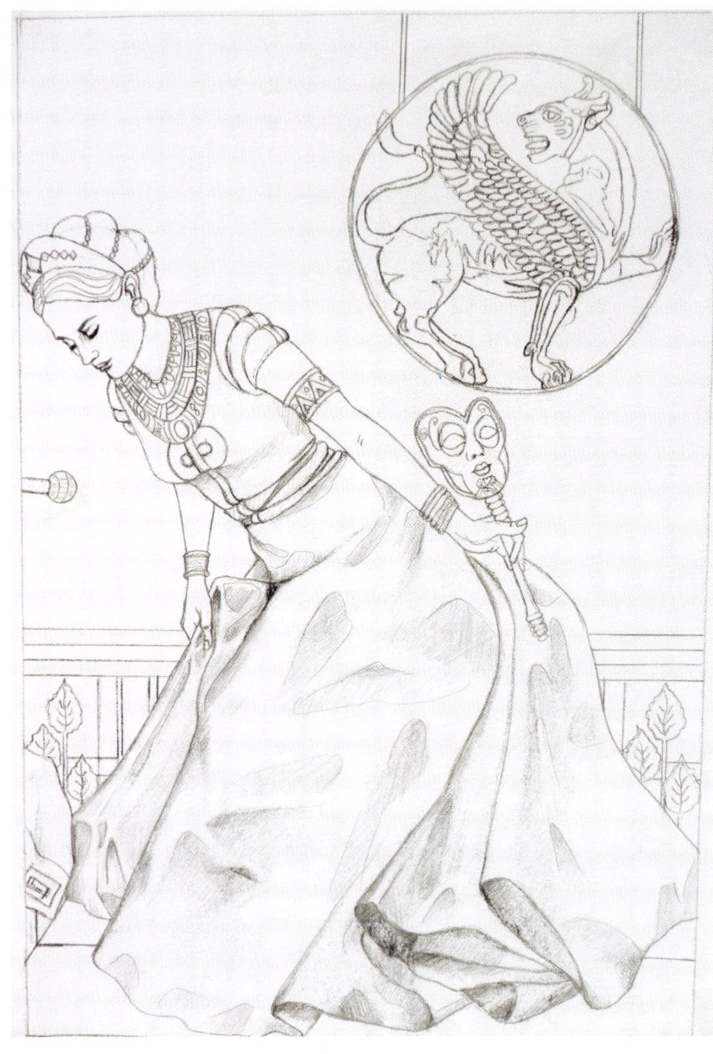

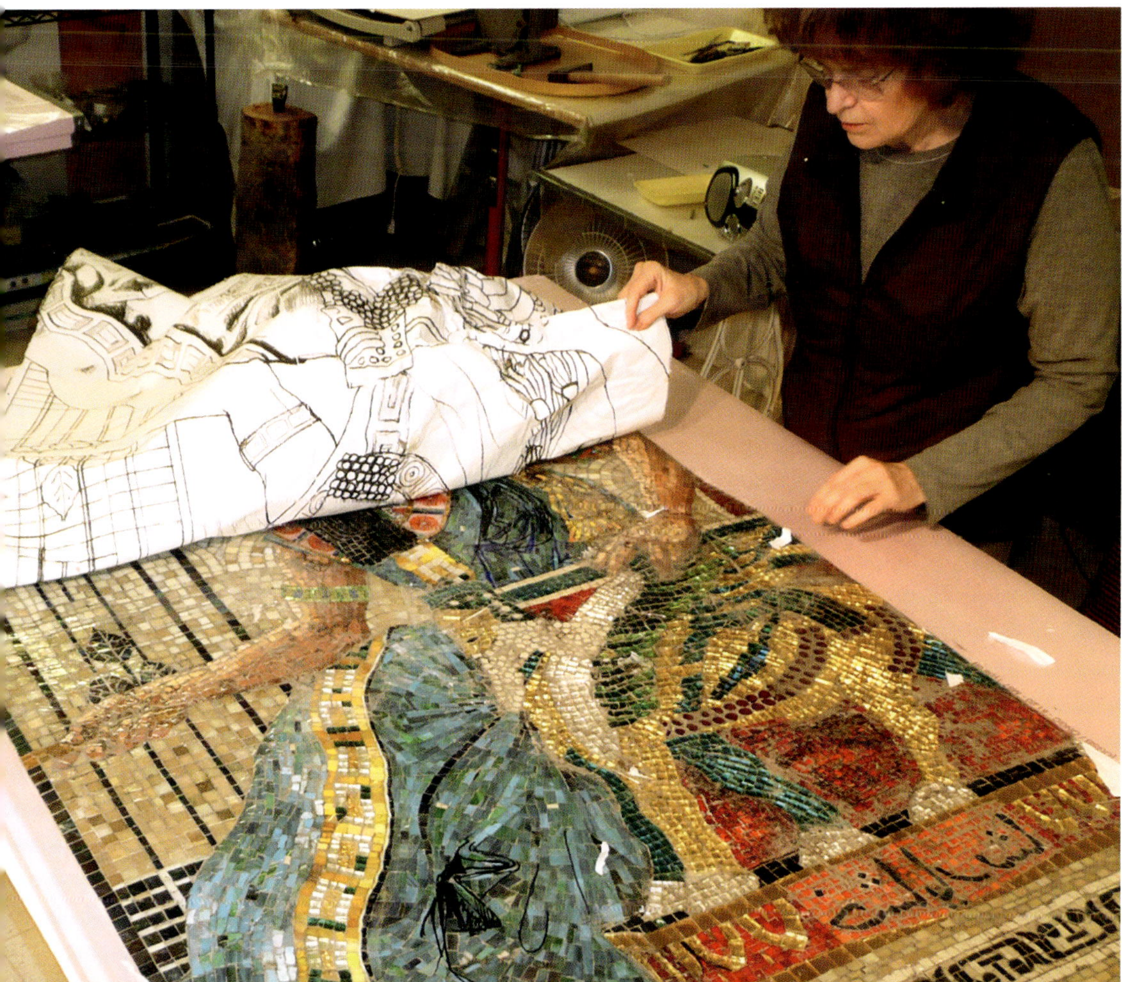

Above left and right
Sketches for *Queen Esther Seeking Permission to Speak,* graphite on tracing paper, 12 x 17 in. (30.48 x 43.18 cm)

Left
Queen Esther Seeking Permission to Speak, work in progress

Overleaf
Queen Esther Seeking Permission to Speak, diptych, 2009
Smalti, gems, Venetian glass, gold smalti, and millefiori on honeycomb panel
64 x 88 in. (162.56 x 223.52 cm)

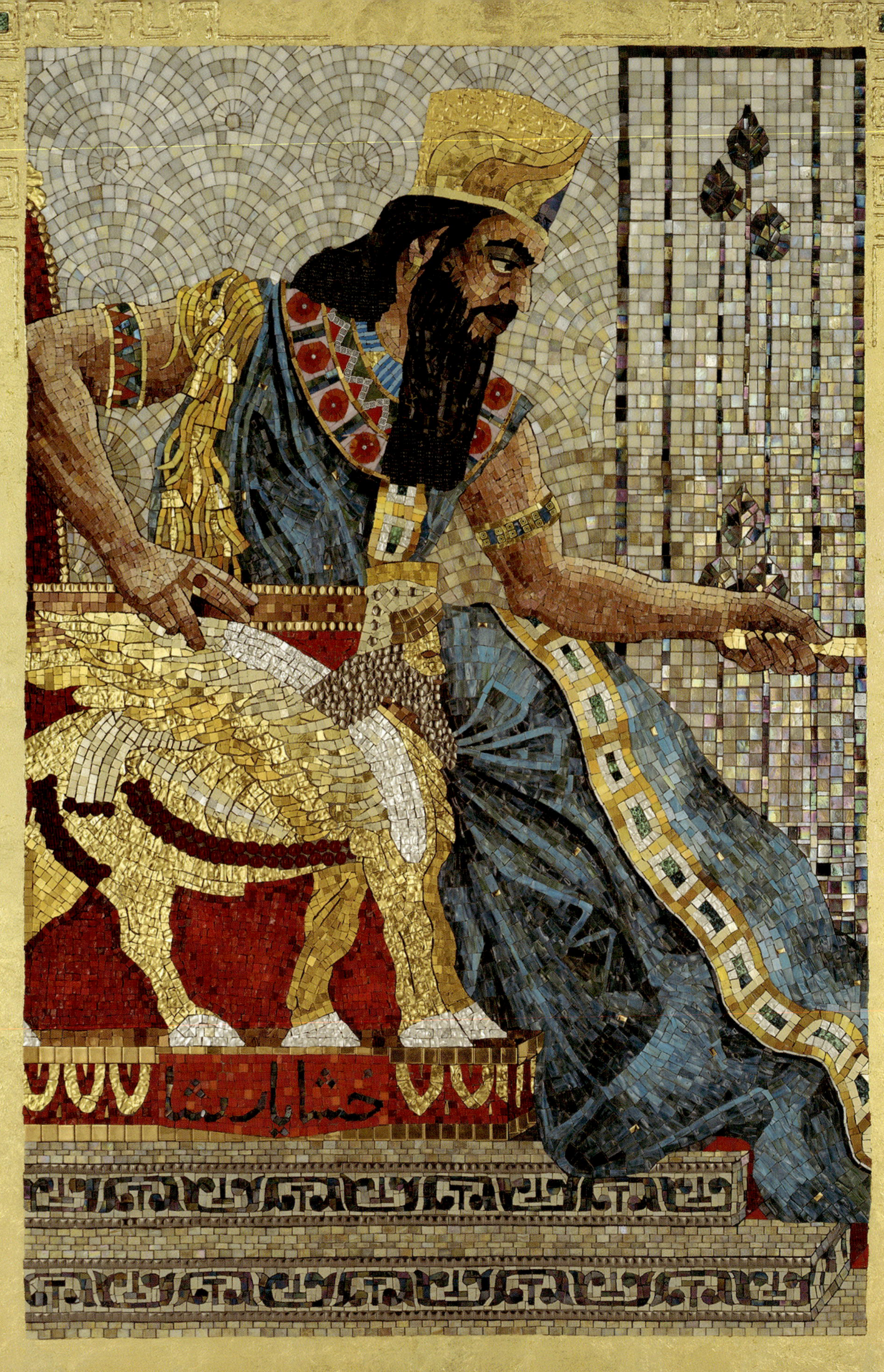
خشایارشا

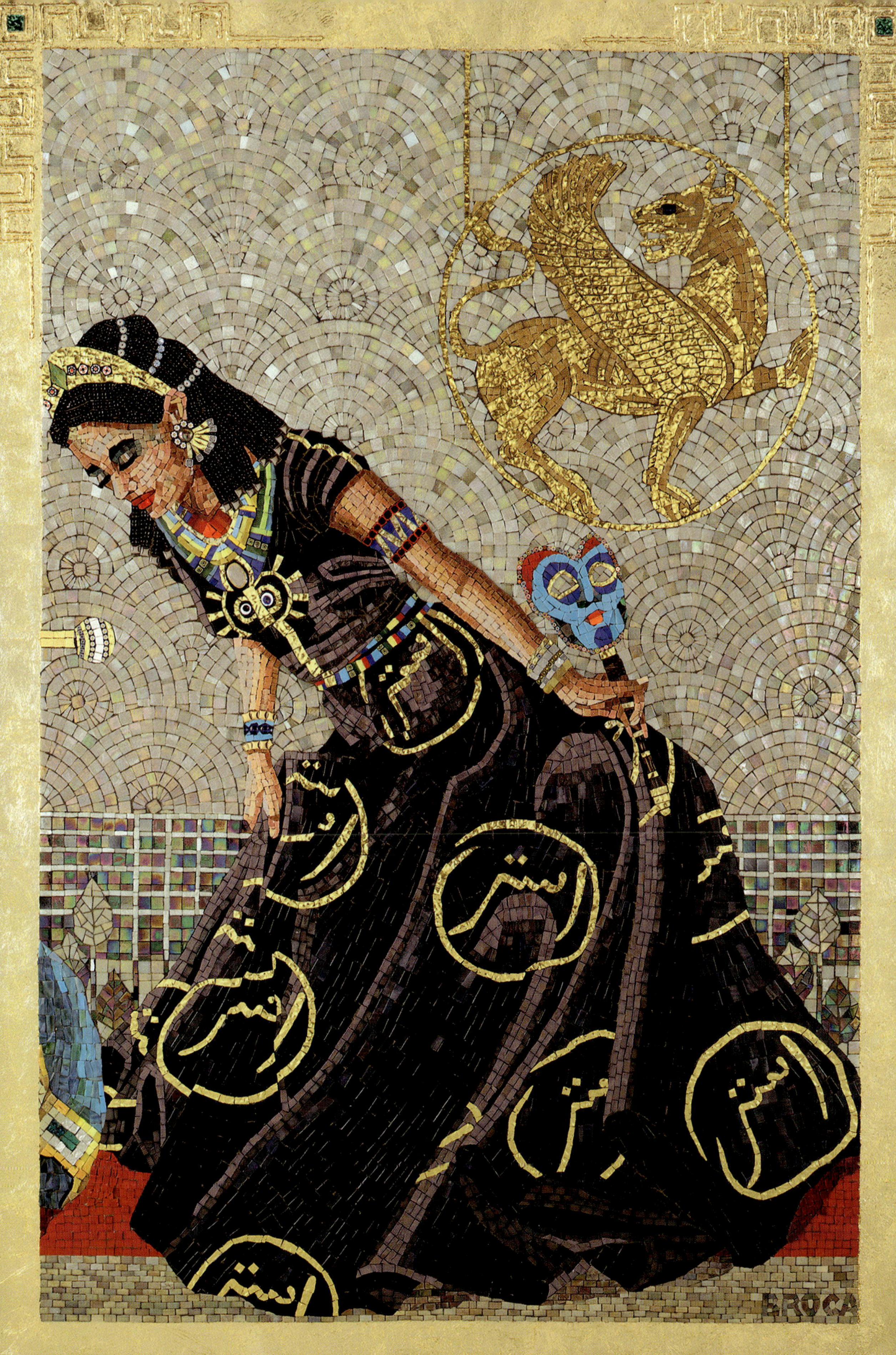
BROCA

Queen Esther's Banquet

In *Queen Esther's Banquet,* I portray the story's second banquet, which the queen had proposed the king hold and which, besides themselves, only Haman attends. A diptych, the two panels when displayed are connected by a piece of actual wrought iron of the same design as appears in the mosaic. The symbolism of this prisonlike iron evokes the fact that women are excluded from the man's world, especially when business and political affairs were discussed. Could it also point to the chasm between the two cultures, though in the story they are connected by marriage?

The mosaic shows both the king and queen reclining on furniture specifically designed for dining, a custom shared by the ancient Romans and Jews. In the highly charged scene, Esther points toward Haman, accusing him of plotting genocide in the kingdom. The royal couple both stare out at the unseen Haman, the king with a doubtful look on his inebriated face and Queen Esther with a determined and accusatory expression. This mosaic implies that her serious accusation can result only in Haman's execution. Nevertheless, as the Jewish Agency website tells it, Esther faces a further challenge:

> Esther emerges highly successful from her plan, but her role does not end here: the decree has not yet been annulled, although the major obstacle has been removed. After Haman is hanged, Esther once again has to approach the king [probably at some personal risk] in order to seek the annulment of the decree. Her willingness to sacrifice herself in order to save her people is boundless.[9]

Queen Esther's Banquet echoes the floor mosaics of antiquity, but with a twist. Like its antecedents, the peripheral ends of the mosaic feature monochromatic tesserae, heavily outlined. These, however, burst toward the center of the mosaic with bright contemporary glass colors. This combination of an ancient monochromatic treatment with a contemporary one expresses mosaic-making's long heritage.

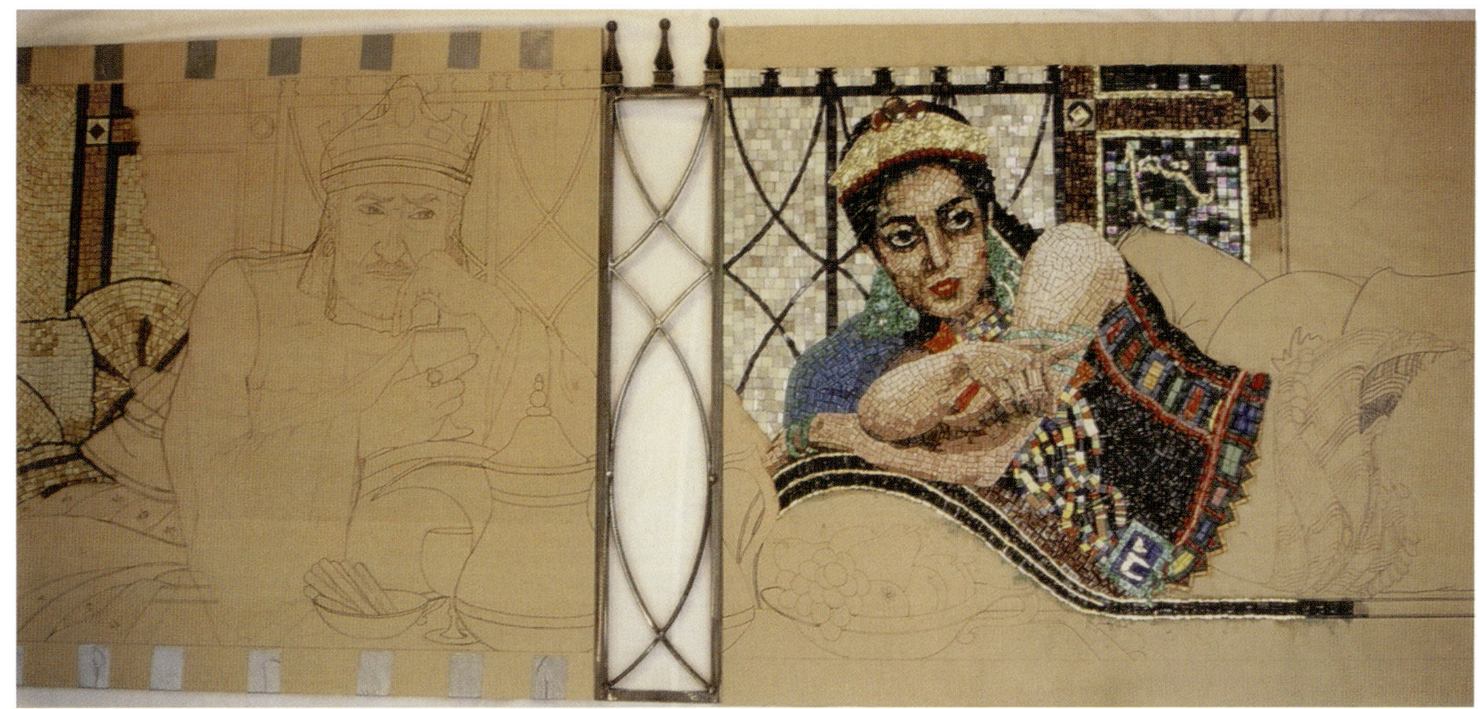

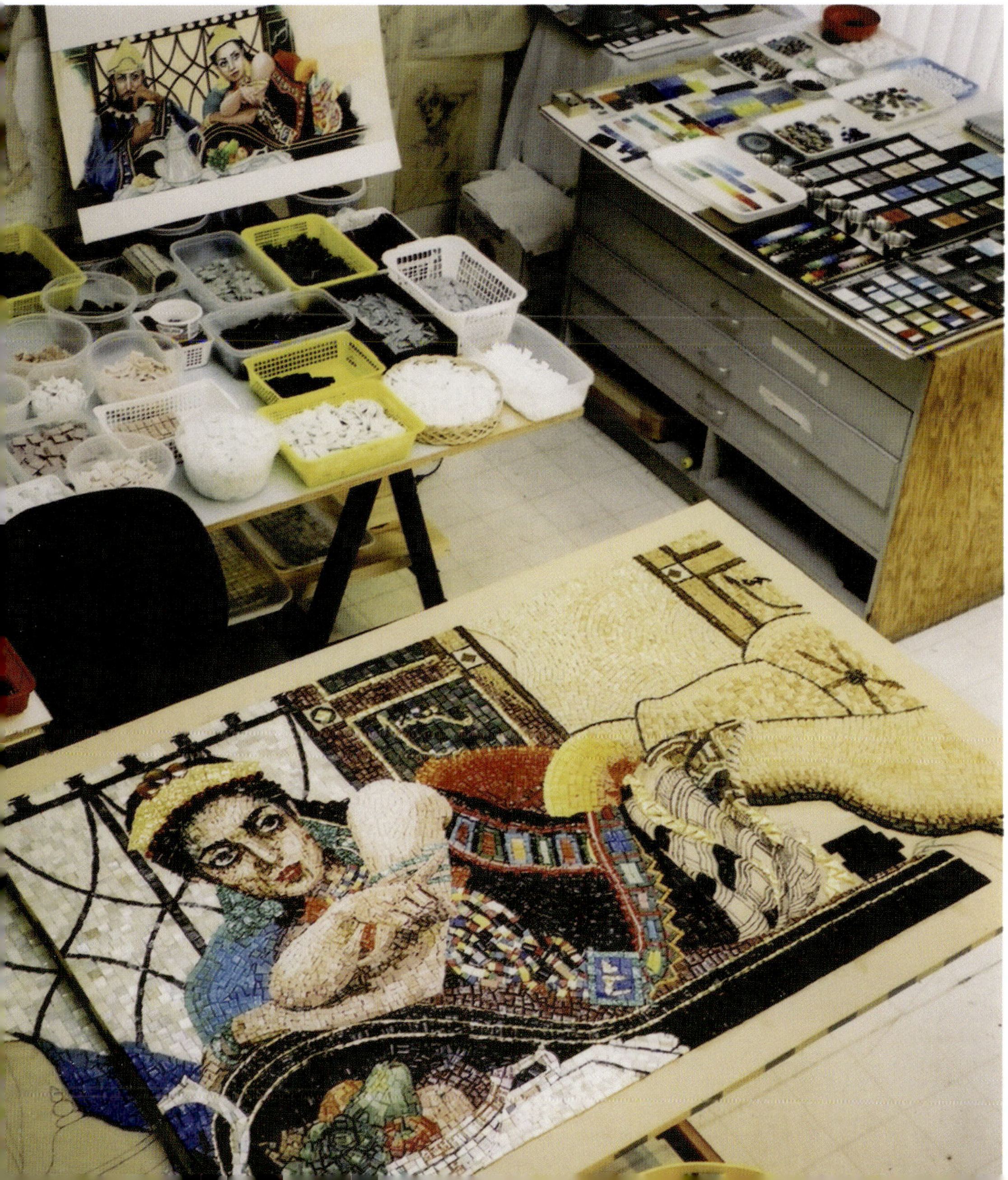

Above and left

Queen Esther's Banquet, work in progress

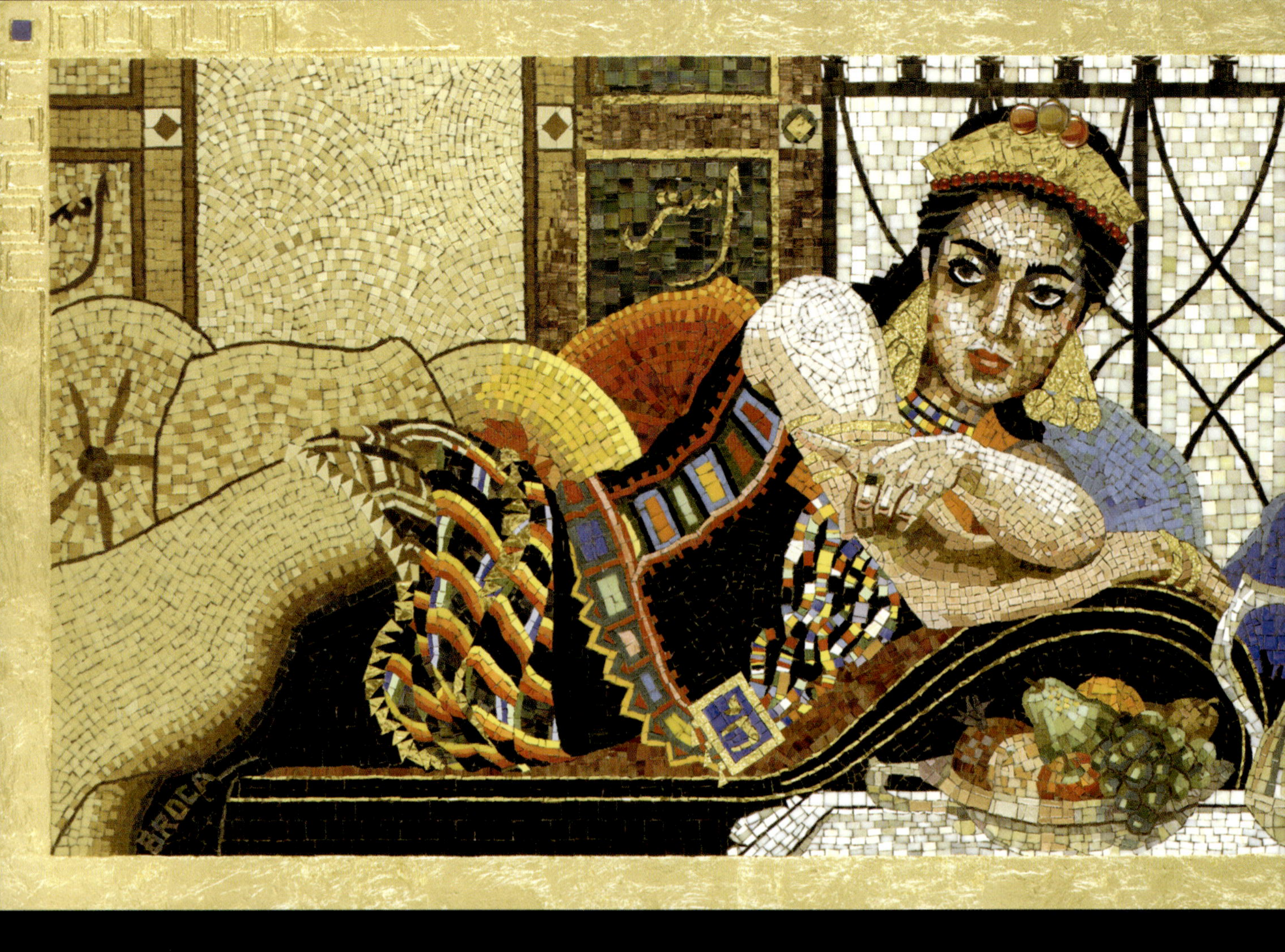

I feel reluctant to discuss any finished artworks, preferring instead to allow the viewer the pleasurable and creative act of personal interpretation.

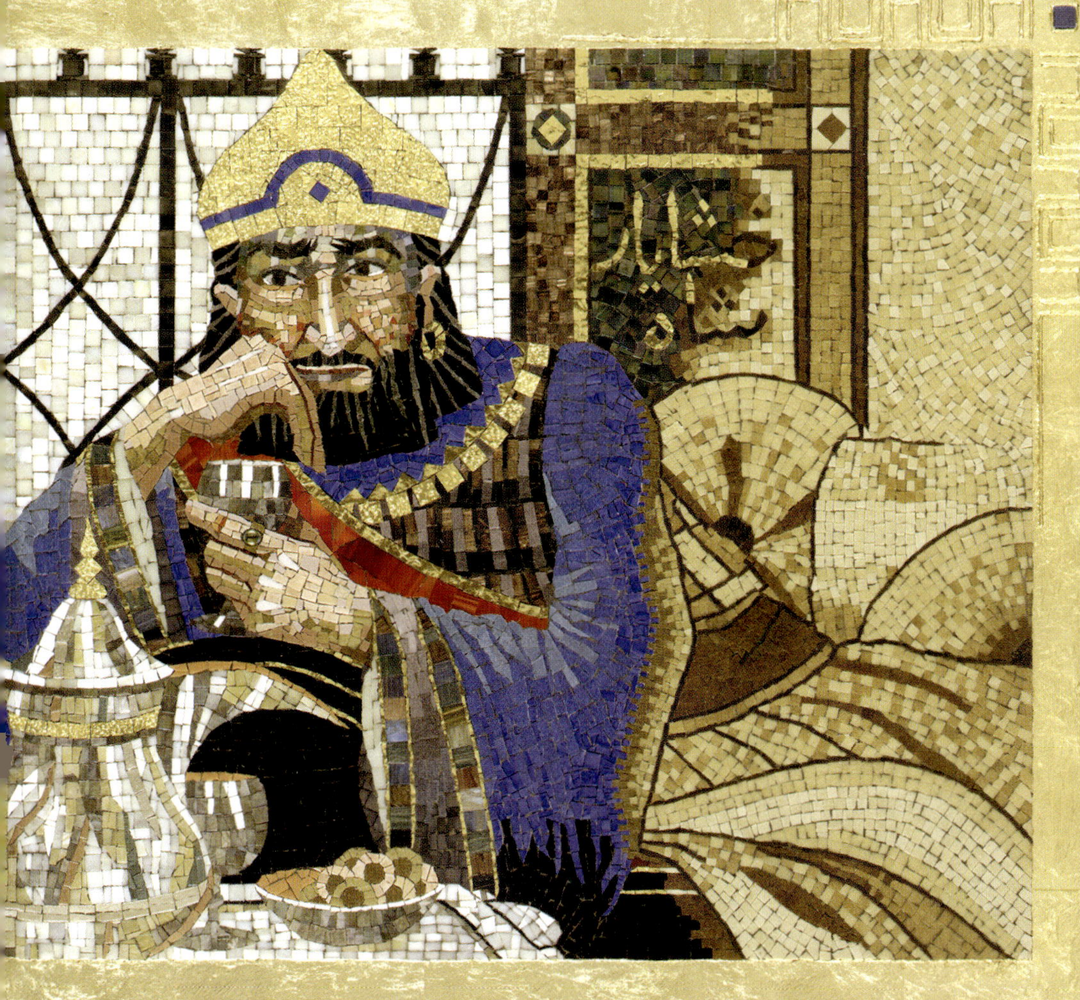

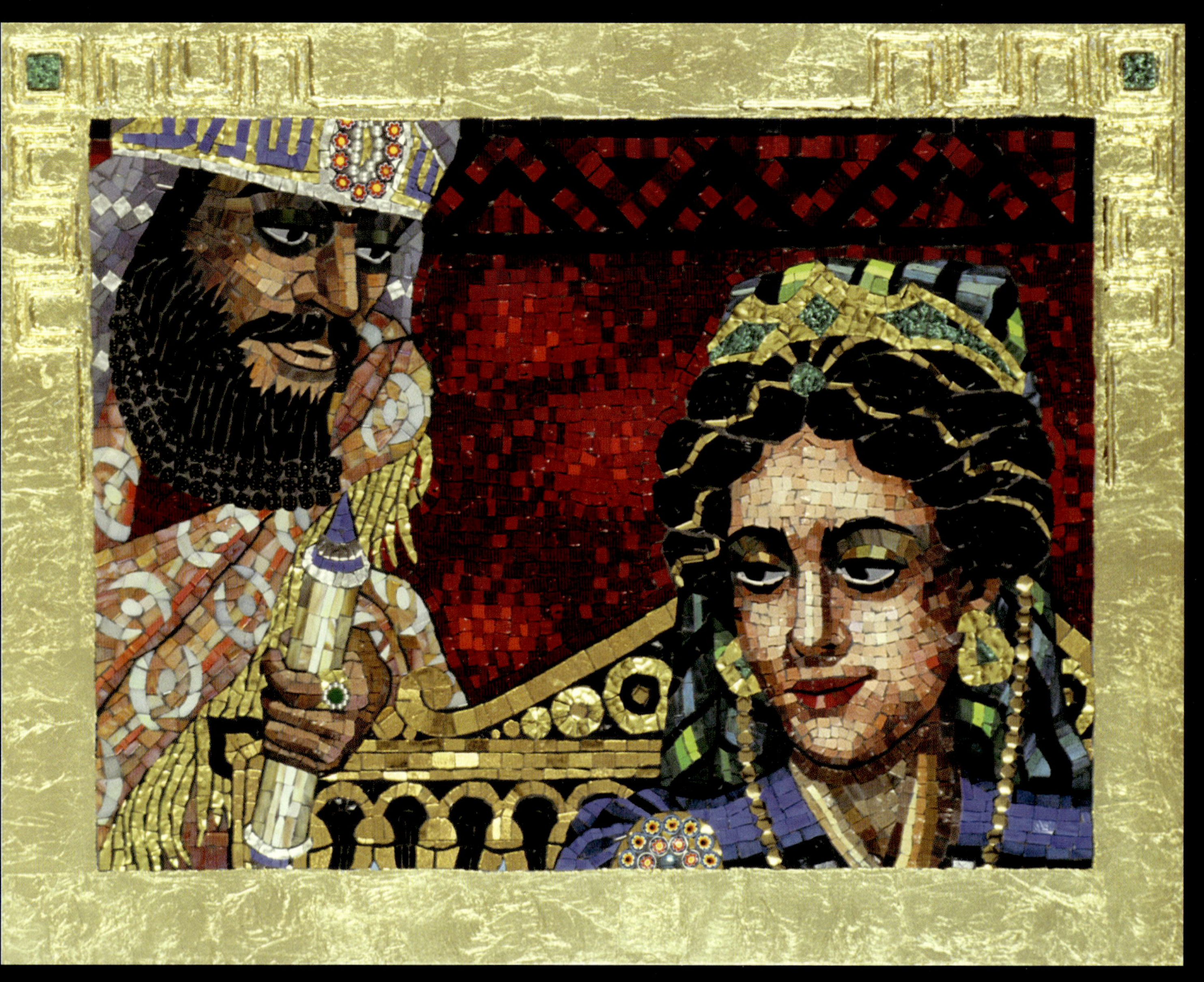

Surreptitious Dialogue, 2007
Millefiori, pearls, Venetian gold glass,

Surreptitious Dialogue

Mordechai and Esther must now plot a further move, and as depicted in *Surreptitious Dialogue*, his suggested maneuver seems to appeal to the queen. Together, the two plan how to stop the massacre of the Persian Jews, the result of Haman's deviously arranged royal proclamation. (According to the Bible account, royal decrees once issued could not be rescinded, an interpretation since challenged by some historians but that still applies to this story.) Once again, her cousin tells her, Esther must seek the king's permission to speak and this time ask that a new edict be sent to all corners of his kingdom announcing the right of Jewish citizens to defend themselves on the day the first decree had designated they be slaughtered.

The conversation between the cousins is secret. What the future will bring is unknown. Mordechai whispers his idea in Esther's ear and she smiles scoffingly, visualizing the next step. The tension of this dialogue is expressed in the diagonal composition and the numerous triangles formed by positive and negative spaces. To further accentuate the dramatically decisive exchange, background distractions are largely eliminated, allowing the viewer's eye to focus on the facial expressions.

The mosaic shows Mordechai dressed in opulent Persian style, now that Haman is dead and he has gained the highest position in court, next to the king. To ensure that the image of Mordechai attired in this fashion and seen communicating privately with Queen Esther is not confused with her husband, the king, Mordechai's headdress features Hebrew letters, albeit cut in the middle and difficult to read.

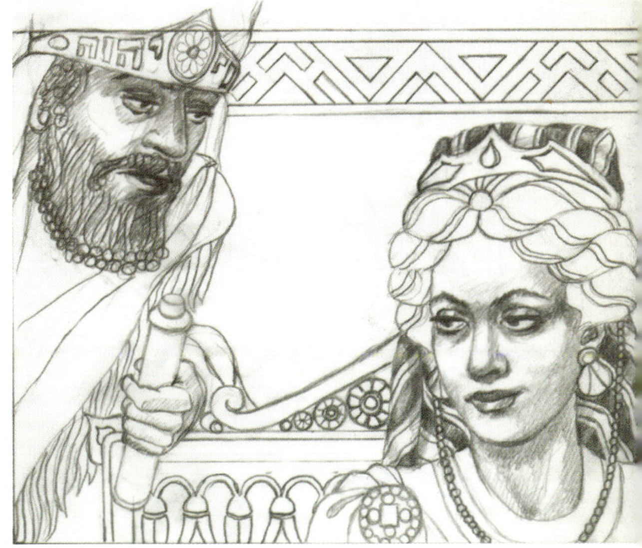

Top
Surreptitious Dialogue, work in progress

Above
Sketch for *Surreptitious Dialogue*, graphite on tracing paper, 6 x 9 in. (15.24 x 22.86 cm)

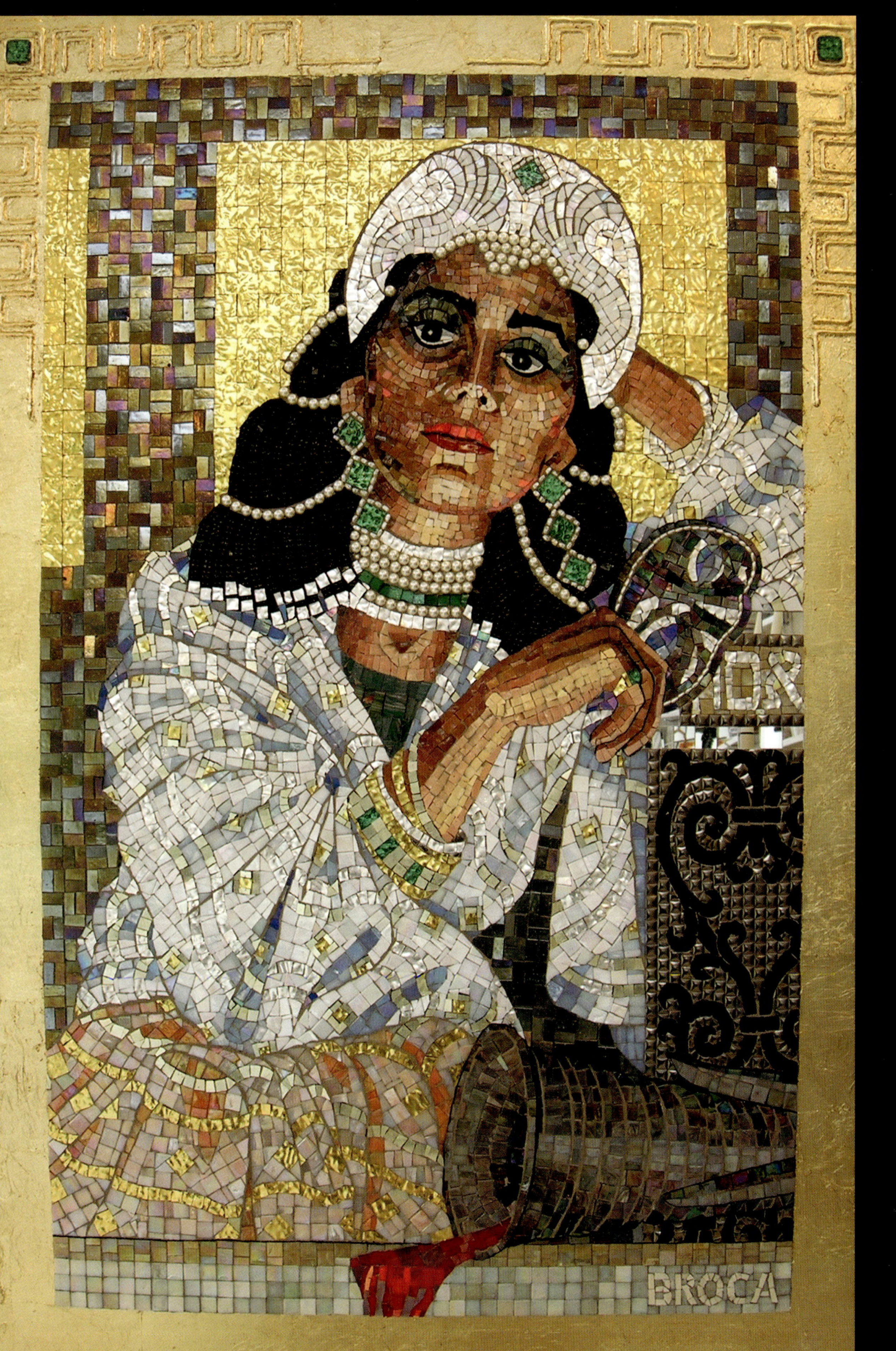
BROCA

Queen Esther Revealing Her True Identity

Queen Esther Revealing Her True Identity, the last mosaic of the series, shows a mature and confident Esther at her ultimate moment, triumphant and victorious, successful in her final appeal to the king. Wearing her most expensive and beautiful attire, she has removed the mask that had symbolically hidden her true identity, revealing now a fully empowered, intelligent, and confident leader. The wrought iron motif makes a final reappearance, but now innocuously so, forming part of the furniture decoration on which she rests her arm, the Hebrew name of Esther written above.

On the table, a *rhyton* (a Persian gold or silver drinking vessel) has been knocked over, spilling its red wine contents. The wine symbolizes the blood of the Hebrew people that would have been spilled had Esther not averted the catastrophe by disclosing Haman's genocidal plan to her husband the king. However, blood will still be spilled during the battle between Haman's Persian supporters and the Israelites, only this time, under the king's second decree, the Israelites in a fairer fight will be allowed to defend themselves.

In this mosaic, Queen Esther is treated iconically as a paragon of supreme leadership, loyalty, wisdom, and vision. In a patriarchal world, both Hebrew and Persian, this unique female figure succeeds in bringing peace through accommodation, cooperation, negotiation, and brilliant maneuvering. Her heroic status enables her to become a role model for all women, both then and now. In typical Byzantine iconic style, Queen Esther would be shown with a gold halo. Although a so-called halo first appears in the Hebrew Bible – above Moses' head when he descends from Mount Sinai with the tablets inscribed by God – I felt unsure of giving one to another Jewish figure. So instead a halo-like square surrounds her head, similar to the treatment in *Esther's Offering.*

In a patriarchal world, both Hebrew and Persian, this unique female figure succeeds in bringing peace through accommodation, cooperation, negotiation, and brilliant maneuvering.

Facing page
Queen Esther Revealing Her True Identity, 2006
Venetian glass, smalti, pearls,
and Venetian gold glass on panel
48 x 33 in. (121.92 x 83.82 cm)

Below
Queen Esther Revealing Her True Identity,
work in progress

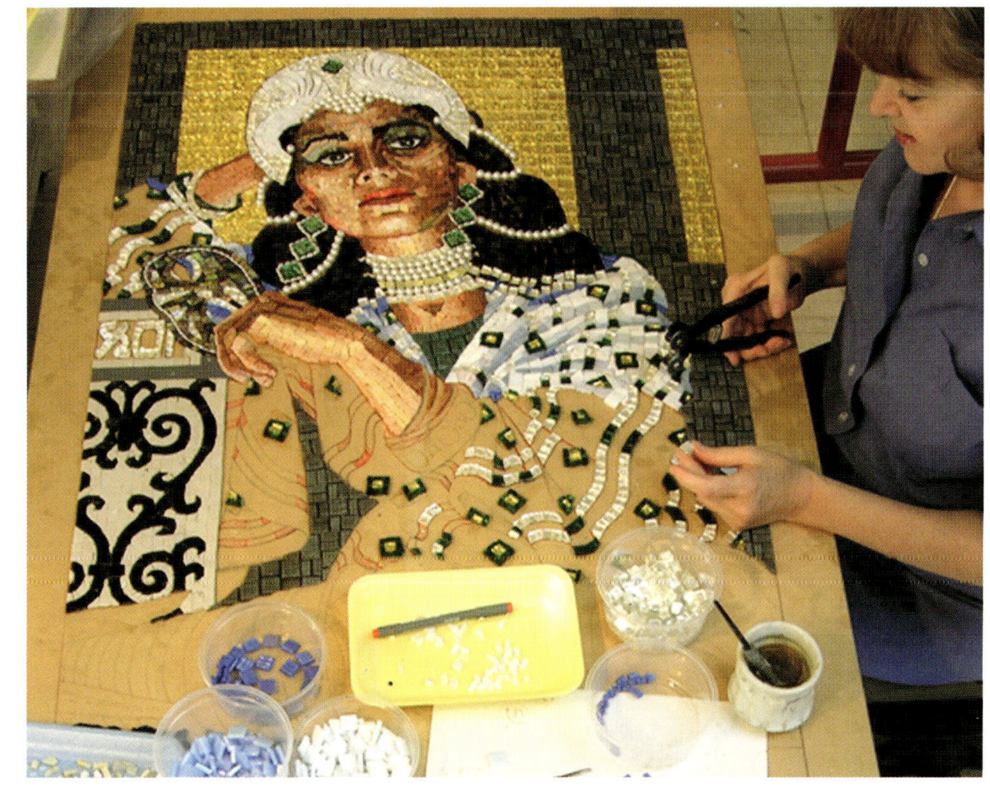

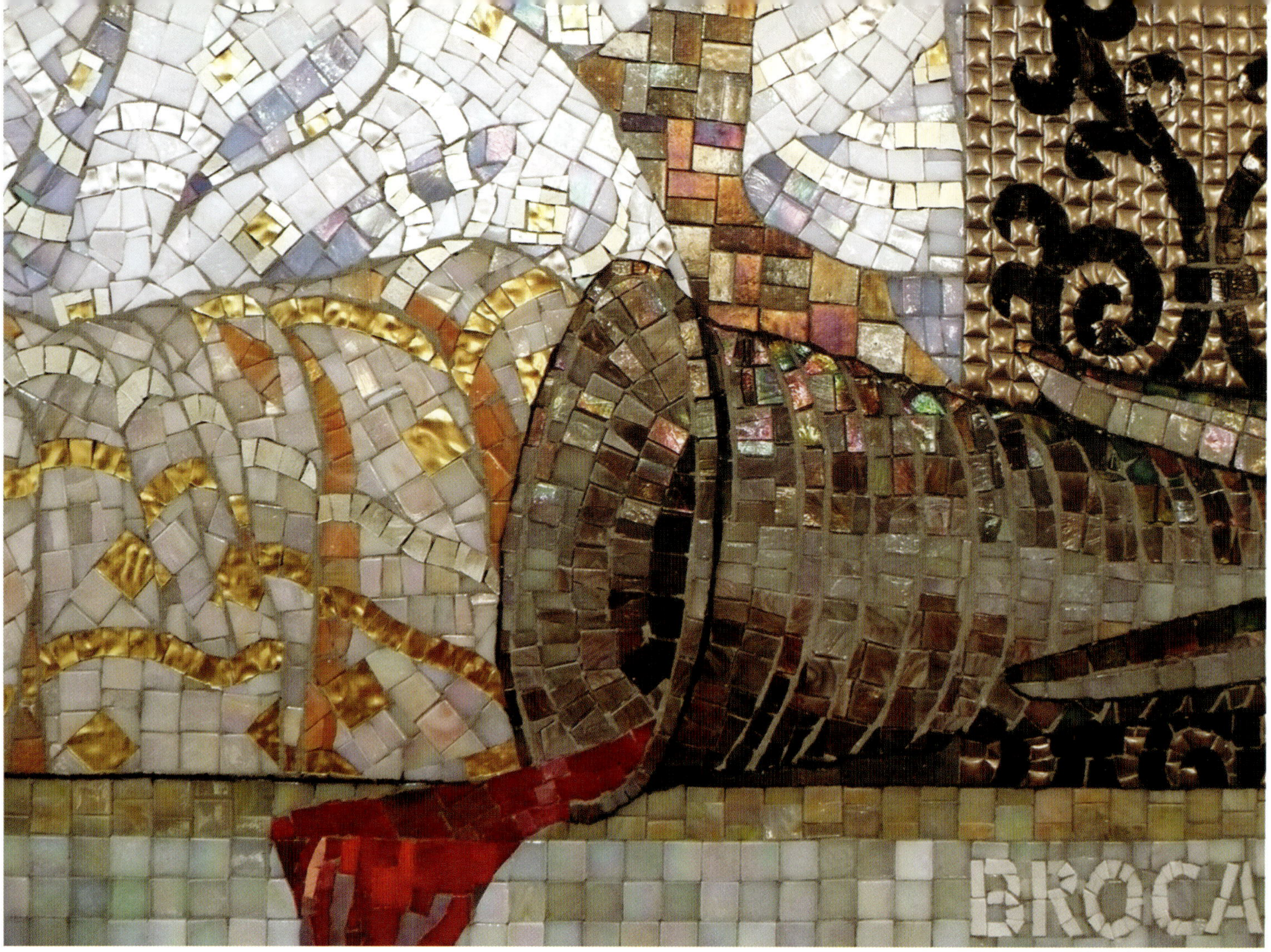

Detail from *Queen Esther Revealing Her True Identity*

In the future, however, I will not hesitate to add a halo over a Jewish figure, for recently I found a photo of a fragment of an ancient floor mosaic made of stone tesserae showing King David playing a lyre, a halo above his head:

> This section of the mosaic floor that decorated the synagogue in Gaza depicts King David as Orpheus, the mythological hero whose music surpassed that of all mortals. David is represented seated on a throne, his crowned head encircled by a halo. He holds a lyre on his lap and is surrounded by an audience of animals enchanted by his playing. To the right of his head is the Hebrew legend "David."[10]

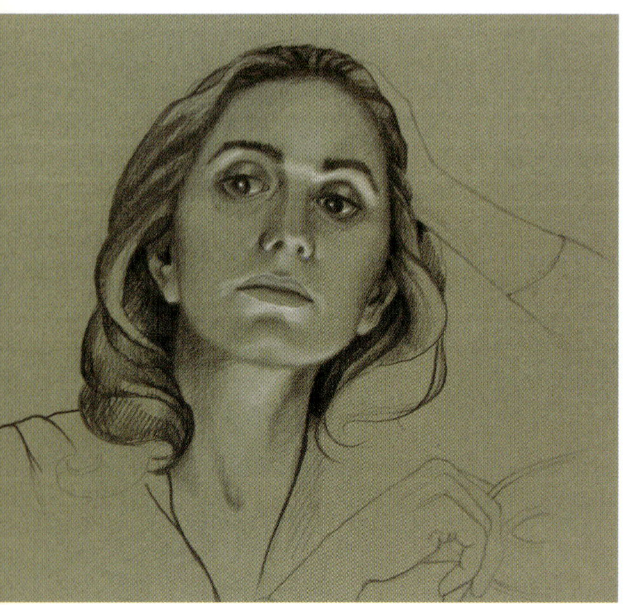

Sketch for *Queen Esther Revealing Her True Identity*, graphite and pastel on paper, 20 x 17 in. (50.80 x 43.18 cm)

Coming Full Circle

My two series on mythical, legendary figures, Lilith and Esther, have formed a spiritual journey as much as an artistic project. The three of us shared an intense fourteen-year odyssey, seven years with each, during which they spoke to me in my dreams. In the end, they became alive through my work. Each became a daily partner who occupied my thoughts and musings, a preoccupation bordering on obsession. Each had a distinct personality, which in the studio seemed to dictate how she wanted to be represented. I shared palpable thoughts and hopes, successes and disappointments, as if we were one entity or a fusion of the two. Saying goodbye to Lilith proved a difficult task. It took a long time to separate us. As I write this, soon I will leave Esther as well, an experience I am not looking forward to. Working on the final mosaic in the Esther series, a diptych, already I felt moments of sadness between us, as if we knew the end was coming.

My two series on mythical, legendary figures, Lilith and Esther, have formed a spiritual journey as much as an artistic project.

Today, I look back at these two emotional connections with pleasure and pride. We bonded, and in our connectedness we created a visual cornucopia of narrative works. The finished oeuvres portray the immense contributions Lilith and Esther both made to our civilization's development.

As I wrote at the start, I was mesmerized as young girl in the darkest days of postwar Romania by the Byzantine images I saw in churches and museums. Later, during my lengthy career in fine arts, I have explored different styles and disciplines. Like the salmon in the Pacific and Atlantic waters of Canada, who return to their inland birthplace each year to lay eggs in the rocky streams, I find myself returning to the artistic origins of my birth country and the world of Byzantium. But now I return as a mature professional artist, better informed, more skilled, but still an eager student of the complex, exotic, and artistic expressions of the Middle Ages, striving to create contemporary mosaic artwork with a Byzantine feel in its heart.

Paintings from *Brides, Goddesses and Heroines* and *The Lilith Series*, the artist's studio, Vancouver, 1993

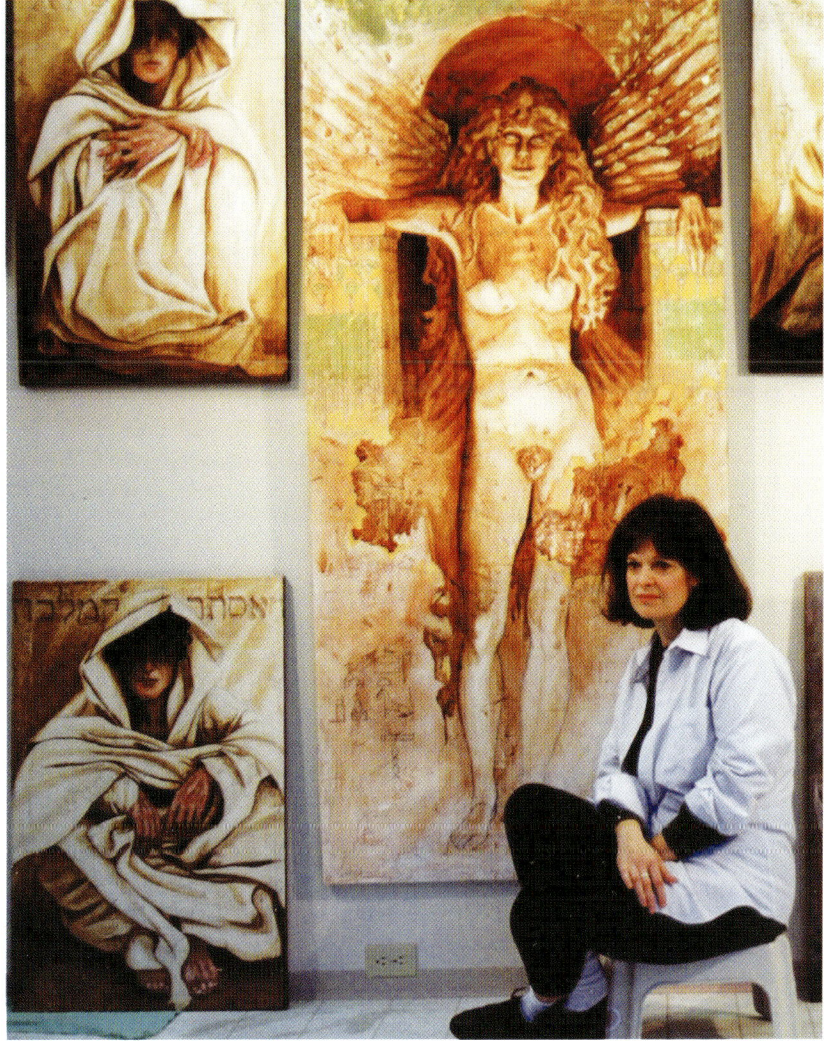

My chosen ancient subject matter, coupled with a contemporary message and a Byzantine approach, has a place in today's critical postmodernist thought.

My chosen ancient subject matter, coupled with a contemporary message and a Byzantine approach, has a place in today's critical postmodernist thought. As the American artist Leonard Koscianski proposes:

> Critical postmodern art is based on the postmodern assertion that all artist perspectives are valid, but unlike postmodernism, the critical postmodern holds that greater understanding of society is possible by viewing it through the lens of individual artworks or narratives… The validity of multiple perspectives does not negate truth. Because it respects the validity of the individual artist's perspective, critical postmodern art pays respect to the integrity of that perspective more than was the case with postmodern art. It values multiple perspectives and the integrity of each individual artist's vision, and by extension the individual self… If individual perspectives are important, then artwork, which expresses those perspectives, must be developed seriously even if the content is humorous. For this reason critical postmodern art is often more highly crafted than postmodern works, and often more accessible and communicative. The critical postmodern artist rightly or wrongly assumes that craftsmanship implies respect for the viewer and enables artwork to communicate more effectively. The critical postmodern artist is ethically engaged in the act of creation rather than ironically detached.[11]

In addition to its artistic perspective, the Queen Esther series allows me to explore my Jewish roots, which during my childhood in Romania were suppressed by the harsh Communist regime. At the same time, however, I feel that the series, with its gold backgrounds and rich colors so reminiscent of the Byzantine icons I saw during my childhood years in Bucharest, derive from a broader heritage.

As I write this in the fall of 2010, I have just returned from a metaphorical "Return to Byzantium." After a fifty-two-year absence, I revisited with great emotion our old family home, built by my grandfather in 1923 in Bucharest, my birth city. During the Communist-ruled years following our emigration, this once majestic residence witnessed seven separate families carving up the interior into a sort of a co-op style residency, still in use today. Old memories flooded my mind, and subsequent visits to the elementary school I attended, the nearby park I used to play in, and, more apropos to this book, seeing again the Byzantine images on churches and monasteries together had a big impact on me. It is strange how particular aspects of the culture from which one originated can linger yet remain dormant for years. However, when one returns to the source, in one swift moment the senses are overwhelmed.

Byzantium left its footprints everywhere in Romania, a land located at the outskirts of that long-gone empire. The old saying "East meets West" is so appropriate here, and only the ancient trees, rivers, and mountains sense the vibrations of horse hooves carrying their riders into endless battles and raids, holding flags that changed every few years.

I tried to envision *The Queen Esther Mosaics* against this backdrop. Although the timeline and subject were, strictly speaking, out of place, I felt a soft aura of familiarity about them, something vaguely connected to my past. I trust that this series, the final segment that completes a circle in my life's artistic creation, would please the old Byzantine masters. And in doing so, I also hope my mosaics have brought new light to the fascinating, multifaceted story of Esther.

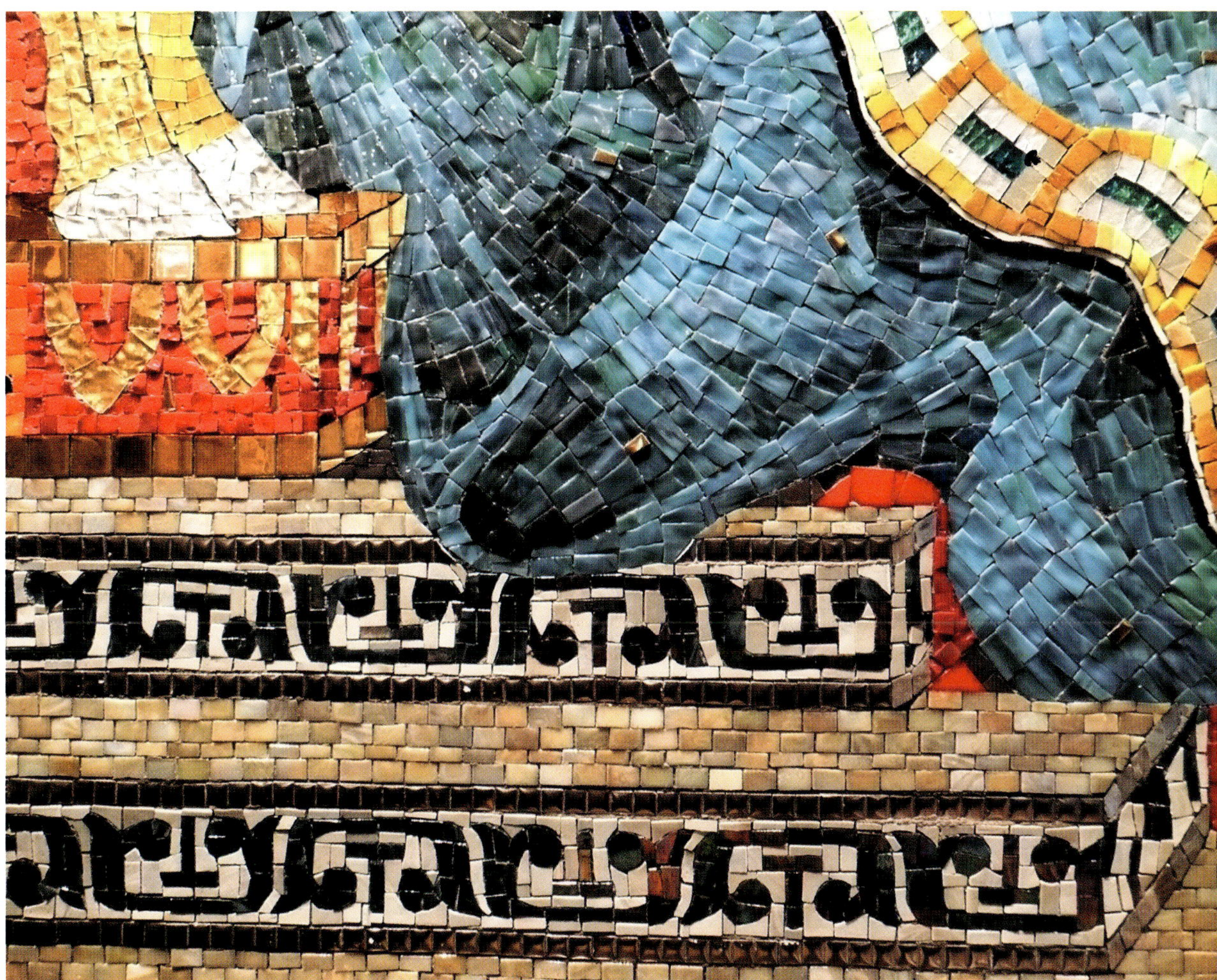

Detail from *Queen Esther Seeking Permission to Speak*

Notes

1 Helen Webberley, *The Book of Esther in 17th Century Dutch Art,* Art Association of Australia and New Zealand National Conference (Sydney: Art Gallery of New South Wales, 2002).

2 "Feminist Aspects of Megillat Esther: Part Two," Jewish Agency, accessed March 3, 2011, http://www.jafi.org.

3 Gili Zivan, "Transformation in the Personality of Queen Esther," The Yaacov Herzog Center for Jewish Studies accessed March 3, 2011, http://www.merkazherzog.org.il/english/.

4 Peter Fisher, *Mosaic: History and Technique* (London: Thames and Hudson, 1971).

5 "Launch of TE21," *Solo Mosaico: History, Contemporaneity, Technologies,* 2009 (April 2010), 130.

6 Patricia Witts, "Proceedings of IV International Mosaic Corpus of Turkey: The Mosaic Bridge from Past to Present," *GROUT,* 28:22 (Winter 2009).

7 Joseph A. deGobineau, *The World of the Persians* (Geneva: Editions Minerva, 1971), 122.

8 Ibid, 129.

9 "Feminist Aspects of Megillat Esther: Part Three," Jewish Agency, accessed March 3, 2011, http://www.jafi.org.

10 *The Jewish World: 365 Days,* ed. Sharon Avrutick (New York: Harry N. Abrams Inc., 2004), 512.

11 Leonard Koscianski, "What is Critical Postmodern Art?" *Tamara: Journal of Critical Postmodern Behavioral Science* (2002).

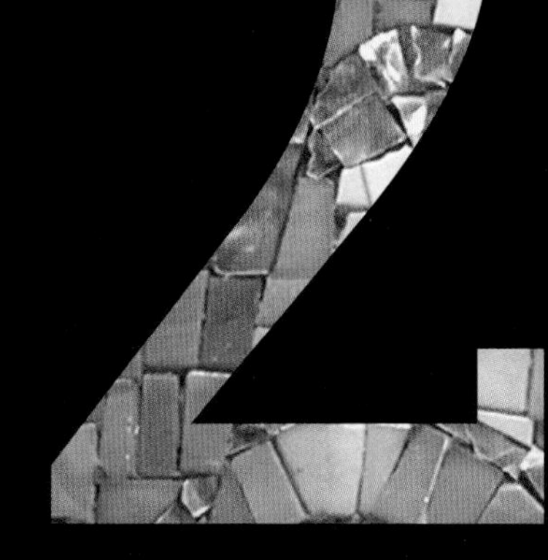

A Biblical Thriller, Told for Centuries

SHEILA CAMPBELL

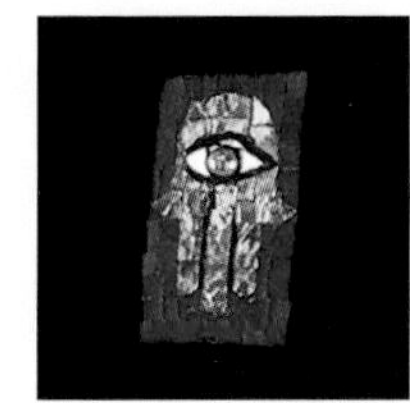

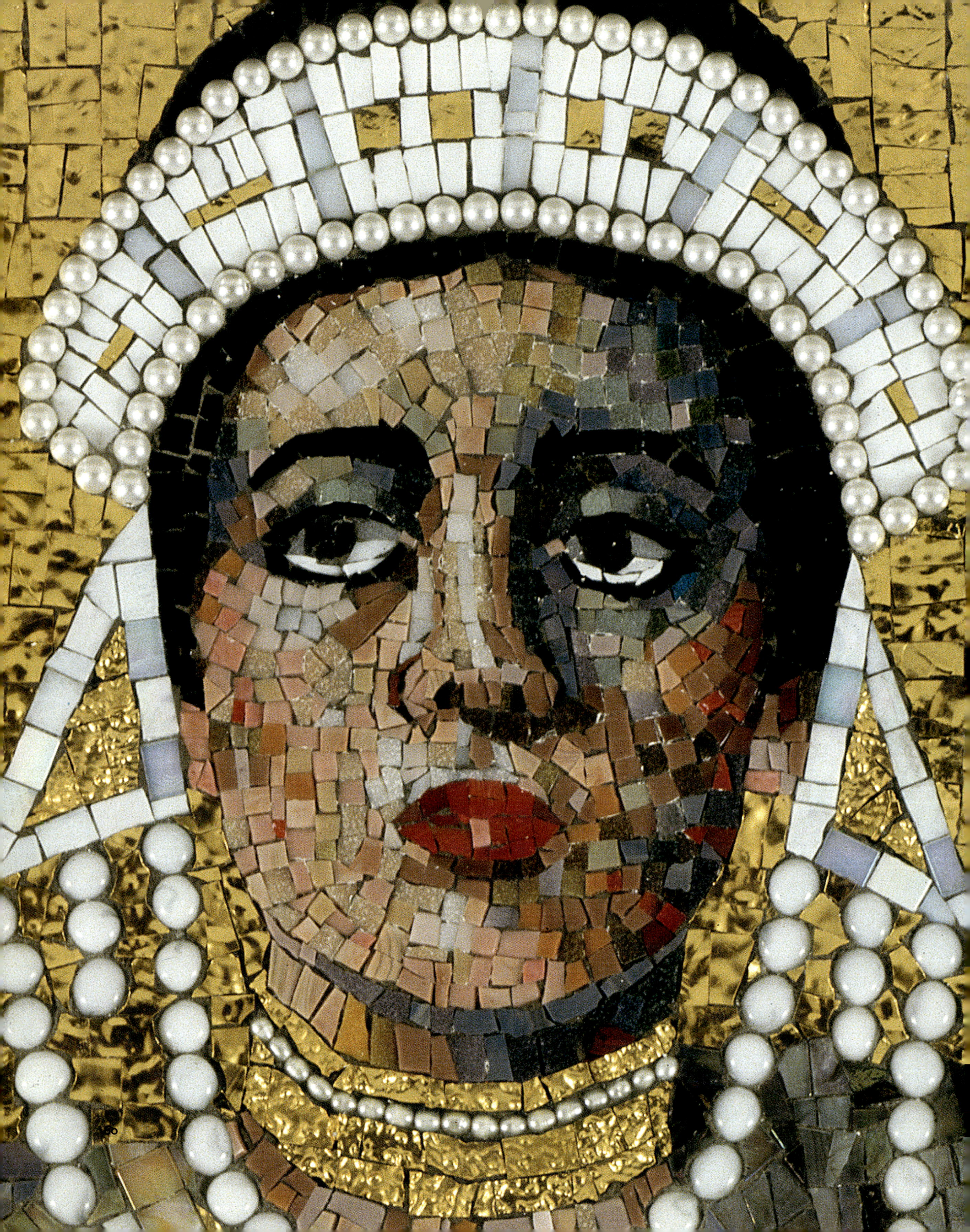

A Biblical Thriller, Told for Centuries

Sheila Campbell

How did visual artists of the past treat the story of Esther and how does Lilian Broca's contemporary mosaic series fit into this tradition? This is my focus here, not issues such as the Book of Esther's authenticity, why it was written, its being truly a religious text, or whether or not it should be included in the Old Testament. Such questions I leave to biblical scholars, philologists, historians, and religious historians.

Certainly, the story of Esther is a good one, true or not. It has narrative, plot and character development, tension, intrigue, resolution, punishment of the wicked, rewards for the "good," and at least a partially happy ending. The exotic Eastern setting gives rise to wonderful opportunities for sumptuous settings and colorful costumes. For all these reasons, artists of past centuries chose the topic, and that alone gives the story validity.

Certainly, the story of Esther is a good one, true or not. It has narrative, plot and character development, tension, intrigue, resolution, punishment of the wicked, rewards for the "good," and at least a partially happy ending.

In fact, the story of Esther has been portrayed by dozens of artists and in works both large and small, private and public, in individual episodes, and in monumental canvases. As painters must select stand-alone segments, not a montage as if it were a video, their choice or choices can be significant. Some artists, such as Rembrandt van Rijn (1606–69) or Gustave Doré (1832–83), depicted more than one part of the story; Rembrandt produced several large canvases of different episodes.

Note that intentionally I do not use the word *illustrated* (as in the artist *illustrated* an episode) but rather *depicted*, since these images are not mere illustrations. They represent a familiar story and remind the viewer of a particular episode from that story. But the artist has chosen specifically what episode to show and painted it in a particular way according to his or her understanding and interpretation of the episode, and within that artist's own time frame. The artist's intent can always be partially ferreted out in his or her selection of which episode

Lilian Broca has chosen to represent ten separate episodes in her mosaic series and in a connected narrative sequence with an underlying theme clearly in mind.

to depict. Or perhaps a patron has influenced the artist's selection. In marked contrast, and as I will address later, Lilian Broca has chosen to represent ten separate episodes in her mosaic series and in a connected narrative sequence with an underlying theme clearly in mind.

An art historian can approach the issue of differing representations and interpretations in various ways. In the manner of a traditional art historian, one could assume a purely iconographical perspective, examining a short or long period of time and making a comparative study of social and stylistic context. For example, should Broca's work be examined as Jewish art in a twenty-first-century context? That, however, doesn't seem to be appropriate for, among other reasons, although the story of Queen Esther and its connection with the festival of Purim are distinctly Jewish, we know that the story is not unique to the Old Testament.

Another approach would be to consider the Jewish-Christian interaction in relation to the art of previous centuries.[1] This, too, does not lead to fruitful intellectual pursuits, as the few pre-nineteenth-century Jewish artists whose works are known seem for the most part to be secular Jews. Their artistic output is best summarized by a quote from the noted late nineteenth-century Dutch artist Jozef Israëls: "In what manner is there a particular Jewish way of painting and a non-Jewish one? Is there a Jewish sea and non-Jewish sea?"[2] Hence, the identification of "Jewish artists" in that context is meaningless. Moreover, Lilian Broca has herself declared that she identifies herself not as a Jewish artist but as a feminist artist. And that, therefore, is the direction I ultimately pursue.[3]

As has often been pointed out, the story of Queen Esther consists of a series of episodes in which information is first hidden and then revealed in the manner of any good thriller. Early in the story, Esther's cousin (and guardian), Mordechai, overhears a conspiracy to depose the Persian king Ahashvayrosh (also called Ahasuerus). He tells Esther, who in turn reveals the plot to the king. Mordechai's role is forgotten and unrewarded until much later in the story when the king calls for the palace diaries and is reminded – that is, the story is revealed to him – and he decides to make a public show of his gratitude. The king then calls in his trusted advisor, Haman, and asks how a true servant of the king should be rewarded. Assuming it will be himself, Haman answers and his answer reveals the extent of his own ambitions.

Meanwhile, Esther has been instructed that to become and remain the king's consort she must exercise great caution and not disclose her true religion. But it, too, is revealed at the end of the story, and along with it her connection to Mordechai. Haman's plot to kill the Jews throughout the Persian empire is meant to be kept secret, but Esther cleverly exposes his devious plans to the king. The Jews of the realm have also, of course, been kept in the dark about their impending doom – that is, until Esther and Mordechai send out an edict in the king's name and with his approval, in effect revealing the dire threat and empowering the Jews to defend themselves.

Underlying all these plot twists is another factor that is only gradually revealed: namely, Esther's personality and character as she evolves from a frightened and shy teenager into a mature and confident queen. Curiously, the character of the king is never directly addressed. Instead, it's revealed through a series of hints. Apart from the introduction to the story, where he acts imperiously toward his wife Vashti, everything else he does is a reaction to someone else's actions. No information is given about him, except as demonstrated by his responses to others. And thus slowly his personality, too, is revealed.

All of these plot twists and turns, these hidden meanings, provide rich fodder for the artist to select and depict story elements, interpreting them according to his or her own perceptions. The story thus offers endless subtle variations in interpretation, one likely explanation why it has been told and retold for centuries and why so many artists have chosen to portray it. A quick search of the Web, for example, lists over thirty artists who have chosen Esther as a topic for their work.[4] In this essay, I consider only a representative sampling of the more prominent ones, especially Dutch and French but also Italian. I examine why so many artists have chosen this topic, what its importance was to them and their contemporaries, and how the story has been adapted to their historical style.

The story thus offers endless subtle variations in interpretation, one likely explanation why it has been told and retold for centuries and why so many artists have chosen to portray it.

As the story of Esther can be read on many levels, examining how it has been depicted visually over the centuries reveals some of these layers of meaning. The significance of the story to a particular artist is demonstrated in which episodes the artist has selected and how the story has been told, namely the settings chosen, how the characters relate to one another, and which story elements have been emphasized. Since most artists have chosen to depict only one or two episodes, these questions can be examined either chronologically by artist, or serially within the story. For the sake of clarity, and since the main focus here is the work of Lilian Broca, I proceed serially within the story, even though this requires moving back and forth chronologically to examine the work of various artists, and each in comparison to Broca's mosaics.

Queen Esther

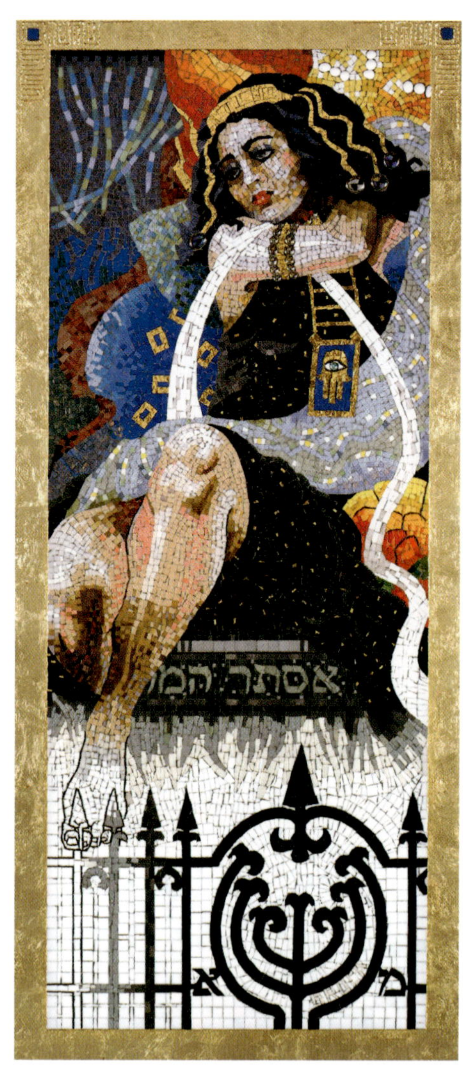

Rembrandt painted at least two panels of a woman being assisted in her toilette by maids. These have been variously characterized as "the Jewish Bride" or as Esther being prepared for the king. One of the two works, later named *Esther Preparing to Intercede with the King,* could portray Esther being dressed by her maids, a portrait of her (for which, incidentally, Rembrandt's wife, Saskia, was the model), or a woman preparing herself mentally for a difficult task. The other figures blend into the background gloom, while all the light focuses on the face, arms, and hands of the woman. Her mouth is set in determination as she sits quietly, mentally girding herself for the task at hand. But could it be said to portray Esther's first meeting with the king or her intention to present herself to the king uninvited, which doesn't occur until much later in the story? The answer to this puzzle is not revealed by the subject's apparent age. While she is clearly not a young teenaged girl who has just moved to the court, depicting her as older looking may only be a convention of seventeenth-century painting.

In the case of Broca's portrait *Queen Esther*, which episodically may be said to correspond to the Rembrandt painting, we see a young woman who, here too not a teenager, is pensive and rather apprehensive, as evidenced by the position of her right arm, as if shielding herself. She is someone totally alone with her thoughts. Indeed, she is seen here literally alone, for she is neither attended by maids nor being advised by her cousin, either of whose companionship might have given her some degree of comfort. She's in a new surrounding, required to hide her identity, isolated – an isolation that sets the tone for the rest of the panels in Broca's series. Moreover, the story is distilled to its essentials, with no unnecessary details. In fact, as Broca makes clear in her artist's statement, each element depicted has specific symbolic meaning. In this sense, the narrative proceeds with the assumption of the viewer's knowledge. In other words, Broca's work is a retelling with a particular slant of an already familiar story.

The mosaics depicted in this chapter are all by Lilian Broca.

Esther's Offering

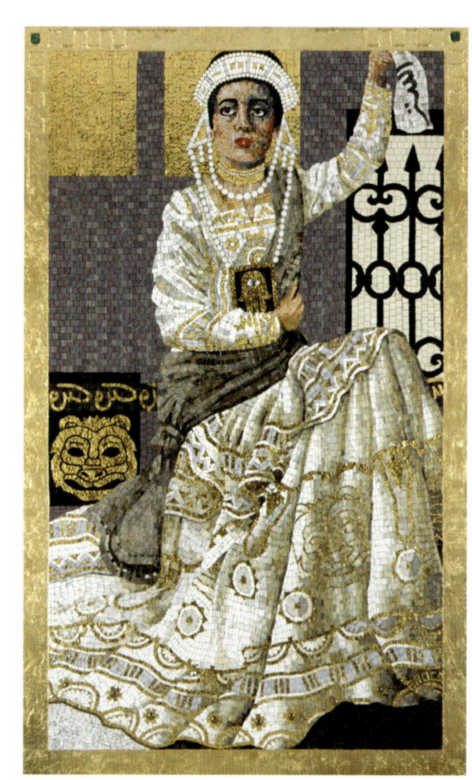

Looking further at the story, I find it surprising that, to the best of my knowledge, no artist other than Broca, in *Esther's Offering*, has chosen to portray Esther preparing for her wedding. The episode presents a distinct opportunity to display lush, extravagant, richly ornamented drapery and jewelry. And that is precisely what we see in the Broca panel. Again, Esther is alone, looking young, vulnerable, and slightly sad. She holds aloft a kerchief displaying her name in Farsi, as if to say that being Persian is now her identity as the wife of the king and that she must obey his will; she has no separate identify of her own. She clutches her side with her right hand, a nervous gesture that betrays her agitated state of mind and emphasizes her solitary state. This very powerful image displays luxury with sadness and impotence yet determination, all in one. Mordechai has told Esther she must follow his instructions to ready herself to protect her people, and at the same time she must also obey the king – a tenuous and difficult mental and emotional predicament for a young girl who has not yet even come to terms with her own womanhood.

Queen Esther with Mordechai

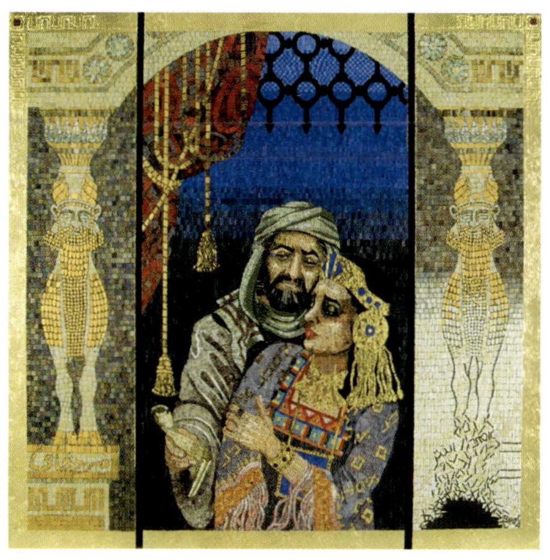

As with Rembrandt, in the painting *Esther Being Instructed by Mordechai* by Aert (Arent) de Gelder (1645–1727), which episode is being depicted is ambiguous. Does it refer to the young Esther who has been taken to the court, with Mordechai telling her to wait and hide her identity as a Jew, or is it the point in the story when Mordechai has gathered evidence against Haman and is telling her that she must find a way to intervene with the king to prevent the mass slaughter of the Jewish people, herself included? De Gelder's Mordechai appears in profile on a slightly lower level than Esther, seated beside her. He gazes intently into her eyes, while she seems to pull back slightly as if in alarm. This hint suggests that the episode is the one in which she must intervene, certainly the more difficult of the two situations. But the depiction is rather low key. She's been interrupted in her reading, and her peace and tranquillity have been disturbed but not shattered. She is alert and listening but not yet an active participant in events. Her right hand lightly touches her chest, a gesture that either declines the request for her to act or expresses her skepticism that she can do anything to help the situation.

The contrast between Esther's state of mind and her sumptuous surroundings and luxurious clothing and jewelry is somewhat dissonant to the scene's high drama, but that too adds to the narrative.

In the corresponding mosaic panel by Broca, the triptych *Queen Esther with Mordechai,* Mordechai has entered the harem and is showing Esther a scroll containing the edict that Haman authored in the king's name and has sent throughout the kingdom, sanctioning the massacre of the Jews. In contrast to de Gelder's work, here which episode is being portrayed is explicit. Esther's cousin has told her she must intervene and that her own life is in danger. Esther recoils in horror, again clasping her arm in a self-protective gesture. She wants to pull away from the whole problem but realizes she cannot. The contrast between Esther's state of mind and her sumptuous surroundings and luxurious clothing and jewelry is somewhat dissonant to the scene's high drama, but that too adds to the narrative. Esther's comfortable, passive, and luxurious life at the royal court is about to be turned upside down.

Queen Esther with Scroll

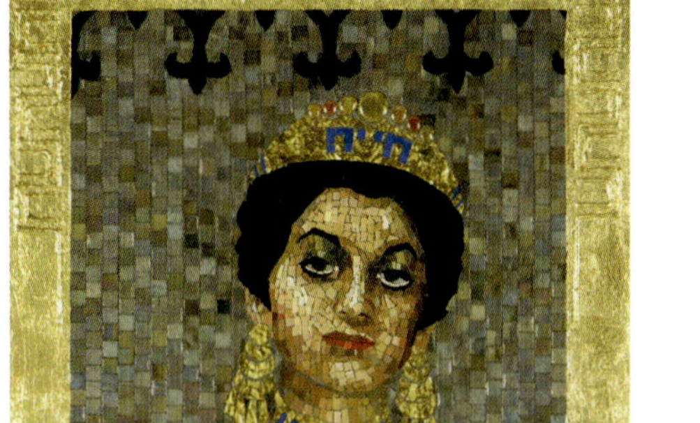

The next scene from Esther, when she contemplates the extreme risk she faces in thwarting Haman's plot, seems not to have been popular with painters of the past. Perhaps the moment is too subtle for a grand statement in the historical style. Not until the late nineteenth and early twentieth centuries would painters portray such a degree of introspection and personal expressiveness. These later artists, too, however, seem not to have turned their attention to this episode.

Broca, however, has tackled it head on in the panel *Queen Esther with Scroll,* using costume and content to highlight the subtleties of the event. A jagged wrought iron motif points down from the top of the mosaic representing Esther's state of captivity. The moment is made all the more tense and dramatic by her isolation and the work's minimal background. She holds the scroll in her hands, but does not look at it. Her superficial trappings as queen are grand yet irrelevant, as she is lost in thought, recovering from the moment of shock seen in the prior panel of the series. Now begins her transition from passive youth to proactive womanhood. The full meaning of the scroll's content is sinking in, and she starts to devise her strategy.

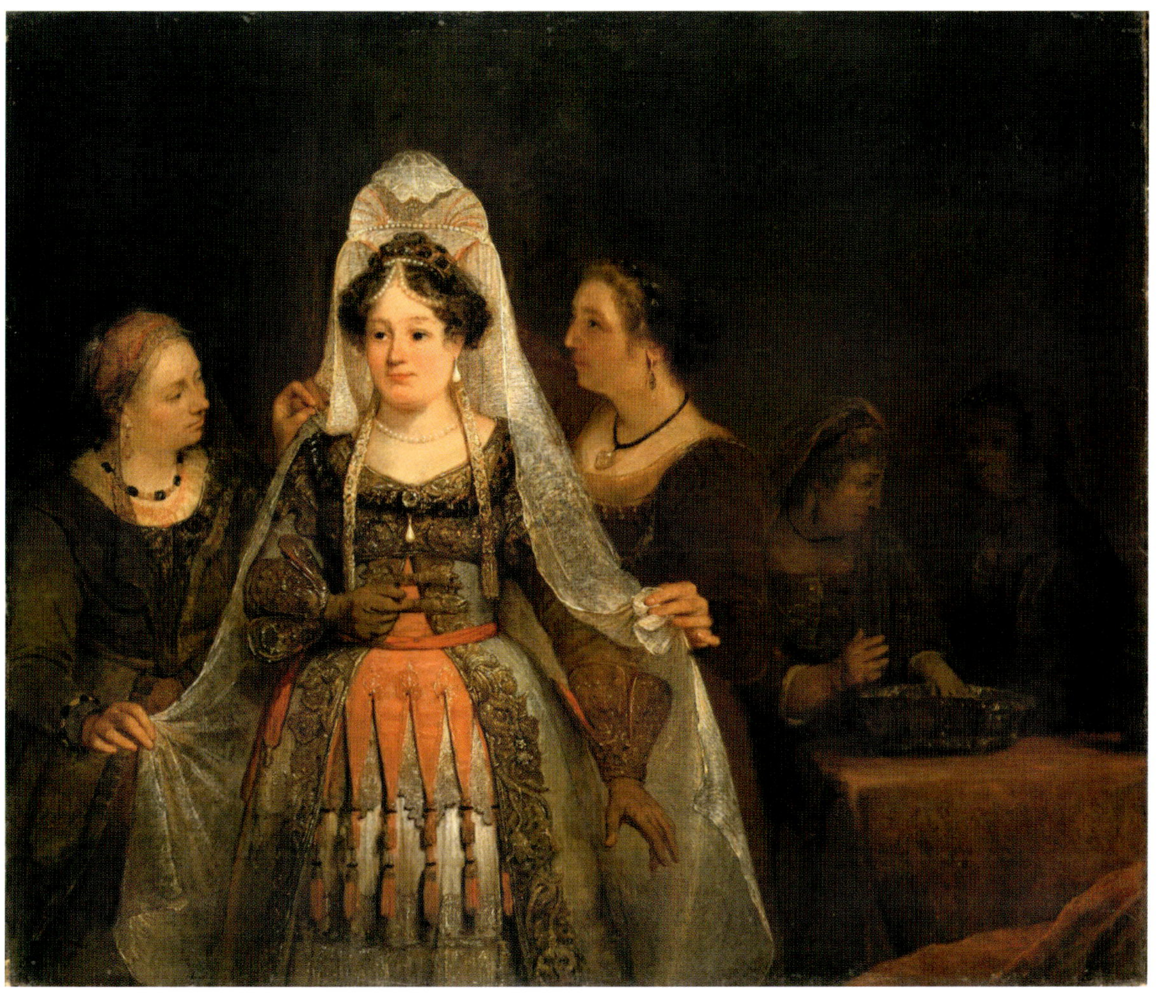

Gelder, Aert de (1645–1727) *Esther Before Her Introduction to Ahasuerus* Painting, 54.9 x 64.3 in. (139.4 x 163.3 cm), Inv. 841 Bayerische Staatsgemaeldesammlungen Munich, Germany

Queen Esther Holding Evidence of Haman's Guilt

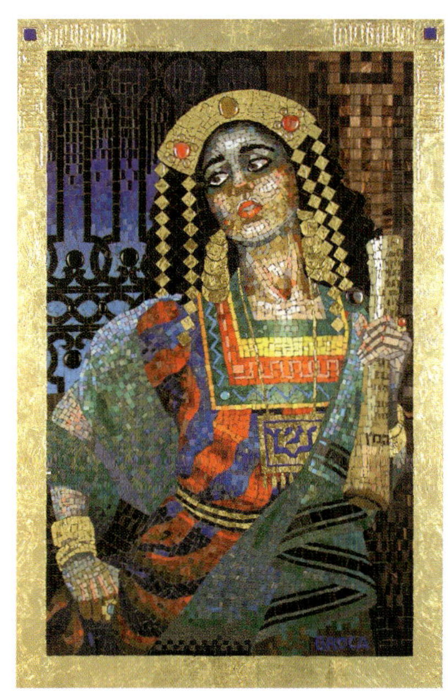

While many artists have portrayed Esther's disclosure of Haman's guilt, most have chosen to do so by depicting the moment when she prepares herself to go before the king. These paintings are a little ambiguous, as we see Esther arrayed in finery, supported by her maids, but without the precise threat being self-evident. See for example de Gelder's *Esther Before Her Introduction to Ahasuerus* (also known as *Queen Esther Being Adorned by Her Maids*). Her anxiety is apparent but not its specific cause.

Broca has omitted this particular scene and chosen instead, in *Queen Esther Holding Evidence of Haman's Guilt*, the moment when the queen realizes not only the danger for her people and herself personally, but also her danger at that precise moment, when she holds the damaging scroll in the confines of the palace, beset with all its intrigues and spies. Once again, the wrought iron work close behind her emphasizes her limitations. She holds the scroll in a way that reveals what she's doing, making the content of the moment clear to the viewer. By showing the surreptitious motion of her slinking in the shadows back to the safety of privacy, the composition also conveys her concern to get away without being seen.

Queen Esther Seeking Permission to Speak

Not just male artists of the past chose Queen Esther as a subject. One female artist who also did so was Artemisia Gentileschi (c. 1597–c. 1651), a rather enigmatic woman with a much-studied personal history.[5] It has been suggested that she made her reputation as a painter of heroic women and female nudes. Does this statement pander to the male viewer, as suggested by some feminist theorists? Perhaps, yet she was a fiercely independent woman who excelled at creativity and foreswore repetition in her work. How to reconcile her with a feminist interpretation has been debated by numerous authors, and the jury is still out.

Here, only her painting *Esther before King Ahasuerus* is considered. In this work, Esther is seen in a fainting pose, supported by her maids, while the king

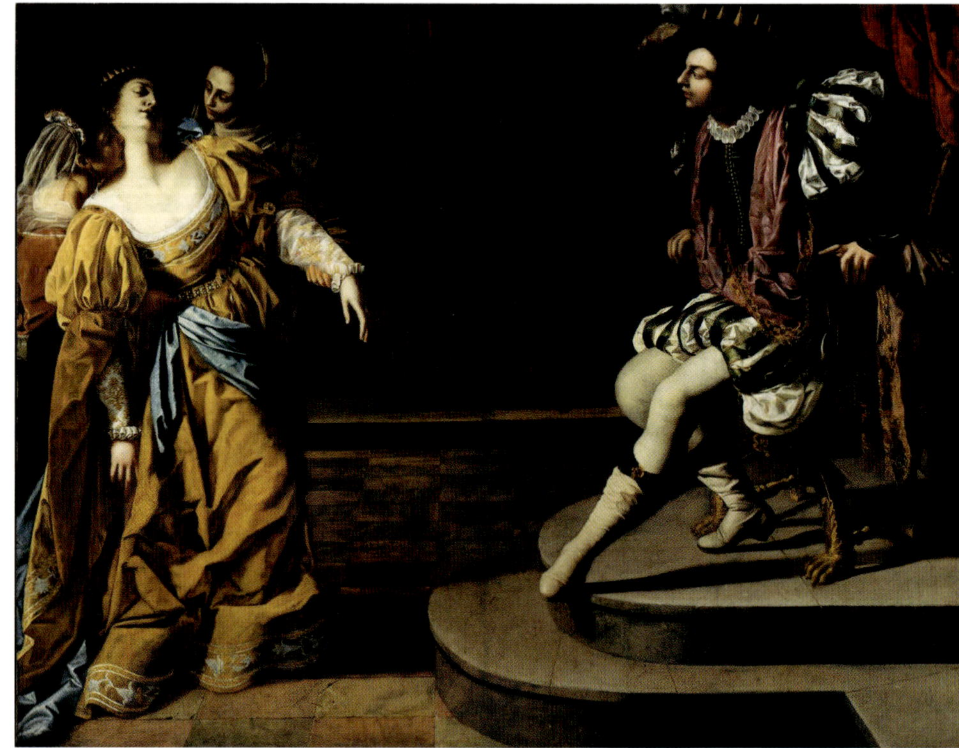

Gentileschi, Artemisia (c. 1597–c. 1651)
Esther Before Ahasuerus
Oil on canvas
82 x 107.75 in. (208.3 x 273.7 cm)
Gift of Elinor Dorrance Ingersoll, 1969 (69.281)
The Metropolitan Museum of Art
New York, NY
Image copyright © The Metropolitan Museum of Art/Art Resource, NY

is shown dressed as a young dandy, about to rise from his seat in alarm at her swoon. Is there symbolic portent in the fact that as she falls he rises? Possibly so. Does the work lend itself to a feminist interpretation? As the art historian Judith Mann has noted, "the painting is very expressive with a pregnant void in the center. The painting lacks real compositional rigor; the beauty of its parts overwhelms the whole."[6] In fact, Artemisia's work doesn't even seem to have a major underlying message. Yes, Esther is shown to be afraid of the king. But she takes up a much bigger portion of the panel than he does and, given also the greater activity on her side of the panel, the viewer's attention is drawn there first.

Perhaps the paramount factor here is that the artist was a career woman who needed to paint to support herself and her family. The story of her rape and the subsequent delayed trial are well known. After the trial she moved from her father's studio in Rome to northern Italy, where she was quietly married off. The marriage was apparently fairly successful, but it seems she remained the family breadwinner. At the time she executed this painting, she was in Venice, where the costumes depicted were much in vogue. It seems evident, therefore, that this work was painted for a particular market, and successfully so since we know it sold quickly.

The "pregnant void" in the work's center is rather odd in such a composition, and X-rays show that the artist changed the painting significantly. However, the changes made in the center – the removal of a dog and a boy – do not alter the work's implied meaning. If anything, the space enhances the drama of the scene, with the queen reacting to her fear and three days of fasting and about to faint, just out of the king's reach. Actually, the pose of the king's legs is rather unstable, and he couldn't rise instantaneously to save her. Rather than reading this as a fault of composition, I see it as a means of enhancing the drama of the moment.

Aert de Gelder, mentioned above, was a male artist working in the Netherlands, roughly contemporary with Artemisia Gentileschi.[7] He produced a number of paintings that, having been subsequently named, are generally presumed to depict the story of Esther. All are very much in the style of Rembrandt, with whom de Gelder had studied. Two of these works are entitled *Esther Being Adorned by Her Maids;* the others are *King Achashverosh Condemning Haman, Haman Begging for Mercy, Esther Being Instructed by Mordechai,* and one not a popular episode with other artists, *Mordechai Writing the Letter in the King's Name* regarding the royal decree that enabled the Jews to defend themselves and forestall their massacre. In each of these works, Esther seems a rather passive creature, an observer rather than a proactive participant in the events.

The French artist Antoine Coypel (1661–1722) created a work in 1697 portraying the popular episode of *Esther Fainting in Front of King Ahashvayrosh.* In a swoon commonly seen in works by other artists, Esther is shown being supported by her maids. In this case, the king has leapt to his feet to help catch her, his left knee bent in obvious concern for his queen. In other words, Esther commands the action in this scene. The light focuses on her, but once again feminine weakness is represented, not strength and mental cunning. The setting is rather dark, with heavy draperies, massive architecture, and voluminous clothing. Interestingly, Coypel painted a scene of the trial of Susanna using an almost identical setting, with heavy dark draperies suspended from the ceiling, similar architecture for both interior and exterior, and the identical style of inlaid marble floor.[8]

Indeed, the marble floor appears yet again in a 1755 painting by Nicholas Poussin, along with the ubiquitous heavy fluted columns, archways, and suspended draperies.[9] This time the queen faints in a direction away from the king, and both she and her supporting attendant form an elongated sinuous S curve.

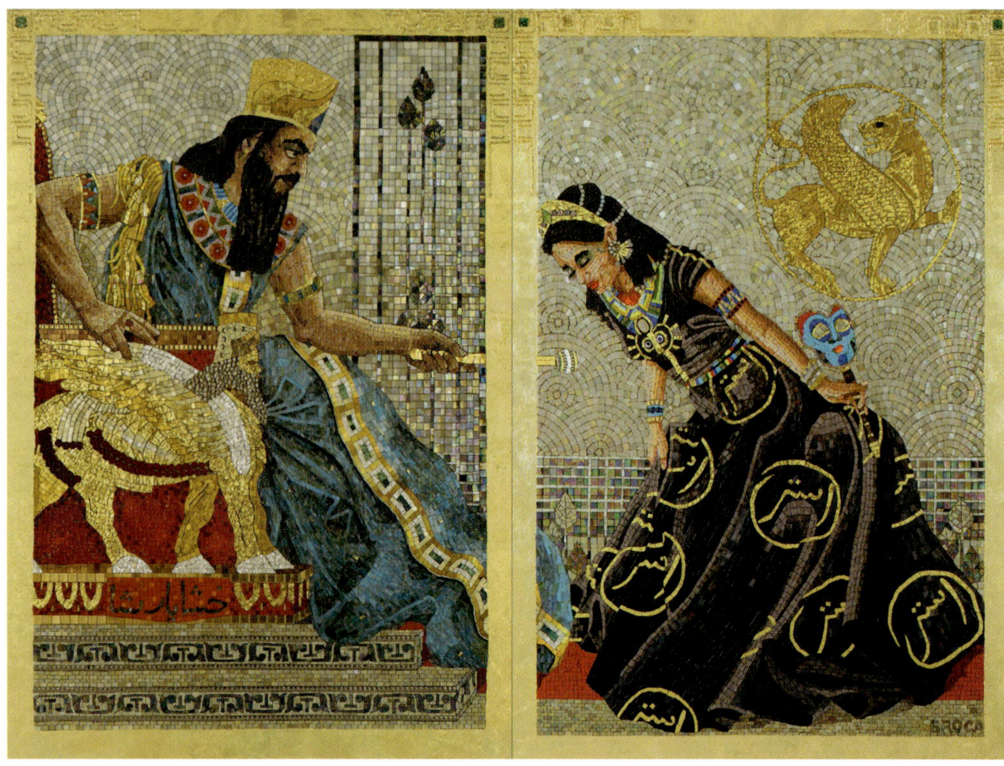

The king, who appears to be wearing a Roman toga, watches the scene with mild interest, only raising his right hand slightly to register awareness of Esther's distress. The composition forms a peculiar inverted triangle, with the peak somewhere between the feet of the king and the knees of Esther.

How do these examples, particularly Artemisia Gentileschi's, compare with Broca's representation of the same episode, in *Queen Esther Seeking Permission to Speak*? Artemisia chose a contemporary setting for her work, with all parties wearing the fashions then current. The actual setting, an Italian drawing room, does not, however, provide a regal stage for the encounter. This is an important moment for Esther, filled with dread and anxiety. According to custom, the king could kill her for approaching without an invitation. Artemisia's work does not convey this context. In contrast, Broca provides a suitable historical setting, with appropriate costumes and décor, albeit according to archaeological investigations not available in the seventeenth century. Broca makes a serious effort to duplicate authentic ancient Persian costumes, jewelry, and *lamassu* (a throne with mythological guardian figures).

Broca makes a serious effort to duplicate authentic ancient Persian costumes, jewelry, and *lamassu* (a throne with mythological guardian figures).

Unlike Artemisia's version, Broca's panel pictures only two figures, the king and queen. The queen is alone, neither supported nor attended by servants, reinforcing her danger and the sense of drama. Dressed in black and purple, the colors of mourning, she has prepared herself mentally for the awesome responsibility that she alone must prevent the forthcoming massacre of the Jews of Persia, herself included. The panel conveys drama and tension in other ways, too: for example, we see Esther not in the customary fall or faint (which, after all, would hardly advance her cause), but ready to speak out. And since Broca's mosaics portray not just one but a sequence of events, the viewer can see that for the first time the king's expression has softened to something almost benign. Appropriate to the story, this suggests that the king's personality has changed under Esther's influence. He's become more gentle, ready to listen to a woman – so unlike the character at the very start of the story who, merely because his wife Vashti refused to obey his command, cast her out without any thought for her.

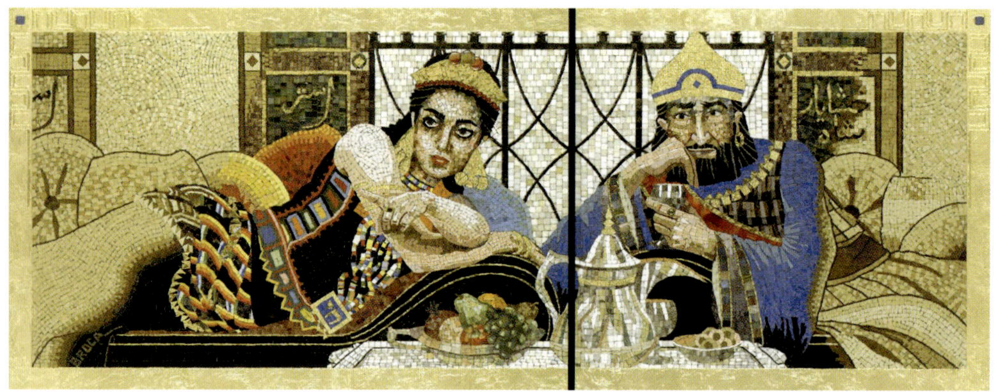

Queen Esther's Banquet

Rembrandt completed several paintings of the Esther story. In *Achashverosh, Esther and Haman at the Banquet,* the light is rather dim, and the two men seem to merge into the background. Esther in the foreground catches all the light and, although small and shown only in profile, she dominates the conversation taking place at the table. She is literally the enlightened one, while the two men withdraw into introspection. Interestingly, even though the title mentions a banquet, no food appears on the table. In *Haman Begging Esther for Mercy* once again the two men seem to merge into a dark background, while Esther in the foreground is a figure full of light. The interaction is between Esther and Haman, while the king, though his scepter gleams in the darkness, is clearly an incidental element.

Just two people are present, Esther and the king, and the necessary third person, Haman, is suggested only through the pointing finger of Esther, a powerful and effective device.

In two paintings by Jan Victors (1616–76), Esther takes a much more active role. In *Esther and Haman Before Achashverosh,* she points to Haman, while the king gently places his hand on her wrist, as if to concentrate better on her words. In a second painting on the same subject, she again points to Haman, this time from the advantage of the central position. The left hand on her hip and the earnest expression directed toward the king tell the viewer exactly what's going on – the exposure of Haman's guilt. This is confirmed further by the king's raised fist and Haman's wringing hand gesture. Esther is no longer pictured as a passive figure, and the other actors are also beginning to show emotion.

Broca's depiction of this episode, *Queen Esther's Banquet,* departs dramatically from those of the artists who preceded her. Just two people are present, Esther and the king, and the necessary third person, Haman, is suggested only through the pointing finger of Esther, a powerful and effective device. Haman, the villain, is right there to the left of the viewer. Just turn to look at him, as she directs! You the viewer are palpably present, experiencing the action. The intense focus also eliminates the need to picture any servants.

The work's intensity is further animated by the king and queen being depicted in brilliant colors in only the top half of their bodies, fading to brown and beige from the waist down. Apart from the content of the moment, all else is irrelevant. The image of wrought iron, reappearing again in this panel, in my view (which differs from the artist's statement) unites rather than separates the two people, the queen appearing on an equal basis with the king. They do not seem, however, to be having a relaxed social exchange. Both parties are identified in Persian inscriptions behind them, but Esther is dominant, the active player, determinedly pointing toward Haman, while the king tries hard to concentrate on her words after imbibing perhaps a little too much wine. He is puzzled and a little surprised that a woman is taking control and directing events in his life, but he seems to accept this.

One other aspect of the story should be pointed out, namely that in the ancient world, apart from weddings, men and women did not dine together, not in the Greek world and not in the Roman world. Only courtesans might make an appearance. Although authorities don't know for sure, the same was likely true for the world of Ahashvayrosh. This point highlights the exceptional nature and drama that Esther's request to invite the two men to dinner plays in the biblical story, and also in Broca's portrayal.

Haman Leading Mordechai on the Royal Horse

The triumph of Mordechai – when a humiliated Haman must lead Mordechai, dressed in the king's own finery, on a fine steed to reward Mordechai for saving the king's life – offers a highly dramatic moment for the artist to portray. And here three works are considered: a 1515 engraving by Lucas van Leyden (1494–1533), an oil painting from 1624 by Pieter Lastman (1583–1633),[10] and a Rembrandt etching executed in 1641.

The van Leyden engraving contains a crowd scene of mostly men and possibly one woman, with Mordechai centrally placed and very prominent on horseback. Haman stands behind the horse's head, nearly invisible among the other revelers accompanying the procession. At least fifteen people are crowded

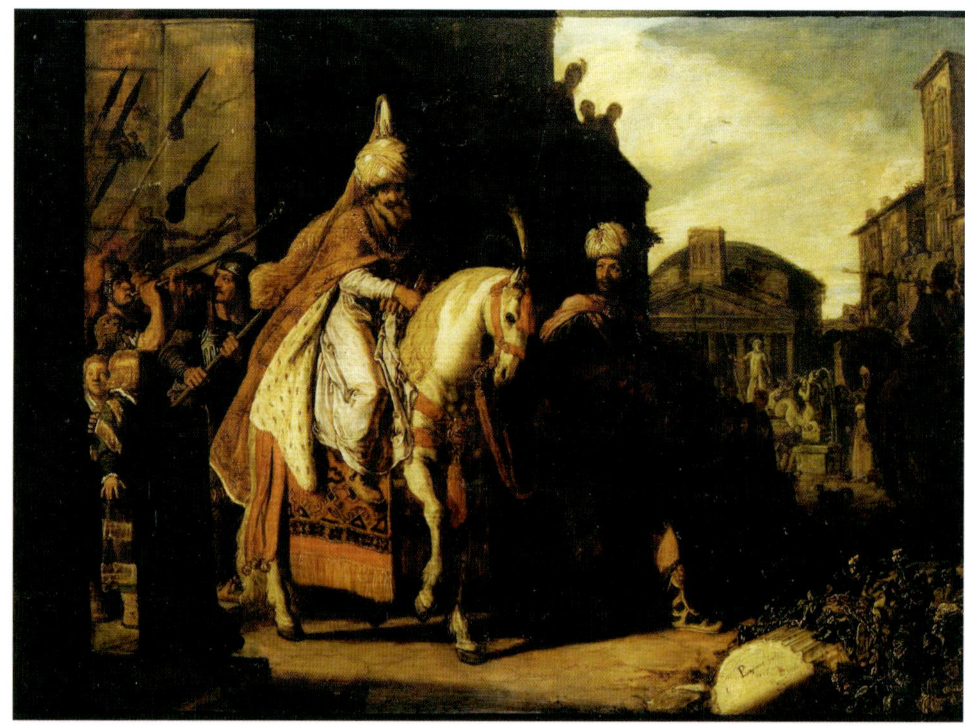

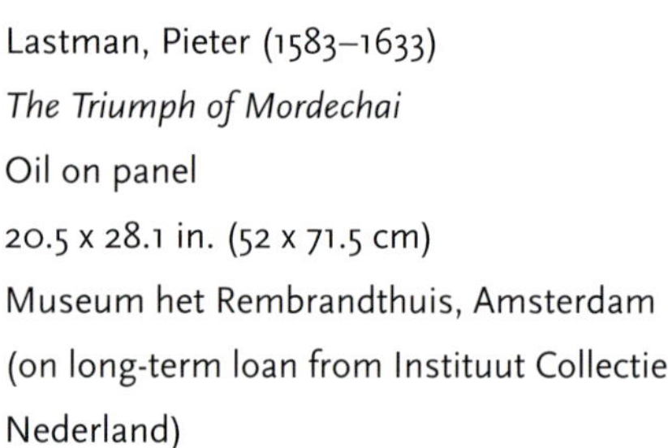

Lastman, Pieter (1583–1633)
The Triumph of Mordechai
Oil on panel
20.5 x 28.1 in. (52 x 71.5 cm)
Museum het Rembrandthuis, Amsterdam
(on long-term loan from Instituut Collectie Nederland)

together, all beautifully drawn with flowing draperies and active poses. Despite the wonderful variety and action throughout, one wonders what the story is about. Mordechai is quite expressionless, and Haman is just one of the crowd, not a courtier who has been put into a demeaning position. Indeed, it seems the artist has not thoughtfully depicted the triumph of Mordechai at all, nor the disgrace of Haman, but rather a display of power and authority, with one or two submissive figures kneeling in the foreground to emphasize just who's in charge. No doubt this setting reflects the artist's own experience of contemporary political display.

In contrast, the Lastman oil painting clearly shows Haman leading the horse on which Mordechai rides, the figure of Haman dominating the scene. Even though in shadow, Haman occupies almost the full center of the work, his head lit up as he gazes back, almost defiantly, at Mordechai. Though seated on the horse, Mordechai in comparison seems quite small, dwarfed by his enormous head dress, and not even seeming to be the hero of the moment. He leans forward on the horse, looking a little nervous about the goings-on. Even more strange, the two principal figures, appearing in pseudo-Eastern dress, are set within a scene of Imperial Roman Triumph, surrounded by Roman soldiers and trumpeters. A building in the background appears to be the Pantheon of Rome, complete with Roman statuary and a fountain. It's a bizarre juxtaposition. Also odd, Haman's face does not suggest embarrassment or shame, nor does Mordechai seem triumphant. While the painting showcases Lastman's facility for picturing crowd scenes with gorgeous costumes and elaborate pomp and ceremony in a traditional style, the work's interpretative content, if any, leans toward showcasing Haman and diminishing Mordechai. All this transpires in a scene of macho display, calling up historical precedent and augmented by anachronistic costumes.

The Rembrandt etching exhibits an intriguing shift in composition compared to the two earlier works described above. Here the figure of Mordechai on the horse proceeds on a diagonal toward the viewer. He and the crowd around him are coming through an archway with a domed structure in the background. Like Lastman's work, Rembrandt's portrays a Roman imperial triumph set within Roman architecture; as well, the two main figures wear Eastern costumes. But altogether different from both Lastman's and van Leyden's portrayals, Rembrandt's crowd comprises a mix of men, women, and children, mostly northern peasant types dressed in northern peasant costume.

As well, this time Haman is prominently placed in front of the horse, not leading it but opening his arms, as if to clear the way and proclaim the importance of Mordechai. And although Haman holds the prominent foreground position, he conveys humility with his outstretched arms and downcast eyes.

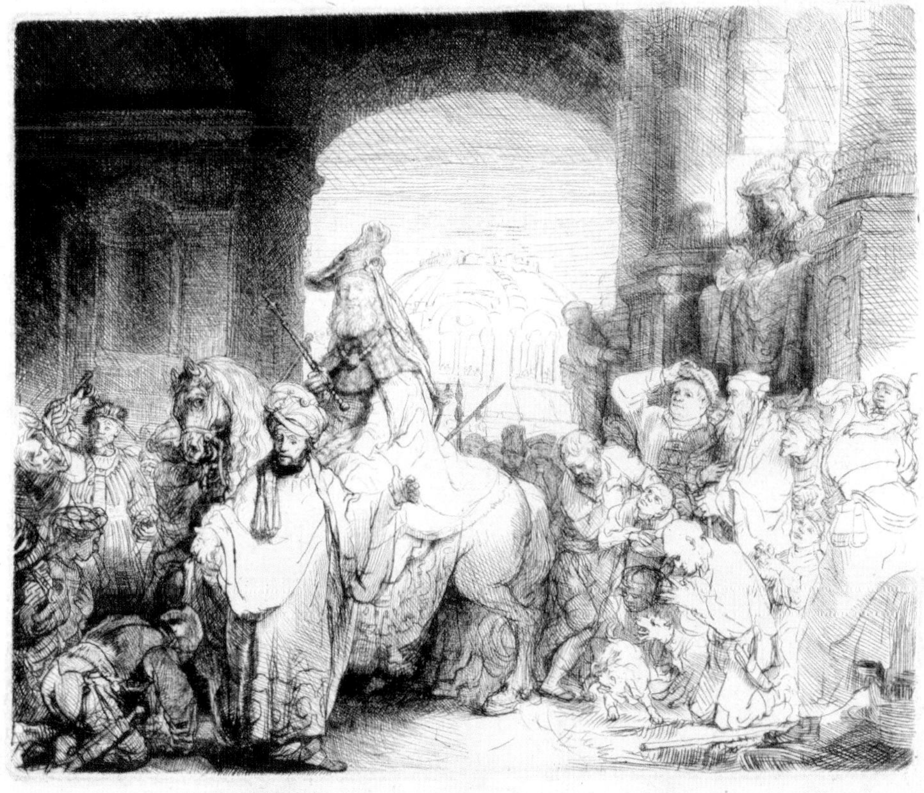

Rembrandt, Harmensz van Rijn (1606–69)
The Triumph of Mordecai, c. 1640 or later
Etching and drypoint on paper
6.94 x 8.44 in. (17.7 x 21.5 cm)
Gift of Mrs. Leo Wallerstein, JM 9–58
Photo by John Parnell
The Jewish Museum, New York, NY

Hierarchically positioned above Haman, Mordechai maintains a solemn expression but sits upright on his horse as if firmly in control.

Rembrandt has played with time here, using contemporary peasants to support an Old Testament story. As well, Mordechai's physiognomy is reminiscent of some of the artist's portrait paintings of Jews in Amsterdam, continuing the use of contemporary people to tell an old story. It has been suggested elsewhere that Rembrandt's religious paintings were not intended to arouse religious fervor but rather to elicit more generic emotions.[11] That certainly seems to be the case in his depiction of Mordechai's triumph.

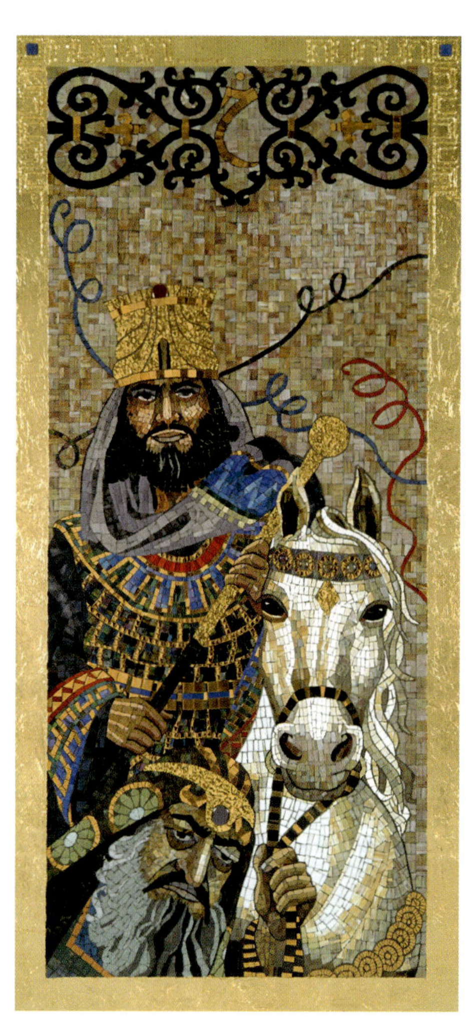

How does Broca's version of the same episode, *Haman Leading Mordechai on the Royal Horse,* compare to these earlier depictions? To begin with, quite different from the broad horizontal compositions of the other three artists, her panel is a vertical rectangle. Only two partial figures appear in the work, plus a horse's head and shoulder – hardly a crowd. As well, the verticality of the piece emphasizes Mordechai's hierarchical position atop the horse. He comes across as serene and clearly in control, even carrying a staff of office and wearing regal costume (which unlike the other three artists' depictions of Mordechai directly follows the biblical text). In contrast, Haman appears in a small head shot, tucked into the bottom corner, appropriately carrying an expression of great unhappiness and humiliation. Meanwhile, colored streamers around the horse and Mordechai's head add an air of festivity, like a New Year's celebration or colorful ticker-tape parade. Tightly grouped together, the two men and the horse move straight forward, out of the panel, toward the viewer. Move out of the way! the work seems to shout, conveying intense immediacy in a very condensed form.

It might seem a little unfair to expect the three earlier works, two of which are black and white, to compete with the brilliant color of mosaic. However, the composition of Broca's work is itself powerful, and the mosaic medium makes it even more so. The significance of this medium is discussed further below.

Surreptitious Dialogue

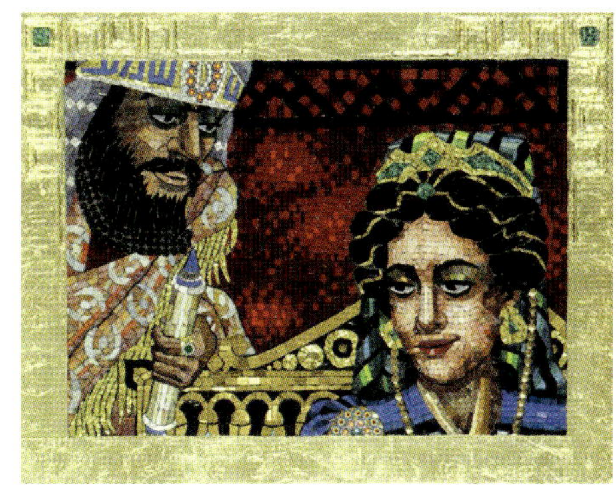

Like the scene *Queen Esther with Scroll,* the episode Broca entitles *Surreptitious Dialogue,* where Esther and Mordechai devise a plan to reverse Haman's plot to annihilate the Jews, has not been a popular topic among artists of the past. There are a few examples showing the two composing a new letter to reverse the effect of the earlier edict, but not many.

An extraordinary tour de force of mosaic skill, Broca's panel relies on the artist's ability to portray expressions, no easy matter using multiple tiny pieces of glass. But Broca has done it with magisterial skill. Esther's expression clearly proclaims, "Now I know what has to be done." She is confident, in charge, prepared. Mordechai, dressed appropriate to his newly elevated rank, holds a scroll case containing the king's earlier edict and gazes at Esther with new respect. No longer the young ingénue he once adopted, she has transformed into a resourceful woman who has fulfilled, even exceeded, his hopes and expectations. The compression of these two partial figures, tightly enclosed by the frame, further enhances the panel's powerful impact. We don't need to see the successful outcome of their scheming: the composition says it all.

Queen Esther Revealing Her True Identity

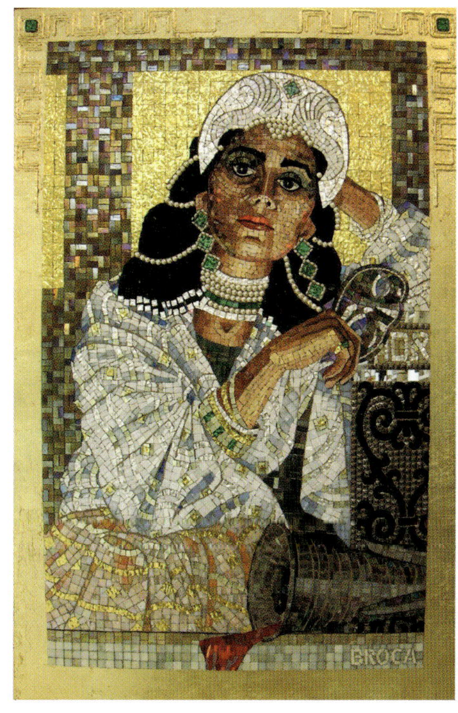

Yet another episode Broca has chosen to depict but past artists have not is Esther's disclosure of her Jewish identity. Here, Broca portrays the queen in the aftermath of her second banquet for the king, the banquet's success implying that the king now knows of her origins. Perhaps earlier artists, particularly those in the sixteenth and seventeenth centuries, avoided the topic because, unless it was a portrait, they were loath to show only one person. Broca's version, however, is strengthened by the composition's singularity. The queen is seen by herself, once again in a pensive mood, holding a mask in her hand while contemplating the triumphal outcome of her actions. She is very much the queen now, a square gold halo behind her head. Instead of spilled Jewish blood, the outcome had Haman prevailed, wine is seen pouring out from an overturned rhyton over the edge of a table.

This last element brings to mind a 1680 painting by Aert de Gelder that depicted an earlier banquet of Ahashvayrosh, the one at which he vainly called for his wife Vashti to attend, where he is shown with a wine goblet spilling into his lap. This image of spilling wine along with Broca's may be seen to form bookends for the story. In his drunkenness, the king took great offense and expelled his wife Vashti for disobeying his request, the very event that eventually drew Esther into the story and led ultimately to her victory in protecting the blood of her people. At the start of the story, a haughty king follows his whims; at the end, a more pliant king submits to Esther's plea.

Looking broadly at how artists have rendered the story of Esther, widely different contexts have been portrayed. Some artists placed the story in a Roman Imperial setting, highlighting pomp and ceremony. Others used settings and costumes contemporary to their era while also adding classical architectural touches for dramatic effect. A few, such as Gustave Doré, used their imagination to achieve a fantasy effect. Most recently and quite distinctively, Lilian Broca has employed archaeological evidence not available to earlier artists to create a realistic architectural setting, costumes, and jewelry.

On the surface, of course, all the artists set out to relate a biblical story. But many more layers underlay their full intent. One might, for instance, interpret the story's popularity in seventeenth-century Holland as an allegory of a small country's struggle to survive against the might of Spain.[12] Or one might investigate the attitudes to Judaism over the centuries, or the strength and prominence of Jewish artists. Certainly, this approach has been taken regarding Rembrandt.

(As a side note, it's interesting that if Esther had to hide her identity at court, then she obviously did not stand out in appearance as being different from the rest of the women.[13] So if what she had to hide was a knowledge of the Jewish rituals, then as an orphan, some woman in her past – Mordechai's wife perhaps? – had to teach them to her. But other critics and art historians have proposed interpretations along these lines and it is not my intention to try to duplicate their work.)

My intention here is not to produce a panegyric on the work of Lilian Broca. As a classically trained art historian, I believe that all art is derivative, and each generation of artists builds on the work of its predecessors. My role is to set the work of one artist within the context of a long lineage of others who depicted the same topic, and to try to shed light on their various approaches.

It should be noted that for a very long stretch of time the art world has not seen narrative and the human form combined. For an artist of the twenty-first century to tell a complex story in multiple episodes, as Broca has done in the Esther series, is almost unheard of (excluding the growing number of graphic-novel artists now using the cartoon form to tell serious tales in small-scale black-and-white ink drawings). With no patron in mind, Broca created the series to express feminist sentiments, sentiments that clearly come through in her interpretation of Queen Esther's life and mission. Broca researched the story extensively and thought deeply about it. In essence, she made it her version of Esther's responses as a woman to the demands of several men, namely Mordechai, Ahashvayrosh, and Haman. In addition, Broca chose to employ a format that has been out of style for some time – using realistic figures in appropriate costume to tell a story. The format is old-fashioned yet still viable. One of few contemporary artists who would dare to work like this, Broca also chose to tell the story in mosaics, taking full advantage of that medium's potential and cognizant of her debt to the world of Byzantium – all this while still being innovative and creative.

Broca also chose to tell the story in mosaics, taking full advantage of that medium's potential and cognizant of her debt to the world of Byzantium – all this while still being innovative and creative.

Esther has long been depicted not just to tell her story but as an allegory, allegory being an age-old device that often employed the female form. The female figure was first used to represent an abstract human quality in the Hellenistic period. For example, the well-known over-life-sized figure of Eirene (meaning peace) as a maternal figure holding an infant representing Ploutos (wealth) demonstrated that wealth comes from peace. The figure of Tyche, an allegorical form used to represent the best features of an ancient city, was also pictured as feminine. Similarly, Esther in the Broca panels is not just the biblical character but, more broadly, an allegorical figure representing womankind as strong, independent, resourceful, an equal partner to the male, and more than clever enough to solve momentous problems. She uses her wits and her position as the king's favorite to influence his decisions and forestall the massacre of all the Jews in his kingdom. Indeed, the king simply handed the problem over to her to resolve, it not being fitting that he should appear to have changed his mind. (Interestingly, the negative aspects of the king's character as weak and easily manipulated are played down in all versions of the story.)

How is Broca's work to be read as Byzantine? To begin with, apart from one or two anonymous servants, the biblical story of Esther comprises only four characters – an abbreviated form of storytelling seen commonly in Early Christian art, in the catacombs for instance. Roman and Early Byzantine floor mosaics rarely depict more than two or three figures in a panel. In the sixth century, when mosaics seem to have moved up from the floor to the walls and ceilings, many more figures are sometimes seen in one work, but still usually in groups of two or three except where the particular story demands more. For example, when a biblical theme is depicted only the principal characters are shown unless the story specifically refers to a crowd or audience, in which case those people are shown with cookie-cutter anonymity.

This stands quite distinct from the post-medieval art period when many figures are added whether they have a role in the story or not. In contrast, Byzantine mosaics feature considerable symbolism and the characters are very much "in your face," with the background devoid of deep or realistic perspective. The settings are quite simple, sometimes totally plain. When the background is entirely gold, the depth of field according to the viewer's perception is either absent altogether or infinite. This characteristic does not, however, indicate that Byzantine artists lacked knowledge of perspective.[14] Rather, the salient fact is that Byzantine pictorial space opens out into what is in front of the particular work, the work having been specifically adapted to fit the architectural form it inhabits, functioning in effect as part of the room. This is quite different from the Renaissance use of the picture space as a window, opening out onto what is behind the architectural enclosure.

The Byzantine style of using space in front of the picture plane is evident in Broca's work, where she intentionally set her characters at the very front of the plane, leaving little depth. As she herself has noted, she had in mind the depth of a stage when composing her panels, and certainly this theatrical aspect is evident throughout the mosaic series. Other Byzantine characteristics that apply to Broca's mosaics include the monumentality of the figures, their static poses, and their strong facial features that are expressive but not emotive. Consider, for instance, earlier representations of Esther fainting in front of the king or "having the vapors" in the scene when she approaches the king uninvited, all representing the supposed inherent weakness of women. Drawing on Byzantine style, Broca depicts the same scene but showing Esther very much in control of both herself and the situation.

A highly dynamic medium, mosaic has qualities that go beyond those of paint. In this, I disagree with the artist and art historian Svetlana Alpers's assertion that, "We look through the pictorial surface to the deeper meaning of the text. It is verbal meaning or the narration of stories that we take away from such pictures. In both the art and the analysis of it, completed composition is asserted over the craft and process of making, and meaning dominates over representation and its functions."[15] In Broca's work, however, the choice of mosaic as the medium enhances the deeper meaning of the text; meaning and medium are mutually dependent.

In Broca's work, however, the choice of mosaic as the medium enhances the deeper meaning of the text; meaning and medium are mutually dependent.

Mosaic also captures the changing qualities of light and the vast range of colors now available in glass. As the noted Byzantine scholar Gervase Mathew wrote in reference to the *Ennead,* "The characteristic conception of the relation between colour and light, and the Byzantine delight in the colour of gold, are already explicit [in the third-century Neoplatonist writings of Plotinus, in the first *Ennead*:] 'All the loveliness of colour and the light of the sun.' 'And how comes gold to be a beautiful thing? And lightning by night and stars, why are these so fair?'"[16]

A number of artists working internationally are bringing mosaic, a centuries old medium, into the twenty-first century. Would their creations succeed as well in paint? I don't believe so. Looking at the Queen Esther series, the richness and luxury of glass and its light effects greatly enrich the setting and the venerability of the story. To see Broca's mosaic panels in natural light is an experience that cannot be duplicated in book plates, no matter how good the quality. This results partly from photographers not wanting to have shadows and thus insisting on full frontal lighting, which completely flattens a mosaic image, canceling out the advantages of glass. Sunshine on the glass creates a three-dimensionality that electric light can never duplicate.

Indeed, mosaics were originally intended to be seen illuminated by candles or lamps, both of which cause a flickering that suggests movement in the figures. Changes in daylight from time to time, day to day, and season to season played a fundamental role in viewing ancient and medieval frescoes, carvings, and mosaics. These factors are often forgotten today. The viewer responds almost emotionally to glass because of the physical depth of the color, its variability, and the light that it traps and sends back. Mosaic is a dynamic medium, the image constantly and subtly changing. In this fashion, the medium Broca has chosen to depict the story of Esther works together with the content and style of presentation to make the queen a provocative, three-dimensional character, more so in my view than was achieved by most painters of the past.

Notes

1 See, for example, Richard I. Cohen, *Jewish icons: art and society in modern Europe* (Berkeley: University of California Press, 1998). Or by the same author, "Exhibiting Nineteenth-Century Artists of Jewish Origin in the Twentieth Century: Identity, Politics, and Culture," *Painting in Nineteenth-Century Europe: The Emergence of Jewish Artists in Nineteenth-century Europe,* ed. Susan T. Goodman (London: The Jewish Museum, 2001), 153–163.

2 Cohen, *Jewish icons,* 161.

3 I am grateful to Prof. Eric Lawee, York University Toronto, for advice on background readings concerning Jewish/Christian relations in the sixteenth century and onward, and to Prof. Natalie Davis, University of Toronto, for suggested readings on the matter of Jewish artists, Christian artists' renderings of Jewish subjects, and so forth.

4 A Web search for Esther, Queen Esther, Esther Bible Art, or Purim, for example, will set the reader along this path.

5 For example, Keith Christiansen, Judith W. Mann, *Orazio and Artemisia Gentilischi,* Metropolitan Museum of New York (New York: Yale University Press, 2002).

6 Christiansen, Mann, *Orazio and Artemisia Gentilischi,* 376.

7 Karl Lilienfeld, *Arent de Gelder, Sein Leben und Seine Kunst* (The Hague: M. Nijhoff, 1914).

8 Nicole Garnier, *Antoine Coypel, 1661–1722* (Paris: Arthena, 1989), plates X, XI.

9 Anthony Blunt, *The Paintings of Nicolas Poussin: A Critical Catalogue* (London: Phaidon, 1966), no. 36

10 Lastman, Pieter Piertersz, *The Triumph of Mordechai,* oil on panel, Museum het Rembrandthuis, Amsterdam.

11 Gary D. Schwartz, *Rembrandt: His Life, His Paintings* (New York: Viking, 1985), 49 and scattered references. (Originally published in Dutch, 1984.)

12 See, for example, Helen Webberley, *The Book of Esther in 17th Century Dutch Art,* accessed March 3, 2011, http://archive.artgallery.NSW.gov.au/aaanz_2002/__data/page/2345/helen_webberley.pdf.

13 Paula E. Hyman, "Does Gender Matter?" *Rethinking European Jewish History,* eds. Jeremy Cohen and Moshe Rosman (Oxford: Littman Library of Jewish Civilization, 2009), 54–71. Hyman on p. 63 also lists several examples in painting and literature where the quintessential Jewish woman is a "distinctly different type" – exotic, mysterious, sexually tempting, seductive.

14 For further discussion of this topic see Gervase Mathew, *Byzantine Aesthetics* (New York: Viking Press, 1964), 31, 32.

15 Svetlana Alpers, "Art History and Its Exclusions: The Example of Dutch Art," *Feminism and Art History: Questioning the Litany,* eds. Norma Brounde and Mary Garard (New York: Harper & Row, 1982), 187.

16 Mathew, *Byzantine Aesthetics,* 19, and footnotes 11, 12; *Ennead* I.6.I. in *Plotinus: The Enneads.* Vol. 7, English translation by A.H. Armstrong (London: The Loeb Classical Library, 1966–88).

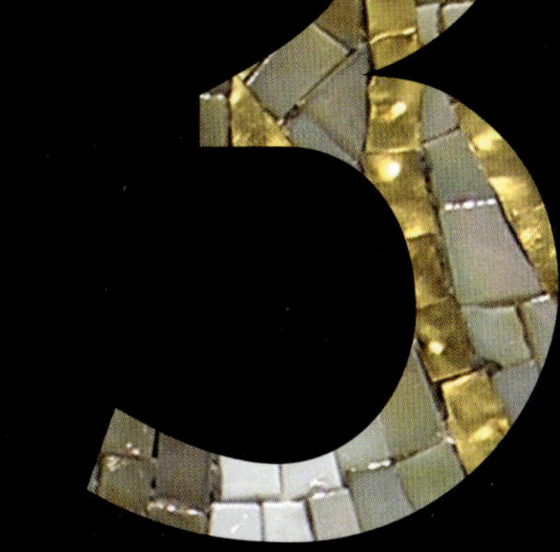

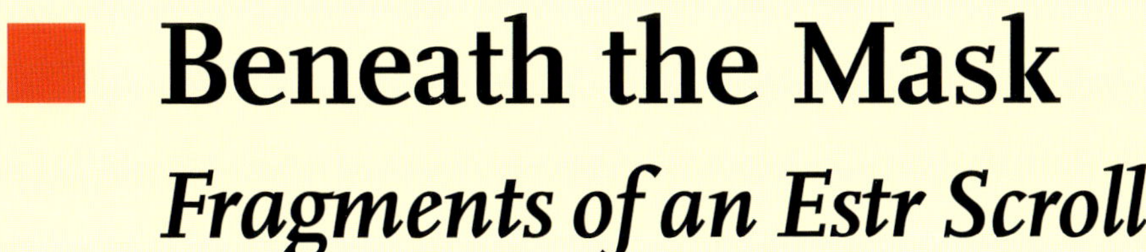

Beneath the Mask

Fragments of an Estr Scroll

YOSEF WOSK

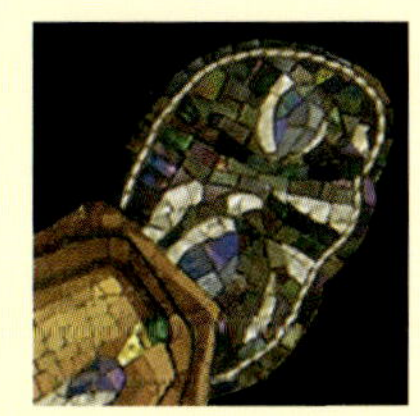

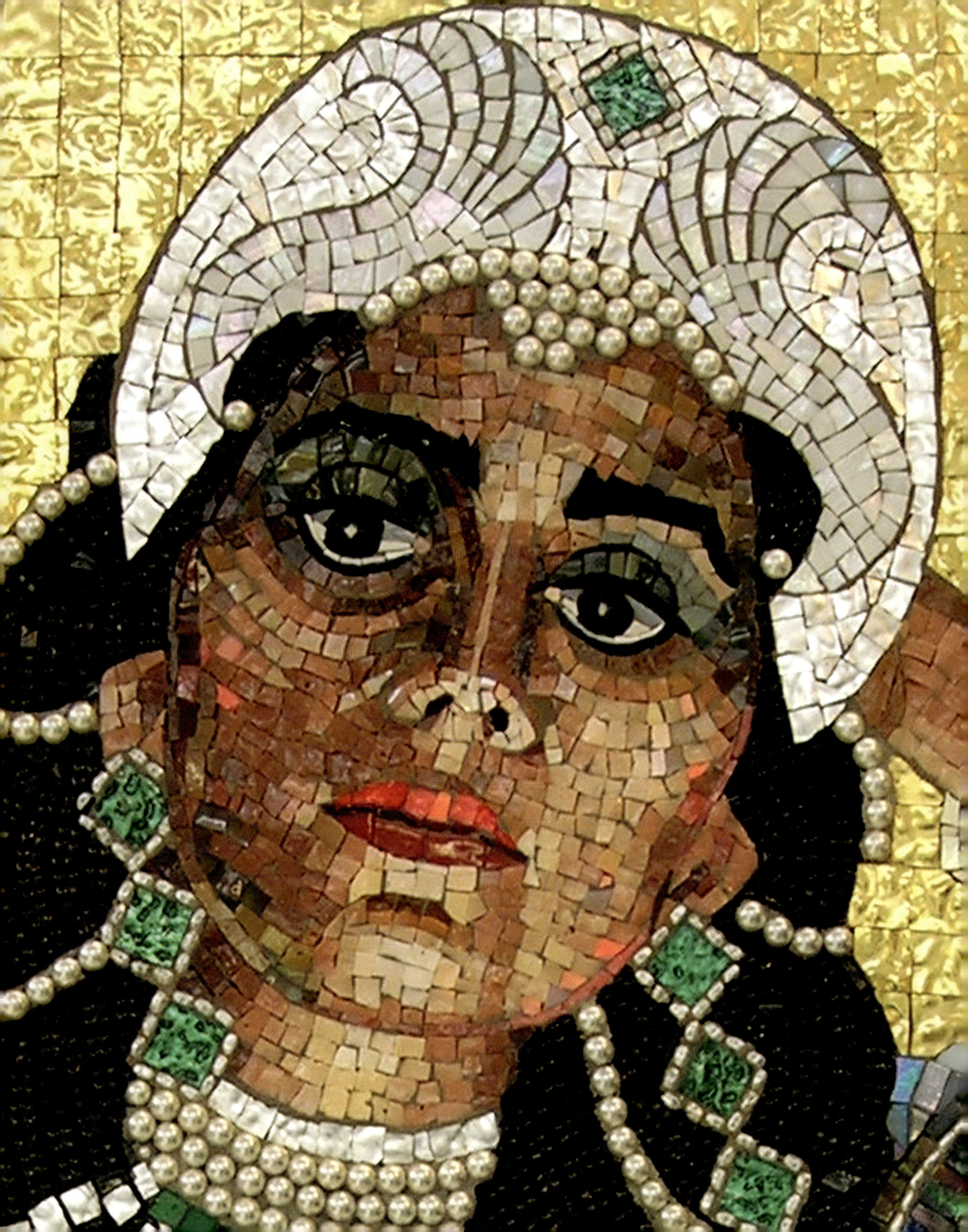

Beneath the Mask

Yosef Wosk

This chapter is a combination of essay, poem, and narrative conversation in which I enter the text of Estr as a kinaesthetic experience, adopt an authentic persona of its heroine, and speak in her voice: not the voice of the young or middle-aged Estr but rather of Estr as elder, woman as sage.

I chose to spell her name as *Estr*[1] instead of the widely accepted *Esther* for two reasons: i) It presents a fresh spelling and therefore acts as an iconoclastic device to remove over-familiar associations with all of their accompanying gravitational detours. It allows the reader to approach the name and character anew: a second chance to make a first impression. ii) The original Hebrew word אסתר has only four letters, so why not the transliteration as well? This lends an air of added authenticity – of weight, shape, and meaning – to the central name that acts as an anchor for the entire text.

The prose poem sprang from an investigation of the Scroll of Estr through multiple lenses, including the biblical text, comparative religious and mythological references, rabbinical commentaries, biblical criticism, modern literary theory, and practical applications.[2] Originally, I planned to examine these aspects in an academic manner, and my lengthy footnotes do so to a limited degree. Research revealed, however, that numerous other authors had already published much in these areas. Heeding the advice of the wise Kohelet, King of Jerusalem, who observed that "there is no end to making many books,"[3] I decided to set out in a different direction.

The resulting narrative constructs a triangulation between Estr, deity, and we the readers (who are also the community). It claims no particular order and flows as a meandering conversation through the various chambers of our heroine's mind. It is Estr's voice, vibrant and self-assured, reflecting on who she was, what became of her, and who she is now. She speaks alternately as Estr the mundane, Estr the historical persona, and as the multi-mythed Estr the goddess. She fluctuates from contemplating herself, to challenging the reader, to engaging the Creator in cosmic speculation. She emerges – like Lilian Broca's tessellated mosaics when viewed by candlelight – as a moving picture of herself. And we see *ourselves* reflected in both Estr's and Lilian's complex lives. We both ache for and admire them as they struggle with exile, beauty, political upheaval, and archetypal creativity, and tell their story in stone and parchment.

Here, then, is Estr's testament: not the authorized version as entered into the canon of biblical literature but rather Estr's hidden words, ones that reveal her beneath the mask that we have been weaving since time out of mind.

The illustrations appearing throughout this chapter are all by Lilian Broca and, except where otherwise noted, are Broca's original sketches for *The Queen Esther Mosaic Series*.

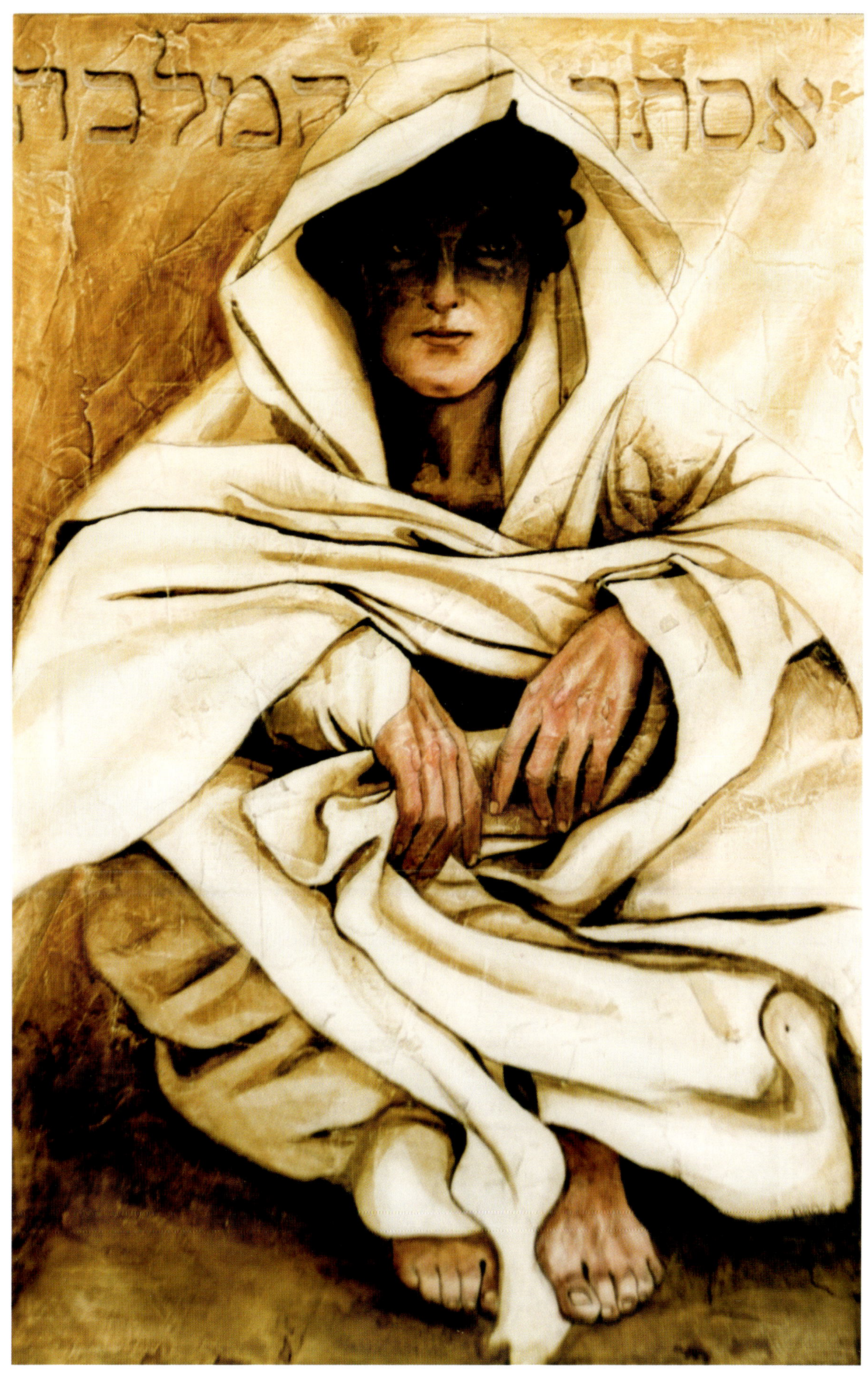

Esther, 1993
Acrylic on panel
36 x 24 in. (91.5 x 61 cm)

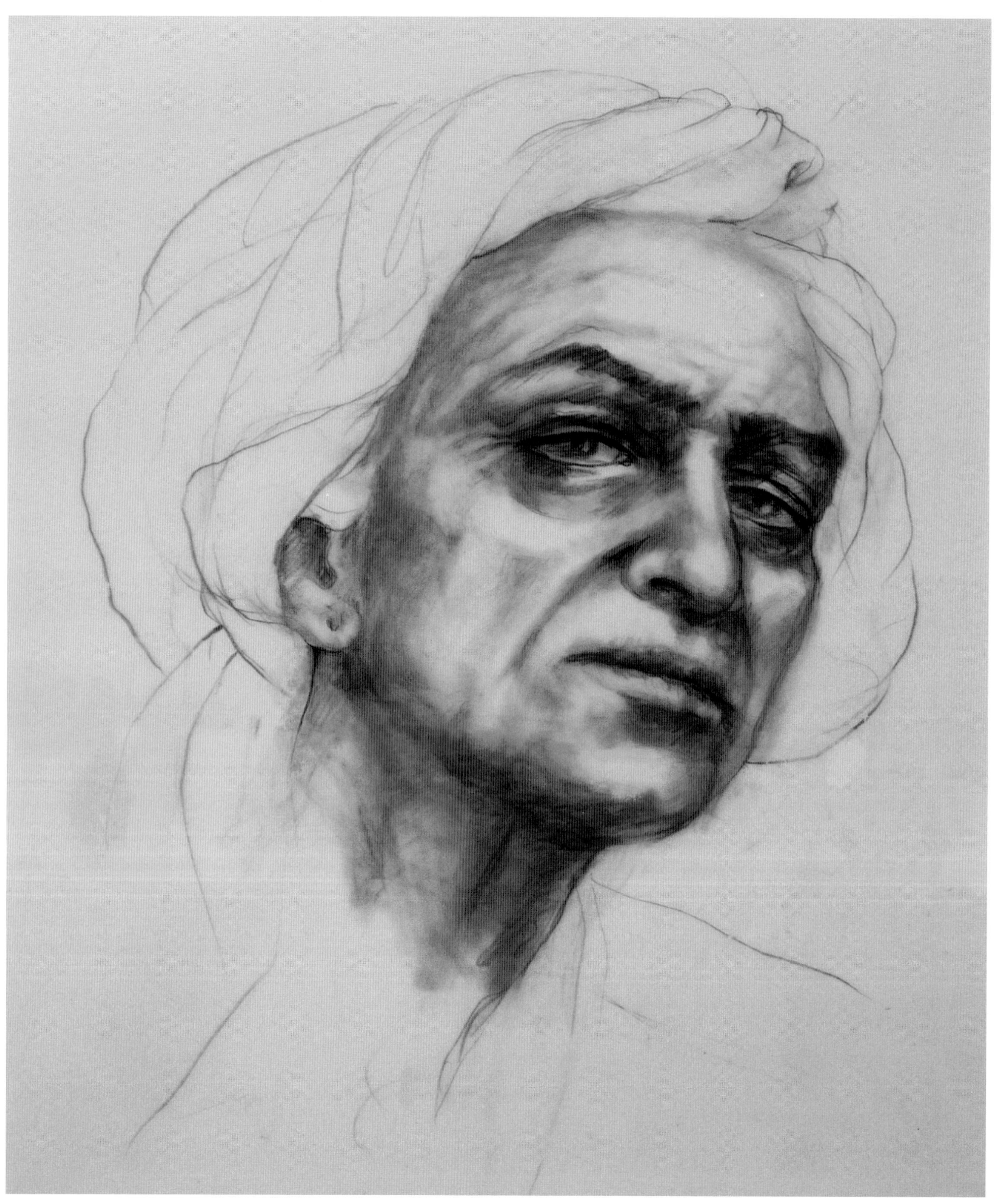

Estr as Sage, graphite on paper, 2011, cropped, at full size 8.5 x 11 in. (21.59 x 27.94 cm)

Fragments of an Estr Scroll

I am Estr,
queen of your
imagination,
that ever-curious agent in search
of its impossible conclusion,
as if something was lost
before it was ever possessed
and you,
you alone,
have been conscripted to
hunger
ceaselessly
for its scattered shards.

Meanwhile,
as if to grant you a
mid-week
Sabbath
in the grip of a tsunami sea,
you grasp at pitiful illusions
floating on eternal winds
artfully disguised
as your distant destination.

In your deluded search for authenticity
you ended up fondling ancient legends,
looking under the wrong set of rocks,
and became surface-filled with today's
empty headlines.

And now,
many hundreds of years since you left home
on this journey beyond memory
of where you came from
or where you were going,
your confidence forsakes you,
like mine did,
that you could make a difference,
that you could influence history,
that they would write about you —
when all that you really wanted to do was
nothing,
to be left alone
in the obscurity of your dire diffidence,
to be veiled beneath reluctant
cloth-covered
eyes
and leave it all
to them,
to they,
to those

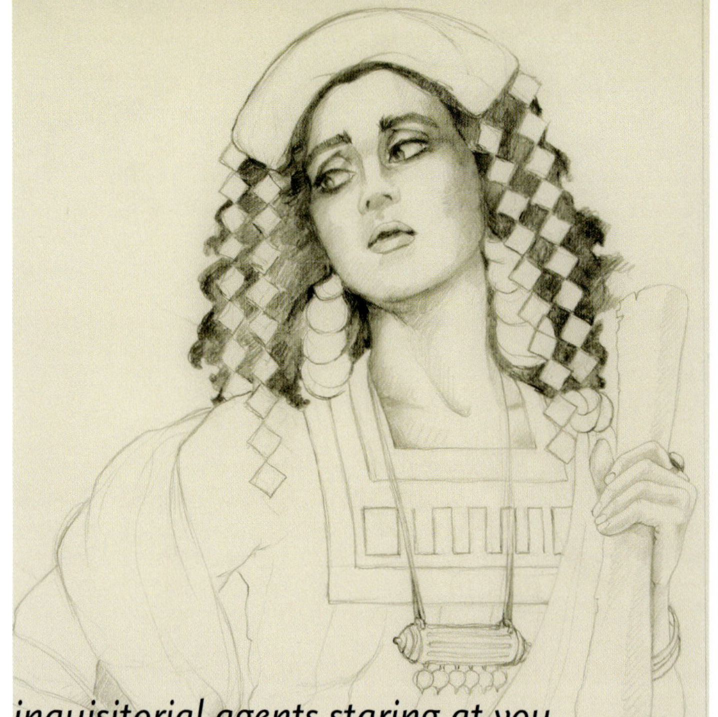

inquisitorial agents staring at you
through censored psyches,
ensconced on gnarled platforms
safely cached behind tilting shades
in an office whose only real furniture
were officially inked and rubbered stamps.

I am the הסתר *of your necessary dreams,*[4]
for if I did not inhabit your private needs,
your daily addiction to idols incarnate,
then you would have tossed my rag sheet
upon the indifferent
trash heaps of long,
so very long ago.
You would not have celebrated
and nourished me all these years
nor dressed and drunk me
as a stairway
to the seven-storied mansion
of your syncopated soul.

You named books
and festivals for me,
minted coins with my likeness,
wrote music, wove tapestries,
painted pictures,
opened entire industries
using Estr as your trademark mask.
Children and great-grandmothers
bear my names.
Before I knew it,
organizations and hospitals
began meeting and healing
beneath the fluttering Hadassahn flag.
Even Israel is spoken of as the people of
Estr,
and ten thousand four-year-olds
costume in my image
every nascent Spring
while their parents
drink,
inhale,
feast
and laugh
as the irreverent iconoclasts that they are,
as ones who have just smashed
another false idol,
in overtime,
with annihilation in its caustic arms.

I am Estr,
or so you say,
and you will continue to use me
as the echo
that sounds in the
quasi-emptiness
of your uncertain
and restless heart.

I am Estr,
heroine of your exhausted projections,
yet you continue
to champion me
because you have no history of your own.
You have been too careful,
too methodical,
clinging to order,
and have not gambled enough to stumble,
to kneel awkwardly,
to reach out,
trembling before death.
You make my story
yours
so that you do not have to
go to all the trouble
of manufacturing your own.

The truth,
sister,
is that
as long as you are not you,
you will not permit me to be me.[5]
You'll only exploit me
as an excuse for not living it yourself;
you'll only maneuver the labyrinth
of my malleable mind
to escape from the prison
of your own making.
You want me to be
your proxy
to cast your every vote,
your key
to open impossibly shuttered doors,
your magician
when there are no more miracles.

Do you realize what you've become?
An insomniac in search of a dream,
a well,
once liquid, wet and deep,
now empty, dry and dead.

Having protested the aura of heroine,
and thrown off the burden
of your persistent projections
for the sake of your bible-bound religion
deep in the Heart of Exile,
I remind you that
you're not the only ones.

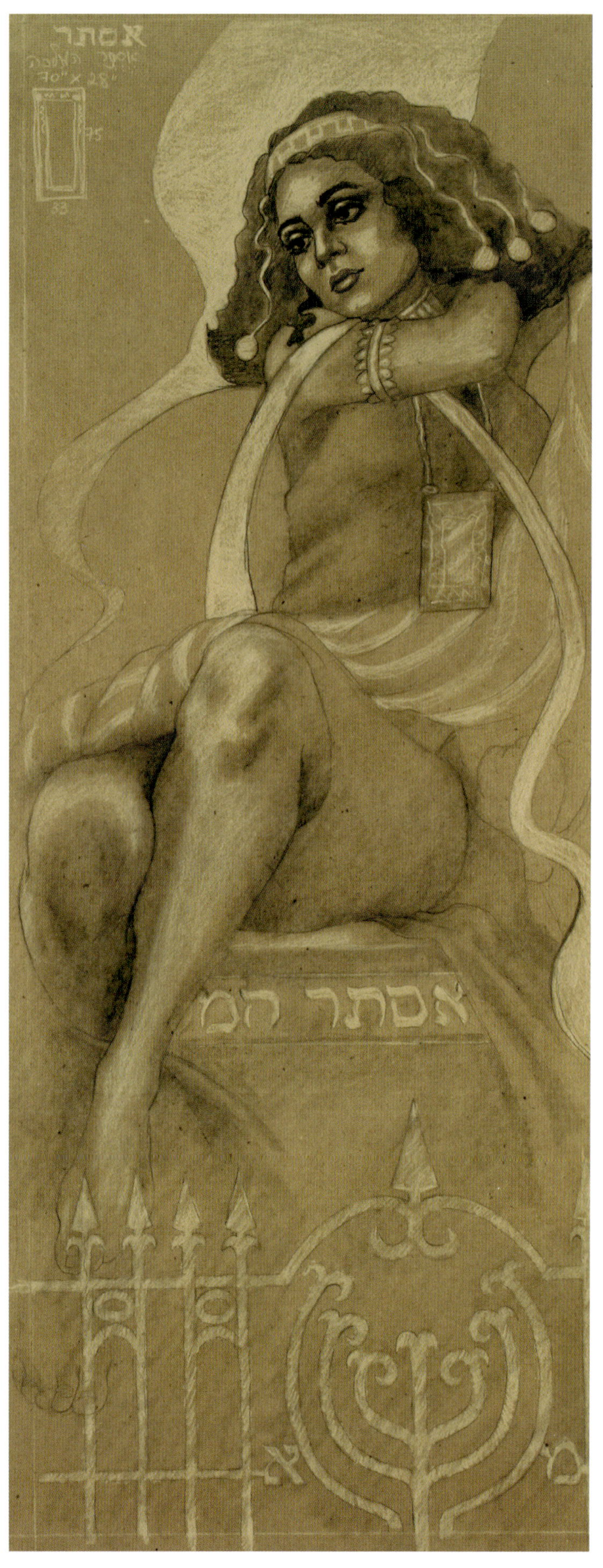

How many more have used me,
manipulated the daughter of Avihayil,
youngest girl child of the youngest son,
scion of the ever-wandering tribe
of the finally-born Benjamin of beloved
Rachel,
wife of reluctant Jacob[6]
who,
like me,
was forced upon the face
of an unforgiving
world.

I was simple,
a typical teen,[7]
an Everywoman,
until challenged with fate
and doused with questions
I could only answer by
not responding,
by hesitating...
then swallowing
what little breath still remained
(it was barely enough).
I called upon allies
from shamayim *to* aretz*,*
in cipher
beneath
a knowing spirit
of enigmatic proportions,
until the answer blossomed
to break a burning brand
upon my cowering name,
my life no longer my own,
forever.

Our lives —
the Hebrews, my peripatetic people,
the ones who left home as elders[8]
to follow the vaporous Voice across
unknown rivers —
our lives are not filled with bliss,
though they may be saturated
with an always engaging animus
that dances us like cosmic puppets
upon the over-groomed
mustachios of every known despot
who laughs into the heart of heaven
with that special joy
reserved for unbridled evil ways.

It is clear that our lives,
although filled with thanksgiving
and pocked by passions,
were marked for sacrifice
two thousand years before we were born.[9]
Some are born to royalty
while others inherit the hunger;
we were born to humanity,
created in a caste-like confine
in the image of Your daily dream.

Just as I, Estr,
cautiously sloughed my limitations
to become the voice
of an abandoned nation,
I wonder
now
when you'll take
your next
stumbling
step.
Perhaps you need an order of pogrom
with a side of zeal[10]
to evolve defiantly into
vigilante villain busters.
Some will participate
with vigor in their gait;
others will be dragged struggling,
their bodies one clenched muscle
protesting every forced foot of the way;
some will be surprised
by their unaccustomed involvement;
many take toddling steps,
falling often on their padded path
as they prepare
for their self-appointed roles
as righteous weekend warriors
versus the viral Man from Megiddo.[11]

All are eventually martyred
for how else can you be born
except through the painful opening
from one world to the next,
always a passage beyond.

Others react to torment
through madness, despair,
depression and doubt;
and then there are those who repent,
cleansing their closets
of salacious secrets
and turning to
Quinta Essentia
to begin yet again and again.
Inexplicably,
in the face of so much conflicting evidence,
they insist that
Evil & Good, Inc.
continue to be held in the
One Great Parenthesis
of Creation.[12]

And what is evil
but an attempt to escape
from Your eternal gaze,
the one that is watching,
forever,
through an omniocular lens
too dark[13] *to gauge the message*
of Your discontent
as You stare with vigilant tenacity
over a universe,
once vacant,
that has recently become abode to
this rather menacing menagerie
of Your ever-emerging creation.

I am no longer just Estr,
the queen formerly known as Hadassah,
and bearer of your fantasy fame.
Listen,
my pilgrim,
my colleague,
my friend —
I've been
renamed, borrowed, justified and explained
like an overjealous footnote in a polyglot
bible.

No longer the maiden,
no longer the girl,
no longer the simple one
who whirls with the winds
upon a child's unconscious awareness.
I now knew that I was
cursed with a Beauty
that became my prison
in a palace of someone else's kingdom.
Perhaps there was meaning
in the parade of unforgiving moments
leading to a royal offer that I could not
refuse.

So Hadassah hid
and Estr was revealed,
one name serving the other
as distant cousins
in awkward ouster from
all sense of native tranquillity.

Hadassah[14] *the myrtle,*
the almond-eyed leaf
held in perfect symmetry
round a royal root
near the waters of Eden's fourbidden[15]
rivers.

Hadassah morphed myrtle,[16]
sweet fragranced
dedicated deeds
that typified both plant and maiden.
Ever pious,
evergreen,
immortal crown of lasting legacy,
cherished charm,
perfume and culinary adornment,
yet, when bit on the bough,
bitter tasting
as the essence of poison
to those who would invade her.

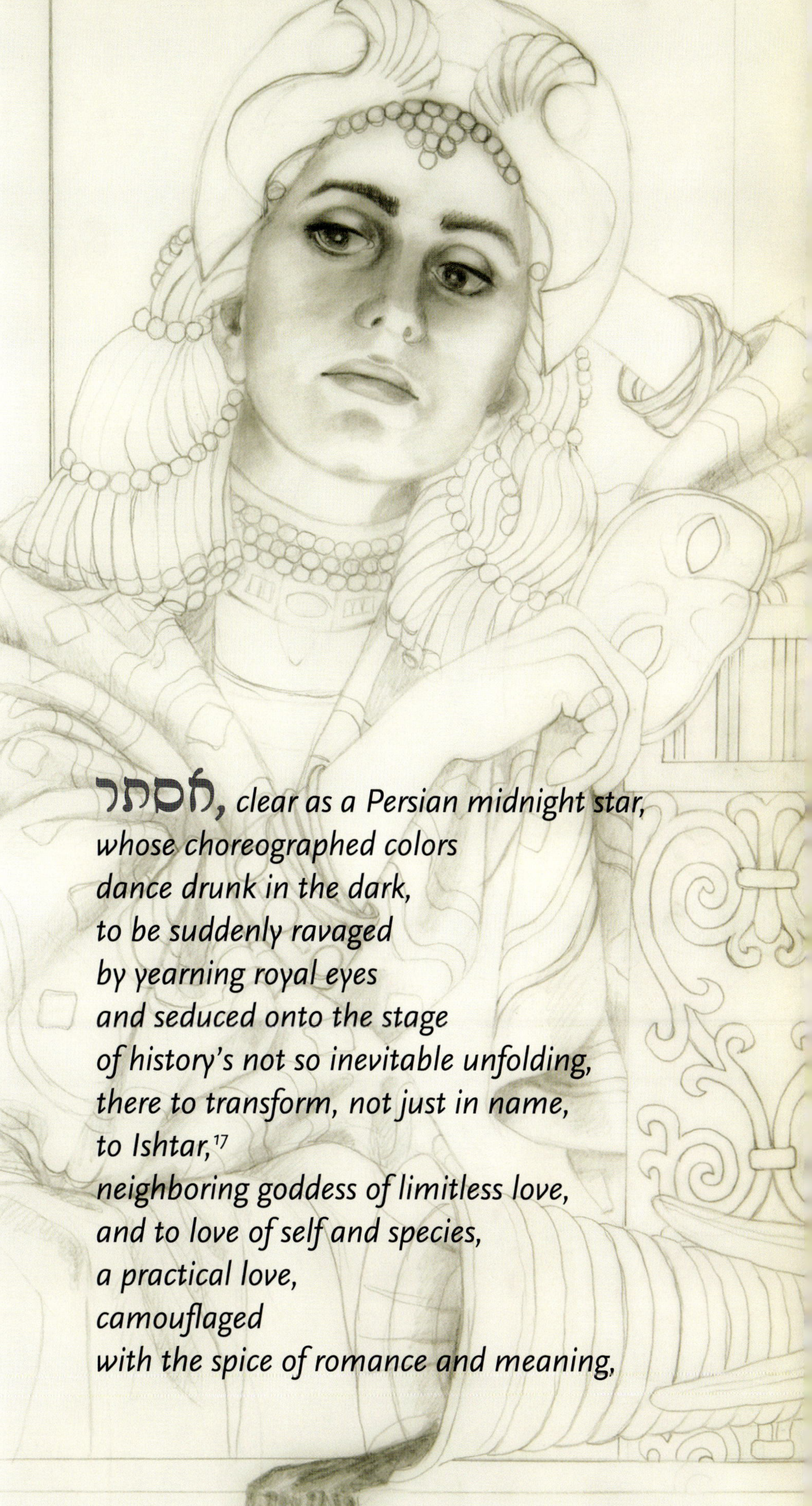

אסתר, *clear as a Persian midnight star,*
whose choreographed colors
dance drunk in the dark,
to be suddenly ravaged
by yearning royal eyes
and seduced onto the stage
of history's not so inevitable unfolding,
there to transform, not just in name,
to Ishtar,[17]
neighboring goddess of limitless love,
and to love of self and species,
a practical love,
camouflaged
with the spice of romance and meaning,

but a kind of love, nevertheless,
one that leads to the fertile increase
of me *over* you
and the incessant replacement
of the dying and the dead
with the infinite hope of the newly born.

I am Stara, Ishtara, Ashtoret,
Astarte, Estara and Stella,
hopeful harbinger of enkindled Spring.
Estarte[18]*—*
one,
singular,
planet or star
(they merge in all this metaphor),
and yet numerous as the stardust
of an unknown evening's paradise.

And I am Venus,
both morning and evening star,
goddess of love and beauty,
who revels in the solar winds
of illuminated shadows,
whose morning light persists
when all other orbs have ceased to shine.
They say that I, too, am a model
of perseverance,
perpetually present
in the darkness of every generation's
rising up
to fulfill Haman's[19] *diabolic desire.*

I am Estr of the Ether,
arising from the eastern shores of Elysium's
morning gate
filled with the blush of dawning light,
augur that the dark of death,
sleep and night have been stirred,
have begun their release
from a season's hold,
have escaped the insistent weight
of gravity's pull.

Slowly,
as the immense orbital ship
spins its weighty way
through inner oceans of outer space,
wisps of seemingly disinterested clouds
reflect the sun's infant light
as it escapes its impregnable prison
to be reborn
as if for the very first time.
It is I, Estr, promised princess
of earliest Spring,[20]
who enters the king's chamber unbeckoned
as I must from year to year
to banish the Hamanic darkness within.

I am Estr of the Easter,[21]
decimated by three days of
fierce fasting[22]
during which I tasted nothing
but the bitter fear of death's rotting spectre.
Three days of death,
starving in the tomb of an earth
that gave and took and gave again.

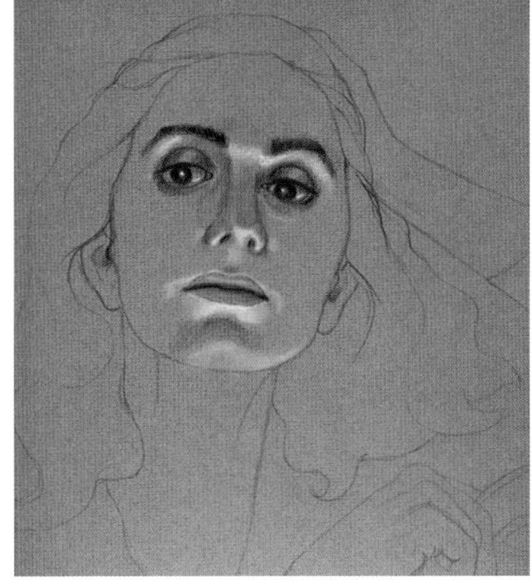

Having already died
I was no longer afraid to live,
so I arose from my wounded womb,
anointed by the diligent dew
that hung like a necklace
upon my weary head.
Acknowledging my new life,
I was inaugurated in the presence of
His Majesty Ahashvayrosh's[23]
one hundred and twenty
and seven kingdoms.

It is only now,
through my death,
that I can be revived again.
The journey seems truly long and impossible,
not the itinerary for most.[24]
If I had never died —
painful as it always is
with its depleted spirit
and discarded soul,
no longer feathered,
no longer winged —
I could never have returned.
If I had not dared hitch a ride
on aurora's gilded steeds
then fallow darkness would still prevail.

And I am Estr the hidden moon-one,[25]
she who swaddles the eclipsed light
until its chosen nativity;
who hides[26] from king and court,
from haremed friend and plotting foe.
I am she who must conceal
so that others never have to,
who hides to avoid confrontation,
who hides in the image of God,[27]
who hides in hiding,
the pilgrim immersed
as an agitated fugitive —
awkward, accented, forever the outsider —
garbed in wrinkles,
with a heart that yearns
with every unnatural beat.
She hides to survive in history's hollow,
always laboring,
always birthed,
until,
at the moment of her crowning
it is revealed that
she is not born into freedom
but into struggle,
a god wrestler of the highest order.
Now it is Estr who stands her ground:
confronter,[28]
not victim,
any more.

Let me tell you about
the genius
of my
beauty.
I was forced to be beautiful
first by blood
and then to help me survive,
and finally to bear
the salvific role
you demanded of me,
enslaving me to my beauty
because
you are not.

Some, in telling my story,
turn everything inside out:
they do not admit to my beauty
but only to my Grace.
They do not want to credit
mere physical attributes
as the passionate catalyst,
as the defining force.
They favor fear, observance, piety,
and the like
so they theologize, devolute,
attempt to empty beauty
of its tingling good looks,
and re-make the book in their own sorry
image.

I was green,[29]
they say,
witchlike,
yet grace enshrouded my deformities,
becoming a false face
that allowed me to hide in plain sight.
There I was,
the chosen one,
disguised in royal chambers
in the presence
of all that was most revealed.

And I am Estr the storied one
whose life became a scroll
that scholars refute,
about which they say
"It never happened, nor ever could!"
But I know better.
I was there,
time after time after time again,
to live something that never was
but always is[30]
in a land where the once in a lifetime
happens every day.

I have become myth and midrash,
the multi-appellated one,
a coated rack for your millennial garments
carelessly tossed upon my image
after another day
at the high walled megalopolitan zoo.

I am no strutting-fool heroine,
arrogant champion of temporary fame,
nor were my acts premeditated gallantry
in search of scandal-star-status
in your checkout tabloids.
For me, it all started as another one of those
"this is really uncomfortable
and I'd rather not be here"
kind of moments.
I should be filed in the archives
of accidental heroes,
for I simply did what was necessary
on an otherwise slow day
at the plotting palace
of our brewing discontent.

I hesitated,
until challenged by Uncle M[31]
with these disturbing words:
"Do not think in your heart
that you will escape
by living in the king's house
any more than all the others.
For if you remain silent
at this time,
if you don't act,
then saving and rescue
will come to our people from somewhere else,
through different channels,
but you and your ancestry
will be utterly destroyed.
And who knows;
perhaps it was only for this
that you came to royalty!"[32]

So I dared to do,
to enter and ask
when
separation
and
silence
would have been more becoming.
I partied with the king and his Haman,
but those who really know how to listen
understood that my every laugh was a tear.
I knew then that I was the
someone else;
I was the they and the them,
becoming the reflected other
to finally see
myself.

I was the reluctant prophet[33]
protesting barefoot
at the desert bush,
stuttering before the court
and practicing for three dreaded days
what I must then declare.
It was Sinai in the midst of Shushan,
and I,
new and noble at once,
prepared to take my first steps.

Nor did I fast alone:
all my people living in Shushan
crossed the river outside the walls of the city,
crossed the waters as they had the
Sea of Red Reeds,
and gathered there
to observe the fast as one.
Twelve thousand priests
marched in the procession,
trumpets in their right hands
and scrolls in their left,
weeping and mourning in prayer.[34]

There were few means of survival
in foreign lands
where I was born three generations after
the Babylonian empire
disrobed our temple,
sacked the city
and forced us from our laureated land.

Exile: an unnatural state of strangers
where we were portrayed as
semi-slaves and itinerant wanderers,
surreal burlesquers in livid lands,
embarrassed by our own shadows,
frightened by the sound of driven leaves,[35]
nervous, tentative,
awaiting the next disaster.

With few rights of our own
we learned to endure
as only the poorest know,
through any means possible:
Some lived exemplary lives
(perhaps our hosts
would not feel threatened,
would even appreciate and reward us
or leave us alone),
while, for the most part,
seduction, favors, bribery, alliance,
tenuous power,
making ourselves useful,
learning, lying and assimilating
were all we really had.
We also relied on the spiritual technologies
of what turned out to be
our eminently portable religion.
We invoked heart-labors
such as prayer, fasting, bowing and believing,
observing a thousand divine directives,
giving charity to holy beggars,
studying, always studying,
and repenting from
dictive desire.

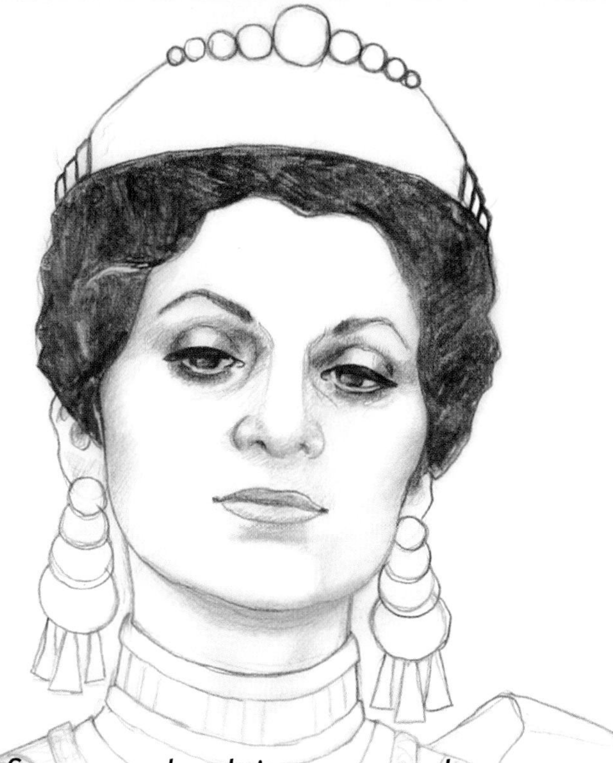

As far as my book is concerned,
this Scroll of Everyday Estr,
there is more here
than innocent words
colliding with alien eyes.
Some call it a romance, a novella,
a subterfuge, mythos
or simply anachronism.
They know it, however,
only for its primp and prop,
its imagined affectations.[36]
They see only an erudite critique
on a predictably tired theme.

What really happened was this:
all the king's critics and all the king's men —
after an orgy of dismemberment
and a procession
of metamechanical autopsies —
may have found a few extra,
or perhaps not enough,
spare parts
but they never could put
Estr together again.

They say the book was written
as an excuse to party,
that it was simply an apologetic,
a new year's vehicle
to import a pagan's inebriated holyday
into the arthritic sombreness
of a nation's ancient bones.
Estr Book was intermarriage,
they say,
an impaired infusion
of vital blood,
grafted branches upon the Tree of Life,
instructions of a distant document
thrust upon a bewildered people
in the metamorphosis
of their strangely outspreading lives.

At first,
even pedantic patriarchs
and wily bands of intoxicated oracles —
those readers of omens
and predictors of signs —
were in rare agreement
that Purim was fantasy,
fiction and fraud.
"It never happened,"
they boast.
"It is the outsider, "
they say;
"Everything about it is inappropriate,"
they declare.
"Is it this that would brazenly attach itself
to our lauded literature?"
they complain.

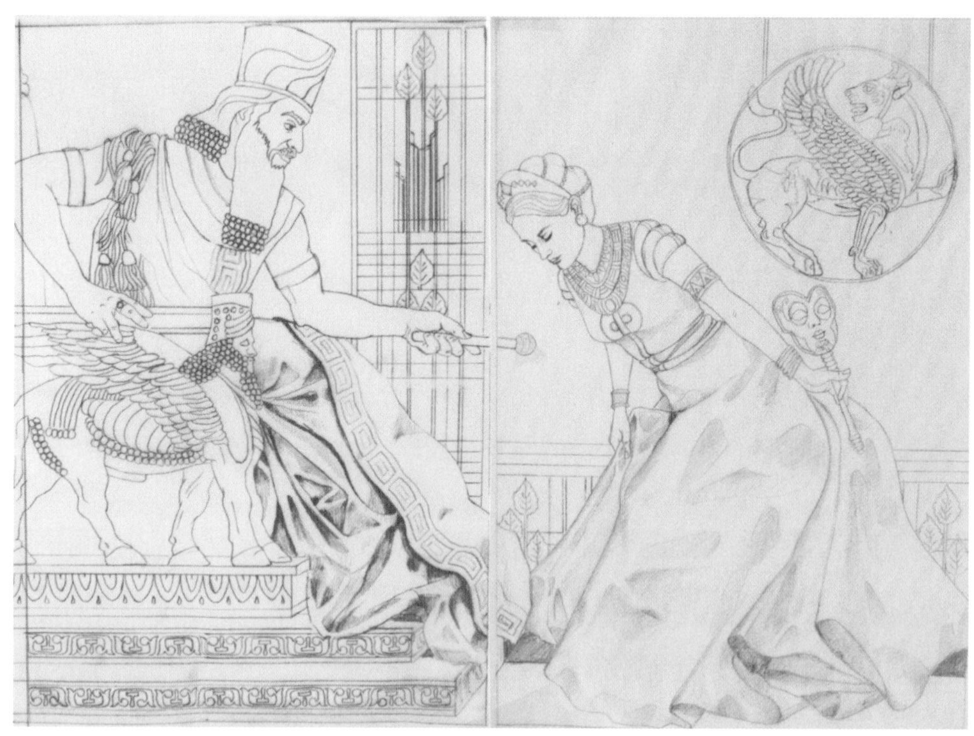

How long did it take
before this nuisance tome
was even allowed on the agenda,
there to be debated among the
fiercely attuned
Fellows of the Great Assembly:
Estr "yeah" or
Estr "nay"
as to whether my scroll
would finally join the contracted canon
of sacra graphia
or be consigned to the untouchable
outer books of false doctrine?

Even then,
twenty-two versions
of my story were not accepted
until they were edited,
washed,
and hung out to dry,
letter by letter,
vowel by variant
with cantillation assigned
to each word and phrase;
they were then massaged,
seeded and asked to bear
deliberate messages from
the hyperbolic front.

The final draft was
a revelation in itself,
product of an emanant age
that spoke of the world in secular terms,
a separation of theocracy and monarchy
or any ocracy de jour.
Bereft of the G word —
it was not even hovering
in the wings of expectant call —
and empty of divine interference,
my scroll simply told its story
and left the rest to us.
No manifest meaning,
this song of mine.
It was no longer Sinai
(when God walked on the winds
and performed miracles
at the drop of a sigh),
but rather Torah of the Absurd
for a covert new world.

When I first told my narrative
of a desacralized humanity
who had denied deity
not three but thirty times
and claimed the planet as their own,
it introduced a new language
of radical reason
unbeholden to covenanted gods
of give and take.
For this to happen,
it, like Eden,
needed the Apple of Eve,
the Eye of Estr,
the woman's birthing suit,
and the subtle serpent of Haman,
incarnation of Winter's darkling death
conspiring to murder
those he had so assiduously seduced
in the seasonal cycle of transmigrated life.
This time not "Ye shall be as gods"[37]
but rather "You shall be human."
Things will be different this time round,
or so we thought,
in the flowering vanity of our singular self.
This reimagined georgic book
whose pages swing precariously
between the antiquarian binding
of an archaic creation,
demands that we embrace the world,
aware and awake,
willingly or not,
battered and burned,
hammered and hit,
simultaneously accused and acquitted,
until our voice calls
in exhausted surrendrance:
Hineini, *"Here I am."*

Your God no longer lives in heaven or hill,
in temple, tower or turret;
It has taken a second,
a millionth, abode,
deep within
our deceptively liberated lies.
It is not just out there anymore
but rather concealed within —
more invisible than breath,
more ethereal than thought,
closer than the beating
of our brave bearded hearts.[38]

Humans,
who like to be nursed —
we still take such a long time to walk
and how rare is it to meet someone who
has fully opened their eyes —
have finally been alerted to a world
overgrown with zealous men
and cultivating women.
Due to low attendance and maturing taste
of what was once considered
a captive audience,
the deities and their angelic entourages
have canceled their terrestrial engagement
and taken the Celestial Circus on the road.
Theatre Earth,
no longer forced to attend
to their daily entertainments,
is now closed
to the Godding Games
of teasing tears and wretched tragedies
produced by,
or on behalf of,
our former Land Lords.
They have absconded
with their infinite powers
and convincing brawn,
although, at times, we do miss their
prophetic possessions
and overt interventions.

After boundless aeons of
demanding, commanding,
rewarding and punishing,
they have finally abdicated,
acceding us our own reveries
that, more often than not,
announce themselves in a series of
pitiful machinations.
How disappointed we were to realize
that we,
ourselves,
(in a kind of child-to-parent ratio),
were no better than the original
Baals, Yahwehs, Allahs and Holy Ghosts,
as we struggled
through relentless frustration
in the depths of a damning dream
to wake up
to the sounds of a barely audible intuition.[39]

Quickened by the extremes
of light and night,
of love and fright,
agitated, cajoled, encouraged,
minded and reminded
by midnight's knock of anticipated terror,
we arose to open the dented door
and found a wizened hand
gloved in tattered textures
holding civilization's crumpled decree
stamped
"Expired."

That is the background to my story,
my story against all odds:
while I was displaced and powerless,
my God seemed to be
in the midst
of an extended administrative leave.
In that double absence
of self and center,
it suddenly occurred to me
what He had in mind.
"Is that what you want of me?"
I suspiciously asked.
"To become your prophet, your face,
your name and blame?
Must I be that burning bramble
walking enflamed in a hostile world?
They would extinguish me,
you would consume me,
but I remain both verdant and ablaze,
holocausted
because now I am mistaken for you,
and you, dear God,
although you banished all the others,
are still not the most popular king-of-kings
in this mutinated neighborhood."

As I crawl out from under the shadow
of my crenulated torch,
I know that I will never enter
that agonizing cave again.
The time has come
to live our lives
as ordinary heroes,
flawed and flayed,
on mundane streetscapes
littered with broken vessels
and remnants of could-have-beens.

My scroll,
like a woman impregnated,
nurtures a complexity
that men could never bear.
So they adopted it
until it became their story,
a journey of forever
in the guise of a masquerade.
Since men give birth through evocative
symbol
and the lingering labors
of their calloused hands,
I became their provocative surrogate
and my scroll their encrypted masterpiece,
the archetypal daughter
they never presumed to have on their own.

*Here is what I think.
No one ever asked me.
I remained loyal to my role
and served as a mirror
for your learnéd commentaries.
My patience has been considerable:
If you accept me as history,
I am two thousand years and five centuries
old;
if you master me as myth,
I am one day older than
three-headed Chronos himself.*

*Come,
lay on my pillowed palanquin,
on silks and satins and sands,
as you listen to more of my story
through the kaleidoscopic lens
of ambered ale,
intoxicating herbs
and the smoldering vapors
of incense-bound bouquet.
Here is what I think,
here is what I have to say
in this conversation with myself
and these far-flung fragments
of an elder Estr Scroll.*

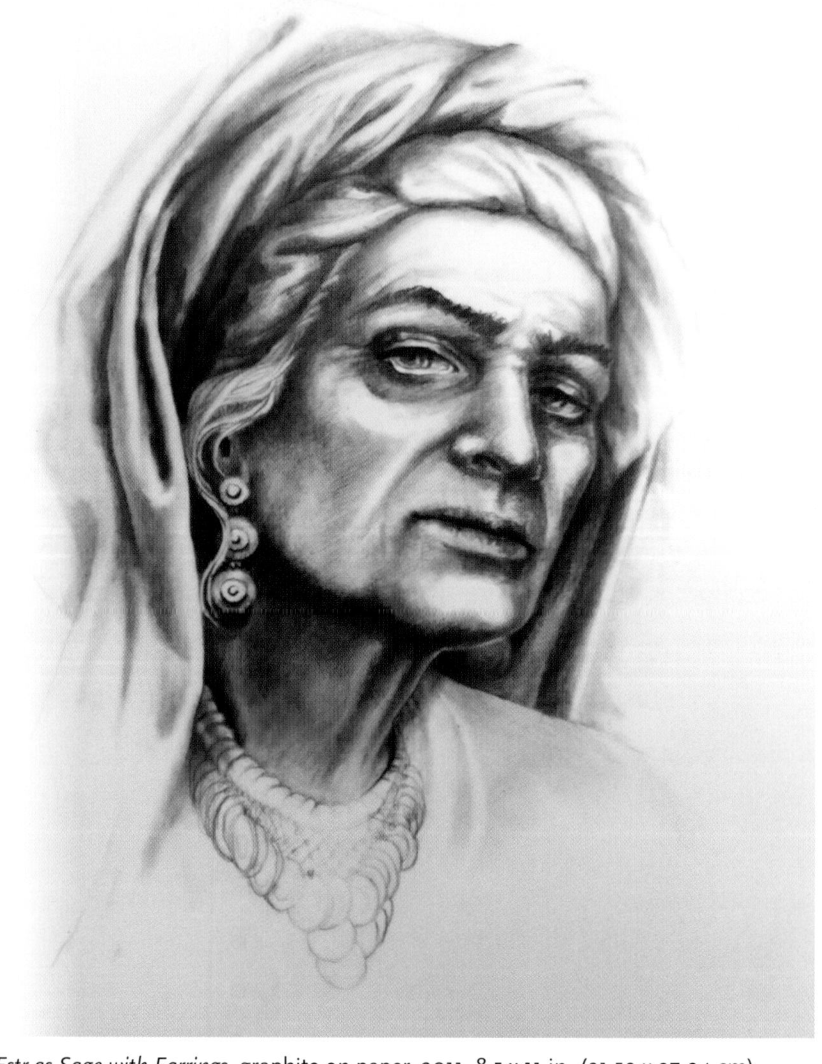

Estr as Sage with Earrings, graphite on paper, 2011, 8.5 x 11 in. (21.59 x 27.94 cm)

Beauty and Grace

They say that I – along with Abigail, Sara and Rahab – was among the most beautiful women in the world[40] and that I was characterized by a combination of a young woman's charm with an experienced woman's grace. My admirers insist that I was born with an abundance of balance, a gift from above, and that I wore it not as a disembodied halo but as a veil of cosmic threads upon the idealized head of a star goddess, so captivating that it was as if the air was suddenly swept from the room and one was left to swim, weightless, in an attar ocean of jasmine and geranium. Some say I was actually old and ugly, with sickly green skin[41] but that people were bewitched in my presence and enchanted with my charm. These were not attributes that I cultivated; they were endowments that accompanied me since birth. I thought it normal but finally, when installed as queen, I realized that there was something peculiar about me. Later, my enemies used witchcraft against me in an attempt to sabotage my efforts but angels assisted me in saving the people. Even the Holy Spirit embraced me when it was so inclined. I was merely the medium, body of beauty, astonished at what my life had become. I often longed for peasant anonymity, to escape my history and conceal my fate, to be normal, once again, just once.

Seductress

Not that I wanted to be, but it helped us survive; this, too, is a power that we women have learned to employ in time of need. Even the earth calls rain to her bosom, heavenly seed that penetrates her valleys in life's great Dance of Love. I used my beauty, sexuality, royal garments, jewels, and perfumes, as well as a false innocence and seductive charm. I seduced the king and his first minister, made them jealous of each other for my sake, for our sake, for yours. Perhaps there were other ways but not then, not under those circumstances. Could it be that I, Estr, wore the greatest mask of all? "Under this mask, another mask. I will never be finished removing all these faces."[42]

Politics

I am from the tribe of Benjamin, named for the youngest son of the favorite wife of a banished father of my ambulant nation. Although our tradition instructs that it is the eldest son who is to be honored like the father and who is to receive a double portion of inheritance, our Torah is filled with the paradoxical phenomenon of ascendant youngest sons and last-born daughters, of the vindication of character over birth, of the anointing of the subservient son as opposed to the expected heir to the throne, the temple, the estate. The roll call of last-born heroes is a temperamental ribbon that runs long through the ever-surprising chronicles of our people: Abel, the second son and first murdered man, was favored by Heaven; his younger brother, Seth, became the progenitor of humankind since Cain was cursed and Abel dead. Isaac was chosen as were a hundred other young ones, including Jacob, Rachel, Joseph and Benjamin, Moses, David, Solomon, and me, Estr, the only child, early orphaned.

There is more: the last created during the six days of Genesis was woman. As such, woman is both the youngest and the ultimate being, destined, in her time, to assume the mantle of leadership. With my ascension to Persian royalty, and with my being descended from the primal royal tribe of Benjamin[43] – the youngest son of the last-borns Jacob and Rachel – as well as with my daring decisions to arise in the face of imminent disaster, I became the first woman to combine monarchy and messianism, the model of a female redeemer, woman as messiah!

We are all the youngest children, a parallel tribe of Vernal Emergence, neotenous and ever-persistent, chosen precisely because we were out of place, humble, stuttering, unexpecting, shattered by divine intervention, offered an invitation to partake in history, to transcend our own limited lives, to escape the leftover spoils of last-born to become the vehicle of the Still-to-be-Born.

Modest

One of my names, Estr, **אסתר**, although it is Persian, relates to the Hebrew word meaning "the hidden one." I was hidden for four years before the king's mercenaries discovered me and then I hid my religion and my nation from the royal court. It is a name I share with the Creator, who also needs to hide, not only from us but also from himself, especially when exasperated with our rebellious ways.[44]

If he did not hide, my people would have been annihilated long ago. Although we suffered and have been decimated, we still survive as a misjudged minority among the nations.[45]

Orphan

I have been told that my mother died giving birth to me: she was the real heroine and I dearly miss never having known her. My father died even before I was born, so I was entirely orphaned before taking my first breath.[46] My uncle and aunt raised me. Eventually, this motherless child became mother to her nation. Decades before I was born, Yerushalayim was butchered by the Babylonians. When the Jewish people cried out: "We are orphans and fatherless," God responded: "Indeed! The redeemer who I will send to you in Media shall also be an orphan, fatherless and motherless."[47]

Hostess and Partygirl

I developed a reputation for throwing the best banquets in Shushan, aka Banquet City. My guests were strictly A-list: the king himself and his prime minister. Actually, I really didn't have the time or the personal inclination for the social scene: I was too busy running a palace, saving my nation, and surviving in hiding. Ah, but so many of you copied me, all those other feasts – the joyous and generous Purim celebrations – millions of them, each one franchised to every home and repeated year after expectant year.

But I am glad that you feast with bold insistence and are not just a nation of rough cloth and enfeebling fasts. Nor do you feast alone: you give money to the poor, food to your friends, and joy to the universe. I have heard that some otherwise staid teachers even instruct you to drink so much that you no longer know the difference between blessed Mordechai and cursed Haman.[48] Others, in their enthusiastic endorsement of both the actual events as well as their esoteric undertones, have even declared that of all the festivals only Purim and the Day of Atonement will be celebrated in the time to come. Some even say that Purim, in its secular disguise, is *already* the holiest day of the year and that even the Day of Atonement is only "like" Purim.[49]

Author

The first thing that I said that was recorded in a book was when I reported what my Mordechai overheard at the King's Gate: that Bigtan and Teresh were plotting to assassinate the emperor. I reported it to the court, the conspirators were arrested, and Mordechai's deeds were recorded in the Royal Chronicles.[50] Later, he and I wrote our letters, composed our history and declared our decrees.[51] It was named for me, the Book of Estr, or simply the Megillah, the Scroll. It is read every year and has become a best seller, often illustrated, with thousands of commentaries. It is drama and humor, overtly secular yet clandestinely sacred. It has been said that one who dreams of the Megillah will live to see miracles performed on their behalf. After a while and after a lot of debate, the book was actually accepted as one of the official twenty-four books of the Hebrew Bible. It was the last book to make it. Some also attribute the Great Hallel prayer cycle to me: sure I gave thanks, organized vigils and celebrations, and popularized these psalms but I wasn't the original author.

Confused and then Determined

I did not know how to react when challenged with getting involved in politics. At first I hesitated, fearful for my life; I also felt that I was not the one to lead the opposition. Like Moses, I refused my calling day after demanding day. "Who knows," those around me would argue, "maybe it was for just such a moment that you were chosen as queen?" and "If you don't do it, then redemption will come to the people through other channels," and "You are from the tribe of Benjamin; royalty runs through you. Perhaps you will do a better job than your predecessor. You have tribal amends to make. Perhaps a redeemer may still, and once again, arise from Benjamin. There is still time, Estr. History is long, themes repeatable. There is no 'they' or 'them.' Only you. Now." I rejected everything they threw at me before finally succumbing to the realization that, for better or for worse, I would be the next reluctant ambassador from this mysteriously despised nation threatened with annihilation, yet again.

Conclusion

Uncle M was right: this *was* my moment. By shattering the idol I had made of myself – by sacrificing my beauty, youth, will and way – I was able to serve with transparent clarity. I, as you, made a difference. As story, I will never be forgotten. But as the real person that I've presented to you in these poetic reflections and intimate conversations, my decay and dust have long ago become the scattered dressings for yet another struggling tree or two. As symbol of hope and dawning dew-light, I am ever with you. However, as *Estr bat Avihayil*, "I leave no trace of wings in the air, but I am glad I have had my flight."[52]

Notes

1 I have chosen to use a variant spelling: Estr instead of Esther. Using the too-familiar English spelling of Esther, could confine/enslave the reader to preconceived notions, overly practiced reactions and unthinking encounters with both the persona and idea of our heroine. In addition, by occasionally employing her Hebrew name, אסתר, we have reinserted an anchor of authenticity as well as transported the reader into exotic realms. The overly familiar "Esther" is almost invisible precisely because it is so well known. Furthermore, it is already removed many times, thousands of years, and hundreds of countries from the Persian original. A variant spelling acts as an iconoclastic event, breaking with the familiar and sweeping away the comfortable. A single letter can awaken one from a centuries-old sleep whether that dream is spelled אסתר in Hebrew, Ester in Spanish, Hester in Latin, Esther in English, French, and German or a more accurate English transliteration of Estr. In addition, the Hebrew word itself has four letters, so using only four letters in the English transliteration creates a name that is more closely aligned with the original in size, shape, weight, and pronunciation. Note: Semitic languages are read from right to left.

2 Following is an overview of the "Four Dimensions of an Eternal Text": i) The Estr story itself; its themes, particularly the hidden and the revealed, and its distinction of being one of only two biblical tomes – the other being the Song of Songs – that does not overtly refer to deity; its literary composition, humor, irony, theological message, and the scroll's unique place in the canon. ii) An appreciation of the story in light of parallel themes in other religions and mythologies; using these comparisons to place the text in both historical and theological contexts; to determine both the similarities and differences with comparative texts and oral traditions, as well as to illustrate how the Estr authors creatively altered the story in order to debunk particular foreign beliefs while emphasizing certain other points that expressed idiosyncratic principles of Jewish belief and practice. iii) An exploration of rabbinic commentaries that not only interpreted the literal text *(pshat)* but also used it for homiletic teachings *(remez* and *drash)* as well as esoteric cosmology *(sod)*; a brief review of more than two thousand years of rabbinic interpretation that illustrates how the Scroll of Estr, along with the fullness of biblical literature, was constantly reinvented through commentary; an investigation into the paradox as to why a story that is bereft of God's name should be assigned the highest rung of all biblical texts outside of the Pentateuch; a discussion of the holiday of Purim, including its peculiar mode of celebration and how it evolved in various communities worldwide; a note on the unique custom of adopting a personal Purim to commemorate a day of one's own deliverance. iv) An examination of how the Estr story is a particular iteration of a universal archetype; its relevance to the modern world; understanding the narrative through the lens of various schools of psychology as well as literary theory and historical recapitulation; other major Estr themes such as another look at the hidden and the revealed, modes of survival in exile, archetypal roles of the feminine and masculine, and the daring call to personal commitment, historical awareness, communal responsibility, and leadership.

3 Eccles. 12:12.

4 Cf. Louis Ginzberg, *The Legends of the Jews* (Philadelphia: Jewish Publication Society, 1938), Index Vol. VII, prepared by Boaz Cohen, s.v. "Esther," 142–43. "Of all the biblical heroines, Esther has enjoyed the greatest popularity among writers, artists, and musicians, representing feminine modesty, courage, and self- sacrifice" (*The Encyclopaedia Judaica,* s.v. "Esther," 6:908).

5 The Kotzker Rebbe (1787–1859) once famously quipped (in Yiddish), "If I am I because I am I, and you are you because you are you, then I am I and you are you. But if I am I because you are you and you are you because I am I, then I am not I and you are not you!" In another daring observation, he maintained that "people must guard themselves and their uniqueness, and not imitate those around them, for initially man was created *in his own image,* and only afterwards in the image of God." Perhaps the most famous quote on the subject is attributed to the first-century-CE scholar, Hillel the Elder, who boldly stated: "If I am here, then everything is here." This is most often interpreted to mean: "If I" [i.e. Hillel, created in the image of God; or "If I" referring to God] "am truly here, then everything is here; if I am not here, nobody is here" (Suk. 53a; Ab. R. N. xii).

One must also appreciate Oscar Wilde's penetrating quote from *De Profundis,* his letter from prison: "Most people are other people. Their thoughts are someone else's opinions, their lives a mimicry, their passions a quotation."

6 Gen. 27.

7 The text does not disclose Estr's age but since she was chosen by the king in a contest for a new queen – a contest in which fresh beauty and natural grace would rank high, with virginity being a prerequisite – conjecture suggests that she would have been between sixteen and twenty-two years old. One didactic rabbinic source claimed she was forty years old, another seventy-five, and yet a third identified her as being eighty. These statements are to be taken symbolically and are based on rules of interpretive hermeneutics. In the most famous romantic play in English literature, Shakespeare's *Romeo and Juliet,* Juliet is just thirteen years old as indicated by the Nurse and Lady Capulet in Juliet's first scene as "not-quite-fourteen."

8 Gen. 12:1–5. In most stories – personal, mythological, or scriptural – it is younger men and women who leave home in search of fame, fortune, or the ineffable.

9 "In the beginning, two thousand years before the heaven and the earth, seven things were created…" (Ginzberg, *Legends,* 1:3; Tehillim [Psalms] 90, 391).

10 "The removal of [King Ahashvayrosh's signet] ring was more effective than the forty-eight prophets and seven prophetesses who prophesied to Israel, for all these were unable to return [the Jews] to righteousness whereas the removal of the ring returned them to righteousness" (Megillah 14a). The king took the ring off his hand to seal Haman's decree to murder all the Jews in the one hundred and twenty-seven states under his rule. It implies that anti-Semitic persecution frightened the people and was more effective as an agent of repentance than all the exhortations of the prophets. This is a timeless principle. Rashi comments that Ahashvayrosh's gesture prompted the Jewish people to fast and repent for their sins. It also elicited Mordechai and Estr's practical involvement. This is reminiscent of Moses at the Sea of Reeds: with the Egyptian army attacking on one side and blocked by the sea at the other, Moses began to pray to God for help. God responded: "Why do you shout to me? Tell the children of Israel to move forward. As for you, lift up your staff and stretch out your hand over the sea and divide it so that the children of Israel can go through the midst of the sea on dry land" (Ex. 14:15–16). "Now is not the time for long prayers," comments Rashi, "when Israel is placed in danger." Now is the time for action, so lift up your staff to divide the waters and prepare a path of liberation.

11 Rev. 16:16.

12 Cf. the idea of *theodicy,* which is a kind of theological apologetic necessary to monotheism. It is defined as "a vindication of the divine attributes, particularly holiness and justice, in establishing or allowing the existence of physical and moral evil" (Dictionary.com). A true appreciation of monotheism must credit the creator God with permitting both good and evil. This is one of the most difficult principles to allow but must be accepted by monotheists, or else polytheism, or at least duality, would be the logical consequence.

13 Perhaps the darkness applies to God's view of the human mind as much as humanity's struggle to know the mind of the Deity or Essence of Nature. Einstein once remarked, "I want to know God's thoughts; the rest are details." In the well-known King James Bible translation of The First Epistle to the Corinthians 13:12, Paul comments on the incessant struggle to understand and experience more of ultimate reality: "For now we see through a glass, darkly; but then face to face: now I know in part; but then shall I know even as also I am known." Even Moses, the greatest of prophets who is described as speaking to God "face to face as one would speak to a friend" (Ex. 33:11), is told that he cannot be granted his request to know the true essence of the Almighty, for, as God reminded him, "No one can see me and live" (Ex. 33:20). Mysteries are only such until known. Some are all-consuming and need to be approached through a series of protective lenses or by struggling with guardians at the gates; others are simply benign, unprotected but relatively inaccessible, humbly waiting to be discovered.

14 Even though the Scroll of Estr identifies Hadassah as Estr's secondary, and, according to some commentators,

her Hebrew name, the name could also be associated with the Babylonian word for "bride," a title similarly connected with Ishtar. Some suggest that Estr was a Persian name given to her upon assuming royalty [cf. Note 25 below]. However, it may also have been a rather common Persian name.

15 Gen. 2:10–14.

16 "Any plant of the genus *Myrtus,* esp. *M. communis,* a shrub of southern Europe having evergreen leaves, fragrant white flowers, and aromatic berries: anciently held sacred to Venus and used as an emblem of love" (Dictionary.com). This definition supports a pivotal and astounding correspondence between Estr's various names: Hadassah, Hebrew for "myrtle," and Estr, now also associated with myrtle through her corresponding association with the Greek goddess of love, beauty, and fertility, Aphrodite, and her Roman equivalent, Venus; see Note 25 below. Further research into myrtle symbology and its place in various mythologies/religions is indicated.

17 Babylonian and Assyrian goddess of love, fertility, and war; Ishtar, or her prototype Inanna, the Babylonian goddess of love and queen of heaven. Many studies demonstrate parallels between the characters and events in the scroll with contemporaneous religions and mythologies. For example, just as Ishtar risked her life to descend into the underworld to appear before its monarch, so Estr risked her life to appear before the king; just as Ishtar put on her royal robes and arranged for a plan if she had not returned in three days – "I am descending to the underworld. If I do not return, set up a lament for me. Go to see the Great Ones, Enlil, Nanna and Enki. Do not let this holy priestess of heaven be put to death in the underworld. Go to see the Great Gods, for surely they will not let me die" – so Estr arranged for the Jews to "take neither food nor drink for three days, night or day," and on the third day she put on her royal robes to approach the king (Est. 4:16–17; 5:1).

18 Also spelled Astarte; note the root of the word "star." According to some, Greek worshippers referred to this goddess as Hera, but she has also been associated with Aphrodite.

19 Haman the Agagite is traditionally associated as a descendent of Amaleik. Just after the exodus from Egypt, as the Hebrews trekked through the Sinai Desert, his ancestors decimated those who were weakened and straggled behind (Deut. 25:17–18), whereas Haman planned to kill all (Est. 3:13). Stark correspondences emerge in that Mordechai and Estr are Benjamites – the same tribe as Saul, the first king of Israel – and Haman is Agagite/Amaleik, thereby recapitulating the episode in I Sam. 15. It is also a reverberation of the Torah's reminder never to forget the destructive character of Amaleik (Ex.17:8–16; Deut. 25:17–19).

The name Haman may be related to the Elamite god Humman. It is also associated with the Persian word hamayun, "illustrious," or to the Persian name, Omanes. In addition, the names of both father and son – Haman son of Hammadatha – have been associated with *haoma,* a sacred drink used in *Mithraic* worship. See additional speculations on the symbolic representation of "Haman" in Note 25 below.

20 This is the Spring equinox.

21 Arising like a new sun in the East, this image alludes to the resurrection of early Spring both in agricultural and mythopoeic terms.

22 To support her resolve and elicit the mercy of heaven, Estr enlisted the entire Jewish nation to fast for three days – she from within the palace; they in their scattered abodes. When it turned out that those three particular days included the Passover festival, Mordechai asked that an alternate date be set. Estr, now awakening to her fate as a leader among her nation, retorted: "Jewish elder! Without an Israel, there would be no Passover!" Mordechai understood and decreed an emergency fast to replace the erstwhile Holiday of Liberation (Est. R. 8:6).

23 *Ahashvayrosh* is the Hebrew rendering of *Khshayarsha,* often identified with the Greek form of the name *Xerxes* (c. 485–465 BCE).

24 Cf. Franz Kafka, *Parables and Paradoxes* (Schocken Books: New York, 1972), 189. Kafka's parable, "My Destination," describes this kind of journey through an absurdly misunderstood dialogue between a master and his servant. It reads, in part: [The servant asked:] "Where are you riding to master?" "I don't know," I said, "only away from here, away from here. Always away from here; only in doing so can I reach my destination." "And you know your destination?" he asked. "Yes," I answered. "Didn't I say so? Away-From-Here, that is

my destination." The conversation continues with the servant, a practical fellow, concerned with his master's provisions. "You have no provisions with you," he said. "I need none," I said. "The journey is so long that I must die of hunger if I don't get anything on the way. No provisions can save me. For it is, fortunately, a truly immense journey."

25 Esta'har could also refer to "moon." The moon is often used as a symbol of the Jewish people, representing the waxing and waning of their historical phases that range from almost disappearing to illuminating the night sky. The Talmud (Megillah 13a) mentions that the name Estr comes from Istahara, which Rashi interprets as referring to the moon. On the other hand, *Targum Sheini* commenting on Estr 2:7 says that it is referring to the Greek word that refers to Venus, a name synonymous with an incarnation of Ishtar.

Some claim that the entire Book of Estr was only written as an apologetic, as an explanation or excuse for celebrating an otherwise secular festival. Some insist that Judaism's adoption of the Estr narrative and accompanying holiday observance was a later imitation of a Babylon New Year's festival. As the days began to lengthen and the renewal of life increased over the death of Winter, it was an obvious time to declare the New Year. The full expression of that idea is that all the main characters in the Book of Estr were variations of cosmic forces in the annual cycle of nature. Another possibility is that the scroll reflects the vestiges of historic rivalries between Elam and Babylon. It has also been compared and contrasted to the Exodus from Egypt: both took place outside the land of Israel; the nature of the Exodus with its Passover holiday was one of the complete dominance and reliance upon the God of Israel, whereas, in contrast, the Purim story is bereft of even the name of deity and is a narrative where people had to act in order to be saved. It was a time at the juncture between biblical and post-biblical history when human, not just divine, action was necessary. In theological terms, it marked the ascendancy of Purim over Pesach (Passover), and described a new, "modern" reality when a more active partnership between heaven and earth was called forth. It is the Torah of exile when the overt presence of God is not always obvious. The Torah relates numerous stories that preceded Estr where individuals argued, wrestled, or allied with God but the deity remained patently present, engaged in dialogue and in charge. With Estr, however, we see the shift to a more mature humanity emerging from its relative cocoon and taking responsibility for its history. In a simultaneous reaction, the deity migrates into semi-concealment, a divine contraction analogous to the kabbalistic principle of *tzimzum* at the time of universal creation. The result of these two shifts – human and divine energy moving in opposite directions but still intimately connected at the other end of the scale – is that Purim represents a recapitulation and continuation of *ma'asei braisheet,* the acts of creation.

It has also been suggested by Jastrow that Mordechai is an allegory for Marduk, the chief Babylonian god, while Estr represents "the Babylonian goddess Ishtar, the chief female deity and as such directly associated with Marduk...Two other names [of main characters in the Scroll of Estr], Haman (Humman or Humbar) and Vashti (Mashti), are Elamite deities." He also points out, but calls it pure conjecture, that the Estr text may be a Judaization of a Babylonian myth in which Marduk (the god of Spring and, as chief god, establisher of order in the universe) and his ally Ishtar (Goddess of Light) are in conflict against Humman and Mashti, hostile powers symbolizing Winter and Darkness, which are themselves local representatives of the uber archetypes of primeval chaos and discord (*Encyclopedia of Religion and Ethics,* s.v. "Purim," Morris Jastrow). This mythic interpretation emerges as a retelling of the annual reincarnation cycle of Spring replacing Winter, life blossoming ascendant over death, light overtaking darkness and hope transcending despair. On a cosmic stage, it describes the primeval drama of order emerging from chaos and creation from the gravity of dark resistance. To the ancient mind, the results were by no means a given. To help ensure that this reincarnation of nature – and, by extension, family, tribe, and nation – would be a success, the people offered sacrifices (sometimes human) to the deities, chanted prayers and engaged in other propitiative behavior.

Rashi (Yoma 29b) also associates Estr with a phenomenon referred to as *Ayeles HaShachar,* which is either the morning star or the very early morning first rouge of light, the dawn and aurora. The Alei Yonah interprets it as the zodiacal light. Also cf. Psalm 22 that begins: "For the Conductor, on the Ayeles HaShachar, a psalm by David." It has been interpreted to allude to Queen Estr's trials. Purim occurs in the middle of the month of Adar, the full moon of the early Spring transition from Winter to Spring. "It is the nexus of darkness and dawn; it is winter's end and springtime's promise" (Rav Aharon Kahn, in a publication of the Student Organization of Yeshiva University, March 5, 1998). So, too, Estr's role as the central character is, as the Morning Star, harbinger in the transition from night to day, from death to life, from Winter to Spring, from dormant nature to blossoming rebirth, from Haman's political genocide to a reversal and salvation. A midrash suggests that "When the dawn awakes (*ayeles hashachar*) the stars set, and so in the court of Ahashvayrosh, as Estr awakened, the stars of Haman and his sons set." Christian tradition, on the other hand, views the psalm as messianic prophecy that was quoted and fulfilled by Jesus (cf. many Web-based works, including the online *The Oxford Bible Commentary*).

According to Jewish belief as well as historical observation, it seems that no matter how often (every generation) or in what land the persecution against the Jewish people may arise, deliverance – even if delayed and bruised – is at hand.

26 Est. 2:1–18.

27 Cf. Deut. 31: 16–18, *hasteir as'tir panai,* "Hide, I will [really] hide, my Face."

28 In the act of self-knowledge, of confronting oneself or others, Estr is finally called upon to reveal herself even to herself, just as the Creator is forced to reveal Itself to Itself, or at least Creation to Itself, to make the invisible visible. It was, in mystical terms, a paradoxical act of giving birth to a universe that is somehow outside "something" that has no dimensions. Creation introduced a complex series of consequences. Revelation – implying duality – was among the costs of creation for if the Creator had not created, it would have "continued to exist" in perfect uniqueness. (Even these words are metaphors because "continued" connotes time, whereas "exist" denotes space. The dimensions of *time* and *space* would not apply to an Absolute Nothing, except in potential. Or in parable's metaphor.)

29 Megillah 13a; also cf. Ginzberg, *Legends,* Index vol., s.v., "Esther, beauty." It seems that later rabbinic sources described Estr's beauty in either hyperbole or didactic terms. The reason they played down her physical beauty and instead described her as unattractive, of sickly green complexion and being older (one source claims forty, another seventy-five years old [like Abraham, Gen. 12:4], another eighty), was to attribute her overwhelming charm and grace to divine intervention. General rabbinic commentaries attempted to reintroduce the overt presence of God into what would otherwise seem like a superficially secular document.

30 One of Jean Houston's definitions of myth.

31 Mordechai is described in Est. 2:7 as "foster father to Hadassah – that is, Ester – his uncle's daughter, for she had neither father nor mother… [W]hen her father and mother died, Mordechai adopted her as his own daughter." Although technically his first cousin and, additionally, after her adoption his stepdaughter, Estr may well have referred to Mordechai as her uncle. The use of this honorific is common in many world cultures and is used as a sign of respect for one's guardian, stepfather, or other respected elder.

Mordechai challenged Estr to step forth and accept her role both for the moment and in history (Est. 4). In a further parallel introduced in Note 19 above, this could be compared to the prophet Samuel's challenge – albeit after the fact – to her ancestor, Saul, first king of Israel: "Even though you may be insignificant in your own eyes, were you not made the head of the tribes of Israel, and [didn't] the Lord anoint you king over Israel?" (I Sam. 15:17). As undeserving and unfit as she may have felt for the role about to be thrust upon her, she was still confronted with having to make this difficult decision: would she accept or reject this sudden call to leadership? Most heroes are everyday folk not looking for acknowledgement. It is their, and our, reaction to sudden crisis, the amplified moment, that identifies them as hero or not. They are ordinary people in extreme circumstances. This theme also relates to "the reluctant prophet" discussed in Note 33 below.

The name Mordechai, or Mardocheus, was exilic in nature and not found in any previous biblical literature. It may be derived from Marduk, the chief god of the Babylonian pantheon. Mordechai was descended from Kish, father of Saul, the first king of Israel, and a member of tribe of Benjamin (Est. 2:5–6). If Saul had not had the kingship stripped from him by the prophet Samuel, then the line of kings would have continued through him. This would result in the inevitable conclusion that the messianic line would be transmitted through the tribe of Benjamin and not, as eventually transpired, through the family of David of the tribe of Judah. Under that scenario, we would be anticipating the future *Mashiakh ben Shaul* and not the *Mashiakh ben David*. That royal line would be intimately connected to the Joseph/Rahel aligned tribes. It would also be consistent with the biblical pattern of youngest sons (in this case Benjamin and Joseph) eventually rising to positions of consequence. (The David messiah model, of course, also adheres to that pattern). When Saul lost his kingship, it was eventually transferred to David, the youngest son of a Judah family. Approximately six hundred years before the institution of kingship was adopted, Judah (Yehuda) proved himself worthy of such a role for his descendants when he, alone among his brothers, defended Benjamin and exhibited leadership that would save the entire family (Gen. 44:14–34). Even Judah could be considered a youngest son of sorts: he was the fourth of Leah and Jacob's sons (Reuven, Shimon, Levi, and Judah) before she stopped giving birth (Gen. 29:35), at least for a few years. He was the youngest of the first group and assumed leadership when Reuven, the oldest, miscalculated in a number of events. Ironically, in yet another twist of events so prevalent in the Book of Estr, it wasn't a representative of the House of David or tribe of Judah who arose in royal fashion to encourage and eventually save the people, but rather Estr and Mordechai – from Benjamin and Saul – who emerged. It is yet another example in biblical literature of the youngest (in this case an orphaned only child) and seemingly the most unexpected – Estr who was elevated from obscurity and made queen because of her beauty and grace – stepping up to an action and office of significance.

32 Est. 4:13–14.

33 Estr is counted among the forty-eight prophets and seven prophetesses in biblical Israel (Megillah 14a). Like most of them, the enormity of the prophetic calling causes her to react by adopting the "reluctant prophet" persona. Cf. Moses at the burning bush, Exodus 3:1–4:17, where the midrash postulates that Moses argued with God for seven days and seven nights in an attempt to deflect his prophetic calling. Prophecy was not just a blissful encounter with the numen (although cf. *benei nevi'im*) but rather a sudden divine invasion into the psyche and soma of the often-astonished individual. Prophecy in ancient Israel did not just imply receiving the transcendental message in dream, trance, or voice form; it was also an imperative to act, to transmit, and to declare the vision to the people. It was this call to action that deterred many prophets. Some denied the calling (e.g., Amos, who protested: *Lo navi anokhi ve'lo ben navi anokhi,* "I am not a prophet nor am I the son of a prophet" [Amos 7:14]); others sought to escape it (Jonah 1:1–3) or collapsed in fear (Abraham [Gen. 15:12]). Estr's inclusion in the prophetic pantheon may be only partly due to her heroic leadership. In fact, since the text does not report that God spoke to Estr and commanded her to do or say any particular thing, we must imply that the scroll introduces a new category of prophecy; that is, emerging from the inner depths of intuition and not from the outer forces of heaven. Her inspired writing (with Mordechai) of the Megillat Estr and declaring that the holiday of Purim was to be celebrated in every place and for all time (Est. 9:20–32), were also considered prophetic acts.

34 S.v. Ginzberg, *Legends,* 4:423 and notes thereon.

35 Cf. Lev. 26:36: "Upon those of you who are left alive, I will instil a fearful faintness in their hearts in the lands of their enemies, and they shall flee at the rustling of a leaf in the wind." Also see Milton Steinberg's *As a Driven Leaf* (Behrman House: N.J., 1996).

36 As Note 2, above, pointed out, multiple levels of interpretation coexist. This seems to be particularly applicable to Estr, a text that, even on the surface, seems to dart from feast to fast, beauty contests to premeditated genocide and hiding everything from personal identity to the name of God. The Zohar – one of the most important books of Jewish mysticism – expressed, in not so veiled terms, its antagonism toward those who insisted on merely a strict and literal understanding of the Hebrew Scriptures. This should be taken as a strong admonition against only interpreting the Scroll of Estr according to its literal sense. It also bears magnificent cosmologies upon its wings (*ha'maivin yavin*). The Zohar (3:152, *B'ha'alotkha*) describes the general principle as follows:

"Woe unto the one who asserts that this Torah intends to relate only commonplace things and secular narratives; for if this were so, then in the present times likewise a Torah might be written with more attractive narratives. In truth, however, the matter is thus: The upper world and the lower are established upon the same principle... When the angels wish to descend to the lower world, they have to don earthly garments. If this be true of the angels, how much more so of the Torah, for whose sake, indeed, both the world and the angels were alike created and exist. The world could simply not have endured to look upon it. Now, the narratives of the Torah are its garments. He who thinks that these garments are the Torah itself deserves to perish and have no share in the World to Come. Woe unto the fools who look no further when they see an elegant robe! More valuable than the garment is the body that carries it, and more valuable even than that is the soul which animates the body. Fools see only the garment of the Torah, the more intelligent see the body, the wise see the soul, its proper being, and in the Messianic time the 'upper soul' of the Torah will stand revealed."

37 Gen. 3:5.

38 Gen. 1:26–27.

39 1 Kings 19:9–13.

40 Megillah 15a.

41 Ibid. 13a.

42 Claude Cahun.

43 The first anointed king was Saul from the tribe of Benjamin (1 Sam. 9–10).

44 Deut. 31:16–18.

45 Deut. 7:7.

46 Megillah 13a.

47 Ginzberg, *Legends,* 5:385.

48 Megillah 7b. Others eschewing drunkenness, suggest that one take a nap: when one sleeps one also doesn't know the difference between Mordechai and Haman; that is, between good and evil.

49 *Yom K'pur, K'purim,* "a day that is like Purim," a day that can be compared to Purim but is not yet on its level. One interpretation of this incredible statement posits that at the present time, in the world as we know it, humans can relate to spiritual life easier through sincere fasting, praying, celibacy, and repenting; that is, becoming somewhat like disembodied angels and removing themselves from desires and inclinations demanded by material life. That is the path of Yom Kippur, the Day of Atonement. Purim, on the other hand, celebrates the revelation of the hidden presence of divinity through feasting and merriment, through a material vehicle. This is considered a more difficult and higher level; it will also be the way in the future. Rabbinical teachings attributed a unique place to the Scroll of Estr, popularly referred to as the Megillah (i.e., the scroll par excellence): "In the time to come [a variant reads: "In Messianic times] all the other parts of the Hagiographia, even the prophetical books, will lose their value and only the Pentateuch and the Book of Estr will retain their worth." See Ginzberg, VI:481, note 194; also cf. Maimonides, Hilkhot Megillah 2:18.

50 This report contributed to Mordechai being honored, Haman being denigrated, and the Jewish people being saved from destruction. This event became the paradigmatic example for the popular teaching that encourages one to always quote the source of information: "Whoever repeats something in the name of the one who said it, brings redemption to the world" (Megillah 15a, Avot 6:6, Est. R. 6:13, Pirkei d'Rav Eliezer 50).

51 Est. 9:20–32. Cf. "I do believe that history will be kind to me. After all, I shall be writing it" (attributed to Winston S. Churchill).

52 Rabindranath Tagore, *Fireflies.*

Selected Bibliography

The works listed here were chosen because each, in turn, provides its own list of relevant texts and thus serves as an additional bibliography for those interested in pursuing the topics raised in this chapter. A number of additional works are cited in the prior notes that provide both literary sources and elucidations on a number of ideas. The reader is encouraged to engage these texts as well as the many articles and volumes that continue to be written on the subject.

A note regarding the various versions of Estr:

"The story of Esther exists in two principal versions. The first is the ten-chapter form we find in the Hebrew Bible and in Protestant translations of the OT. The second is the sixteen-chapter form appearing in the Septuagint (Greek) versions of the Bible and in Roman Catholic translations. The material that appears in the Roman Catholic but not the Protestant Book of Esther is put by Protestants in the Apocrypha, where it is known as The Additions to Esther. The Additions do not appear in Jewish Bibles."
– David J. A. Clines, "Esther," in *Harper's Bible Commentary*, 387.

Babylonian Talmud (Talmud Bavli). London and New York: The Soncino Press, 1990. Originally published 1952.

Clines, David J. A. "Esther." In *Harper's Bible Commentary*. General Editor James L. Mays, with the Society of Biblical Literature, 387–94. San Francisco: Harper & Row Publishers, 1988.

Encyclopaedia Judaica, The. Index s.v. "Esther." Jerusalem: Keter Publishing House, 1972.

Encyclopaedia of Religion and Ethics. Edited by James Hastings. Edinburgh: T. & T. Clark and New York: Charles Scribner's Sons, 1956. Originally published Edinburgh and New York: 1926.

"Esther" in *Encyclopedia of Religion, The*. Editor-in-chief Mircea Eliade, 166. New York: Macmillan Publishing Company, 1987.

Gaster, Theodore H. *Purim and Hanukkah in Custom and Tradition: Feast of Lots, Feast of Lights*. New York: Schuman, 1950.

Ginzberg, Louis. *The Legends of the Jews*. Translated by Henrietta Szold, et al. 7 vols.; Index s.v. "Esther." Philadelphia: Jewish Publication Society, 1909–38.

Interpreter's Bible: A Commentary in Twelve Volumes, The. Vol. 3, 821–74. 31st printing. Nashville: Abingdon Press, 1984. Originally published Nashville: 1954.

Jerusalem Bible – The Holy Scriptures. Jerusalem: Koren Publishers, 1977. Hebrew with English translation.

Jewish Encyclopedia, The. "Esther" (V: 232–37); "Apocryphal Book of Esther" (V: 237–241); "Esther Rabbah" (V: 241–42); "Purim" (X: 274–283). New York and London: Funk and Wagnalls Company, 1903–05.

JPS Bible Commentary: Esther, The. Commentary by Adele Berlin. Philadelphia: The Jewish Publication Society, 2001. This volume includes an extensive bibliography.

World Wide Web. There are numerous articles and opinions on the Web. Although many are biased, nuanced, and unscholarly, others do offer legitimate research, clear insight and stimulating conjecture. *Caveat emptor.*

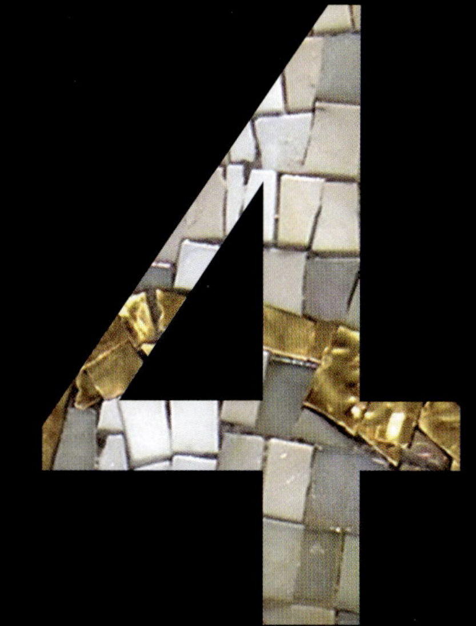

Appendix

Scroll of Esther

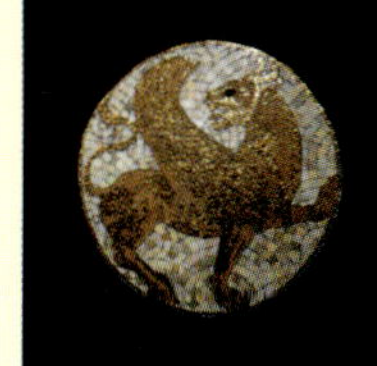

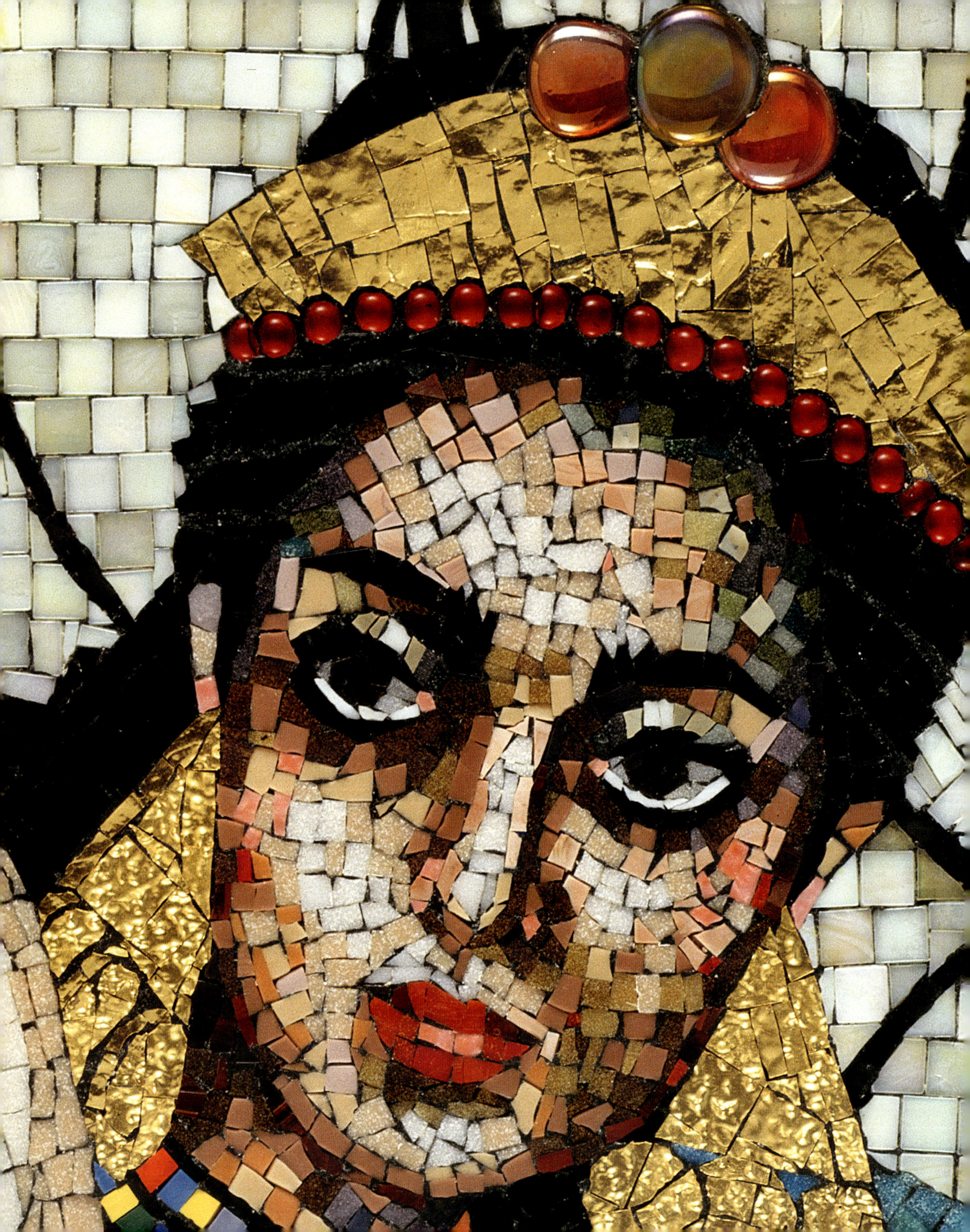

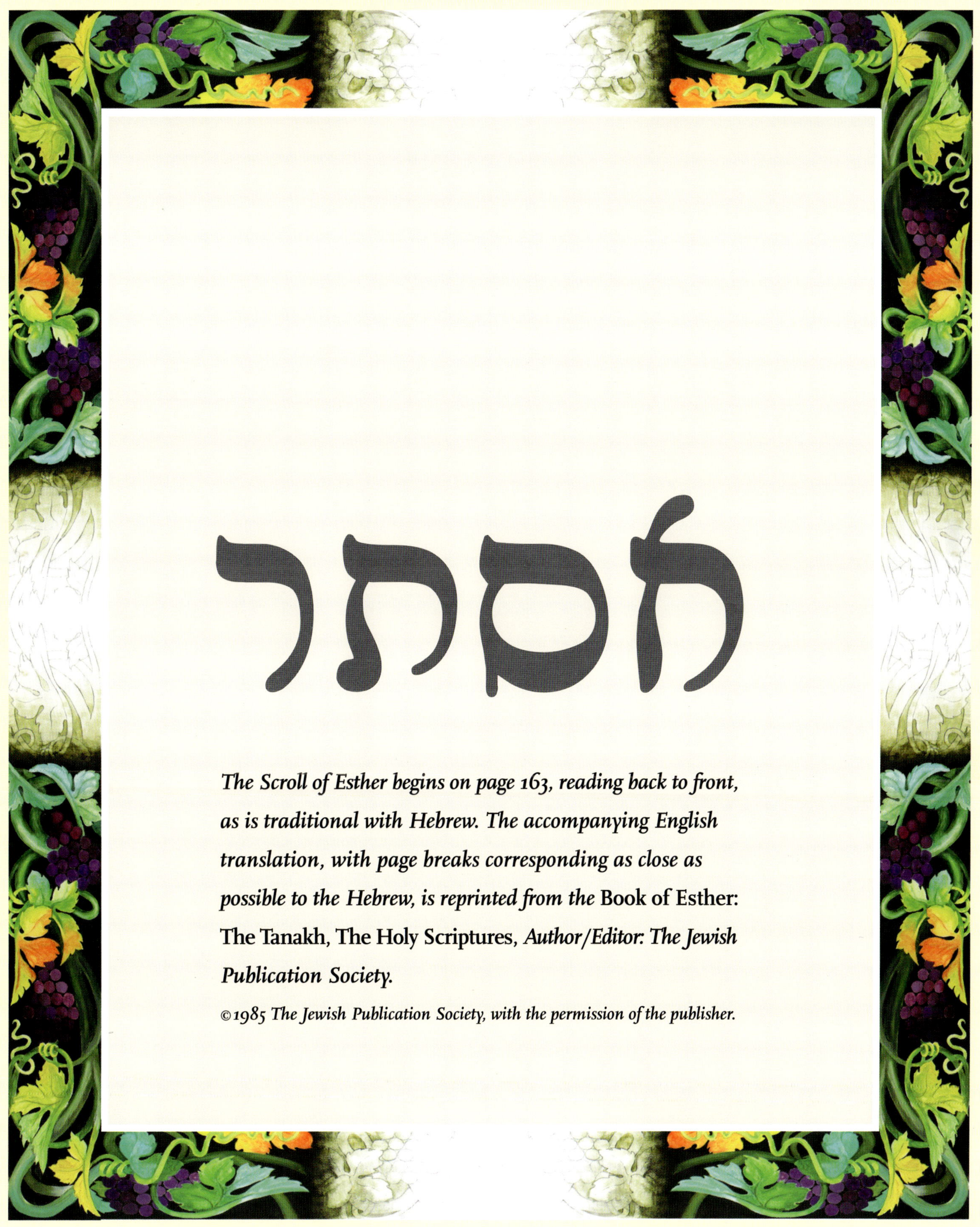

אסתר

The Scroll of Esther begins on page 163, reading back to front, as is traditional with Hebrew. The accompanying English translation, with page breaks corresponding as close as possible to the Hebrew, is reprinted from the Book of Esther: The Tanakh, The Holy Scriptures, *Author/Editor: The Jewish Publication Society.*

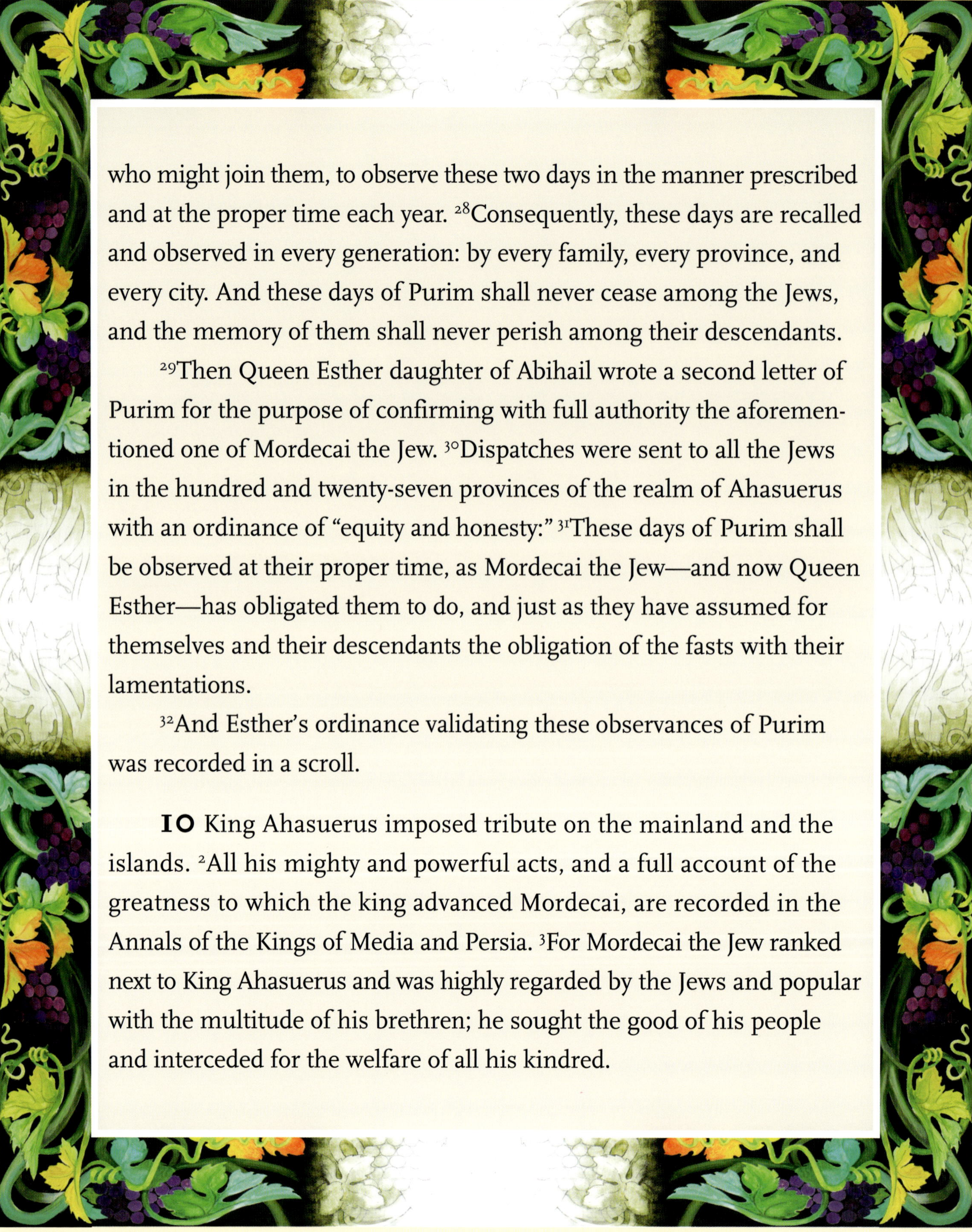

who might join them, to observe these two days in the manner prescribed
and at the proper time each year. 28Consequently, these days are recalled
and observed in every generation: by every family, every province, and
every city. And these days of Purim shall never cease among the Jews,
and the memory of them shall never perish among their descendants.

29Then Queen Esther daughter of Abihail wrote a second letter of
Purim for the purpose of confirming with full authority the aforemen-
tioned one of Mordecai the Jew. 30Dispatches were sent to all the Jews
in the hundred and twenty-seven provinces of the realm of Ahasuerus
with an ordinance of "equity and honesty:" 31These days of Purim shall
be observed at their proper time, as Mordecai the Jew—and now Queen
Esther—has obligated them to do, and just as they have assumed for
themselves and their descendants the obligation of the fasts with their
lamentations.

32And Esther's ordinance validating these observances of Purim
was recorded in a scroll.

10 King Ahasuerus imposed tribute on the mainland and the
islands. 2All his mighty and powerful acts, and a full account of the
greatness to which the king advanced Mordecai, are recorded in the
Annals of the Kings of Media and Persia. 3For Mordecai the Jew ranked
next to King Ahasuerus and was highly regarded by the Jews and popular
with the multitude of his brethren; he sought the good of his people
and interceded for the welfare of all his kindred.

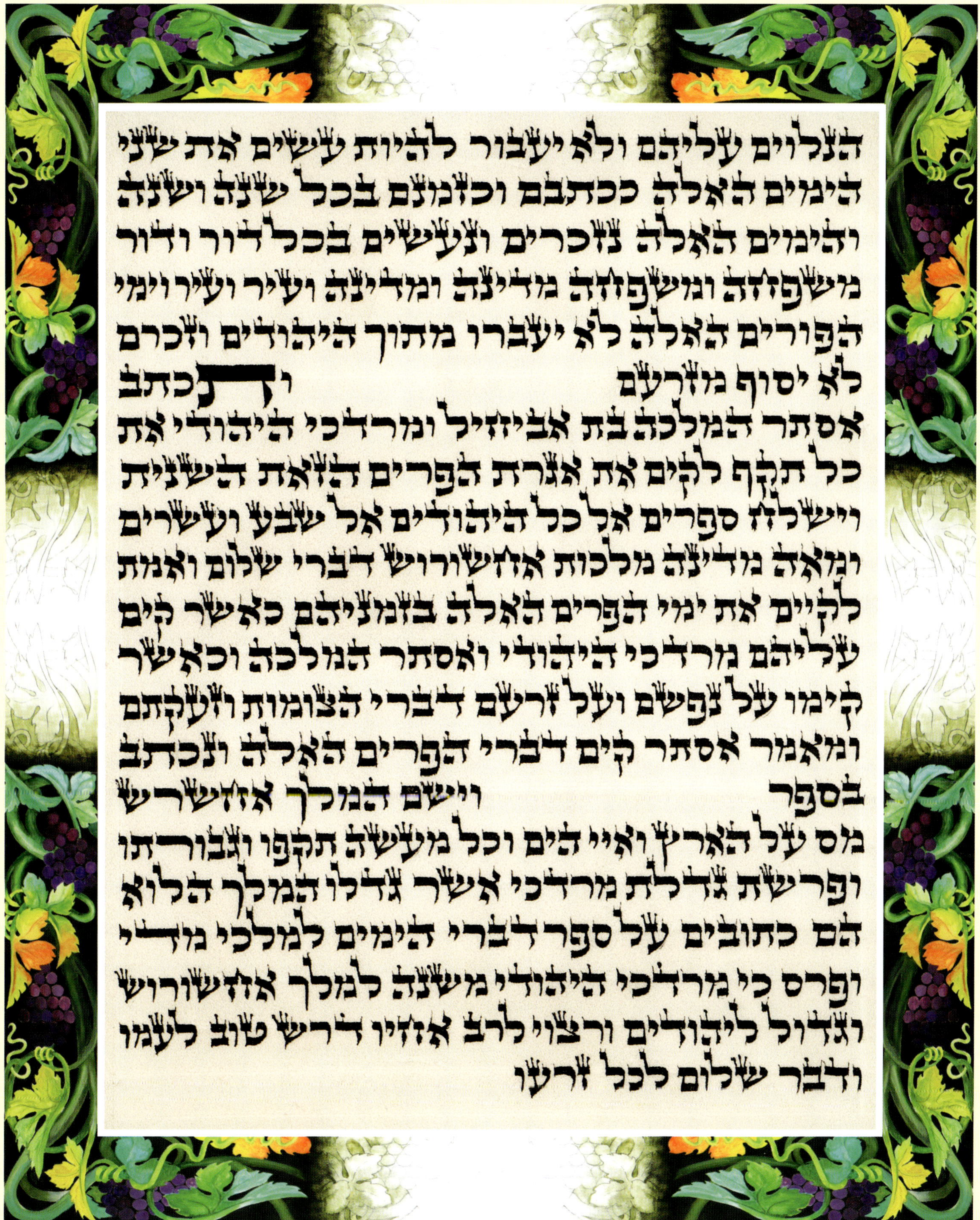
הנלוים עליהם ולא יעבור להיות עשים את שני
הימים האלה ככתבם וכזמנם בכל שנה ושנה
והימים האלה נזכרים ונעשים בכל דור ודור
משפחה ומשפחה מדינה ומדינה ועיר ועיר וימי
הפורים האלה לא יעברו מתוך היהודים וזכרם
לא יסוף מזרעם ותכתב
אסתר המלכה בת אביחיל ומרדכי היהודי את
כל תקף לקים את אגרת הפרים הזאת השנית
וישלח ספרים אל כל היהודים אל שבע ועשרים
ומאה מדינה מלכות אחשורוש דברי שלום ואמת
לקים את ימי הפרים האלה בזמניהם כאשר קים
עליהם מרדכי היהודי ואסתר המלכה וכאשר
קימו על נפשם ועל זרעם דברי הצומות וזעקתם
ומאמר אסתר קים דברי הפרים האלה ונכתב
בספר וישם המלך אחשרש
מס על הארץ ואיי הים וכל מעשה תקפו וגבורתו
ופרשת גדלת מרדכי אשר גדלו המלך הלוא
הם כתובים על ספר דברי הימים למלכי מדי
ופרס כי מרדכי היהודי משנה למלך אחשורוש
וגדול ליהודים ורצוי לרב אחיו דרש טוב לעמו
ודבר שלום לכל זרעו

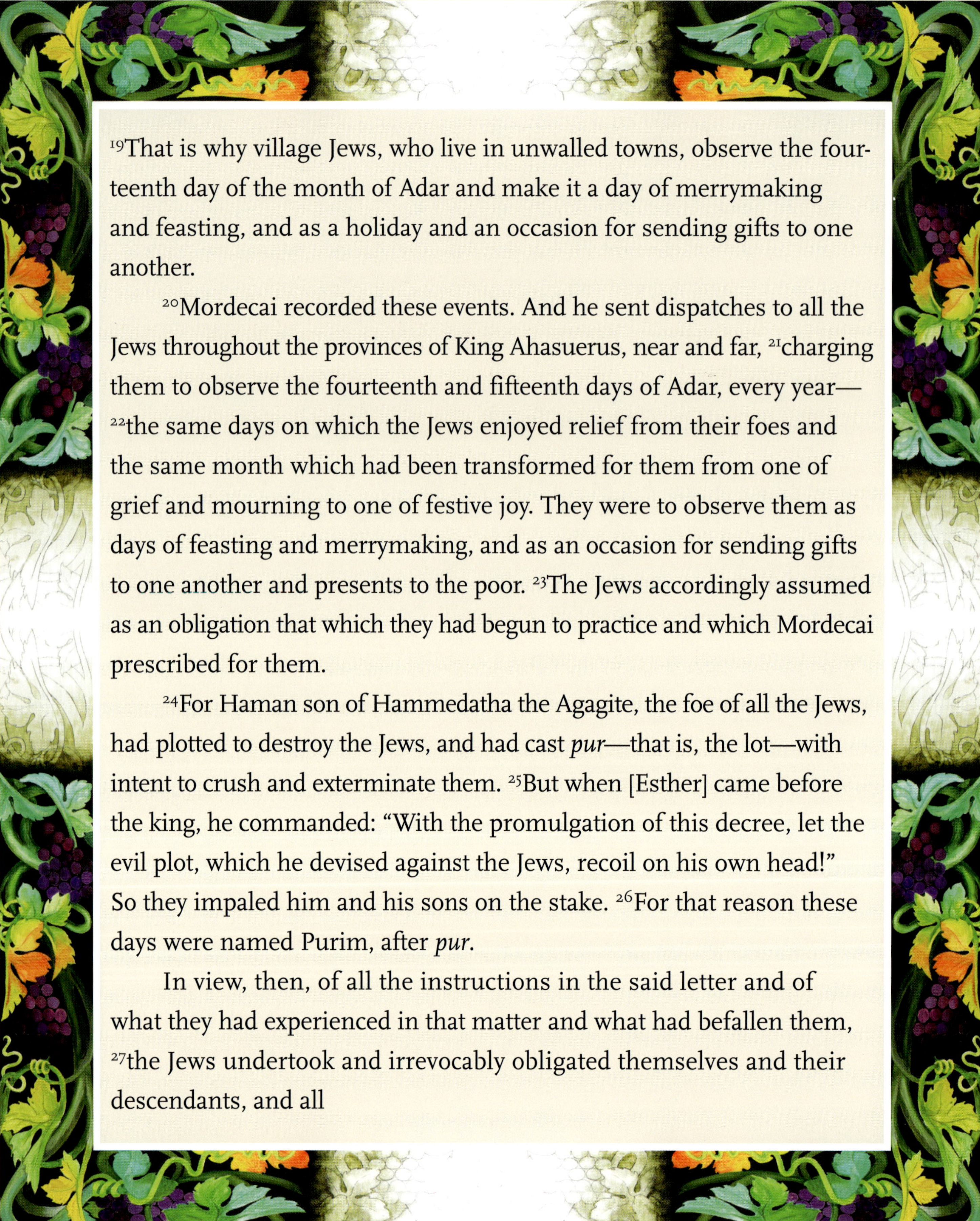

[19]That is why village Jews, who live in unwalled towns, observe the fourteenth day of the month of Adar and make it a day of merrymaking
and feasting, and as a holiday and an occasion for sending gifts to one
another.

[20]Mordecai recorded these events. And he sent dispatches to all the
Jews throughout the provinces of King Ahasuerus, near and far, [21]charging
them to observe the fourteenth and fifteenth days of Adar, every year—
[22]the same days on which the Jews enjoyed relief from their foes and
the same month which had been transformed for them from one of
grief and mourning to one of festive joy. They were to observe them as
days of feasting and merrymaking, and as an occasion for sending gifts
to one another and presents to the poor. [23]The Jews accordingly assumed
as an obligation that which they had begun to practice and which Mordecai
prescribed for them.

[24]For Haman son of Hammedatha the Agagite, the foe of all the Jews,
had plotted to destroy the Jews, and had cast *pur*—that is, the lot—with
intent to crush and exterminate them. [25]But when [Esther] came before
the king, he commanded: "With the promulgation of this decree, let the
evil plot, which he devised against the Jews, recoil on his own head!"
So they impaled him and his sons on the stake. [26]For that reason these
days were named Purim, after *pur*.

In view, then, of all the instructions in the said letter and of
what they had experienced in that matter and what had befallen them,
[27]the Jews undertook and irrevocably obligated themselves and their
descendants, and all

בערי הפרזות עשים את יום ארבעה עשר לחדש
אדר שמחה ומשתה ויום טוב ומשלוח מנות
איש לרעהו ויכתב מרדכי את הדברים האלה
וישלח ספרים אל כל היהודים אשר בכל
מדינות המלך אחשורוש הקרובים והרחוקים
לקים עליהם להיות עשים את יום ארבעה עשר
לחדש אדר ואת יום חמשה עשר בו בכל שנה
ושנה כימים אשר נחו בהם היהודים מאיביהם
והחדש אשר נהפך להם מיגון לשמחה ומאבל
ליום טוב לעשות אותם ימי משתה ושמחה
ומשלוח מנות איש לרעהו ומתנות לאביונים וקבל
היהודים את אשר החלו לעשות ואת אשר
כתב מרדכי אליהם כי המן בן המדתא האגגי
צרר כל היהודים חשב על היהודים לאבדם
והפל פור הוא הגורל להמם ולאבדם ובבאה
לפני המלך אמר עם הספר ישוב מחשבתו
הרעה אשר חשב על היהודים על ראשו ותלו
אתו ואת בניו על העץ על כן קראו לימים
האלה פורים על שם הפור על כן על כל דברי
האגרת הזאת ומה ראו על ככה ומה הגיע אליהם
קימו וקבל היהודים עליהם ועל זרעם ועל כל

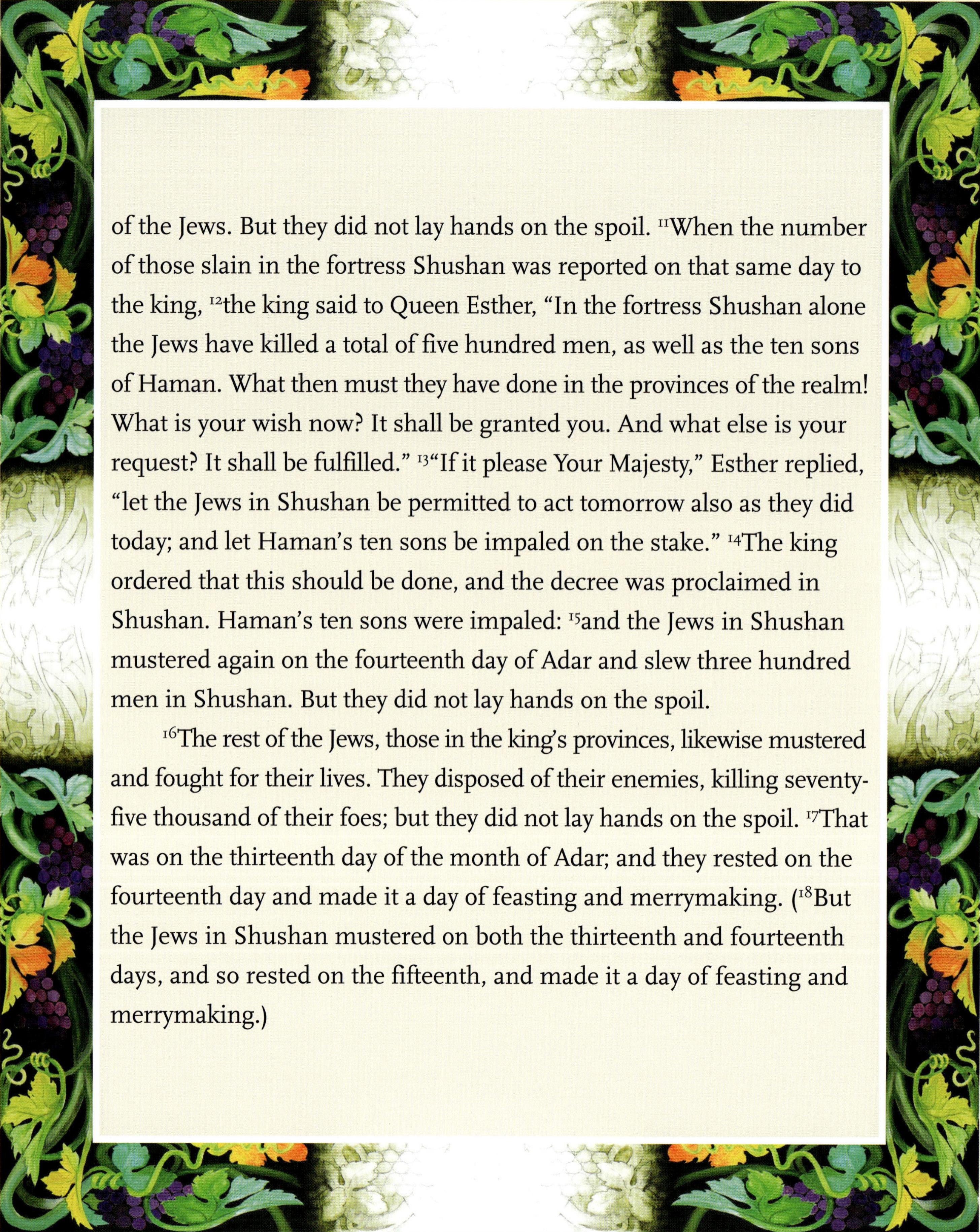

of the Jews. But they did not lay hands on the spoil. 11When the number
of those slain in the fortress Shushan was reported on that same day to
the king, 12the king said to Queen Esther, "In the fortress Shushan alone
the Jews have killed a total of five hundred men, as well as the ten sons
of Haman. What then must they have done in the provinces of the realm!
What is your wish now? It shall be granted you. And what else is your
request? It shall be fulfilled." 13"If it please Your Majesty," Esther replied,
"let the Jews in Shushan be permitted to act tomorrow also as they did
today; and let Haman's ten sons be impaled on the stake." 14The king
ordered that this should be done, and the decree was proclaimed in
Shushan. Haman's ten sons were impaled: 15and the Jews in Shushan
mustered again on the fourteenth day of Adar and slew three hundred
men in Shushan. But they did not lay hands on the spoil.

16The rest of the Jews, those in the king's provinces, likewise mustered
and fought for their lives. They disposed of their enemies, killing seventy-
five thousand of their foes; but they did not lay hands on the spoil. 17That
was on the thirteenth day of the month of Adar; and they rested on the
fourteenth day and made it a day of feasting and merrymaking. (18But
the Jews in Shushan mustered on both the thirteenth and fourteenth
days, and so rested on the fifteenth, and made it a day of feasting and
merrymaking.)

בני המן בן המדתא צרר היהודים הרגו ובבזה
לא שלחו את ידם ביום ההוא בא מספר ההרוגים
בשושן הבירה לפני המלך ויאמר המלך לאסתר
המלכה בשושן הבירה הרגו היהודים ואבד
חמש מאות איש ואת עשרת בני המן בשאר
מדינות המלך מה עשו ומה שאלתך וינתן לך
ומה בקשתך עוד ותעש ותאמר אסתר אם על
המלך טוב ינתן גם מחר ליהודים אשר בשושן
לעשות כדת היום ואת עשרת בני המן יתלו על
העץ ויאמר המלך להעשות כן ותנתן דת בשושן
ואת עשרת בני המן תלו ויקהלו היהודיים אשר
בשושן גם ביום ארבעה עשר לחדש אדר ויהרגו
בשושן שלש מאות איש ובבזה לא שלחו את
ידם ושאר היהודים אשר במדינות המלך נקהלו
ועמד על נפשם ונוח מאיביהם והרוג בשנאיהם
חמשה ושבעים אלף ובבזה לא שלחו את ידם
ביום שלושה עשר לחדש אדר ונוח בארבעה
עשר בו ועשה אתו יום משתה ושמחה והיהודיים
אשר בשושן נקהלו בשלושה עשר בו ובארבעה
עשר בו ונוח בחמשה עשר בו ועשה אתו יום
משתה ושמחה על כן היהודים הפרוזים הישבים

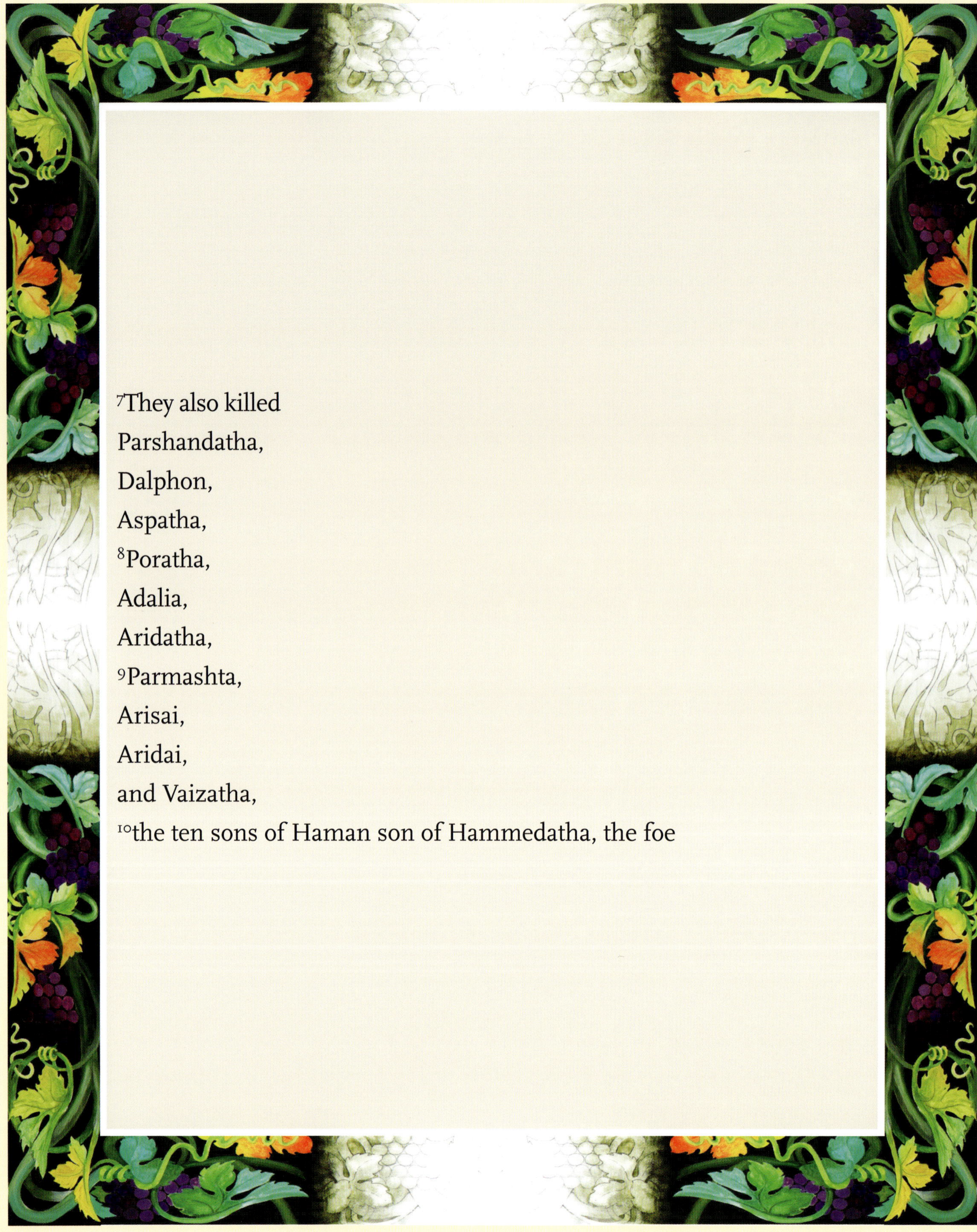

7 They also killed
Parshandatha,
Dalphon,
Aspatha,
8 Poratha,
Adalia,
Aridatha,
9 Parmashta,
Arisai,
Aridai,
and Vaizatha,
10 the ten sons of Haman son of Hammedatha, the foe

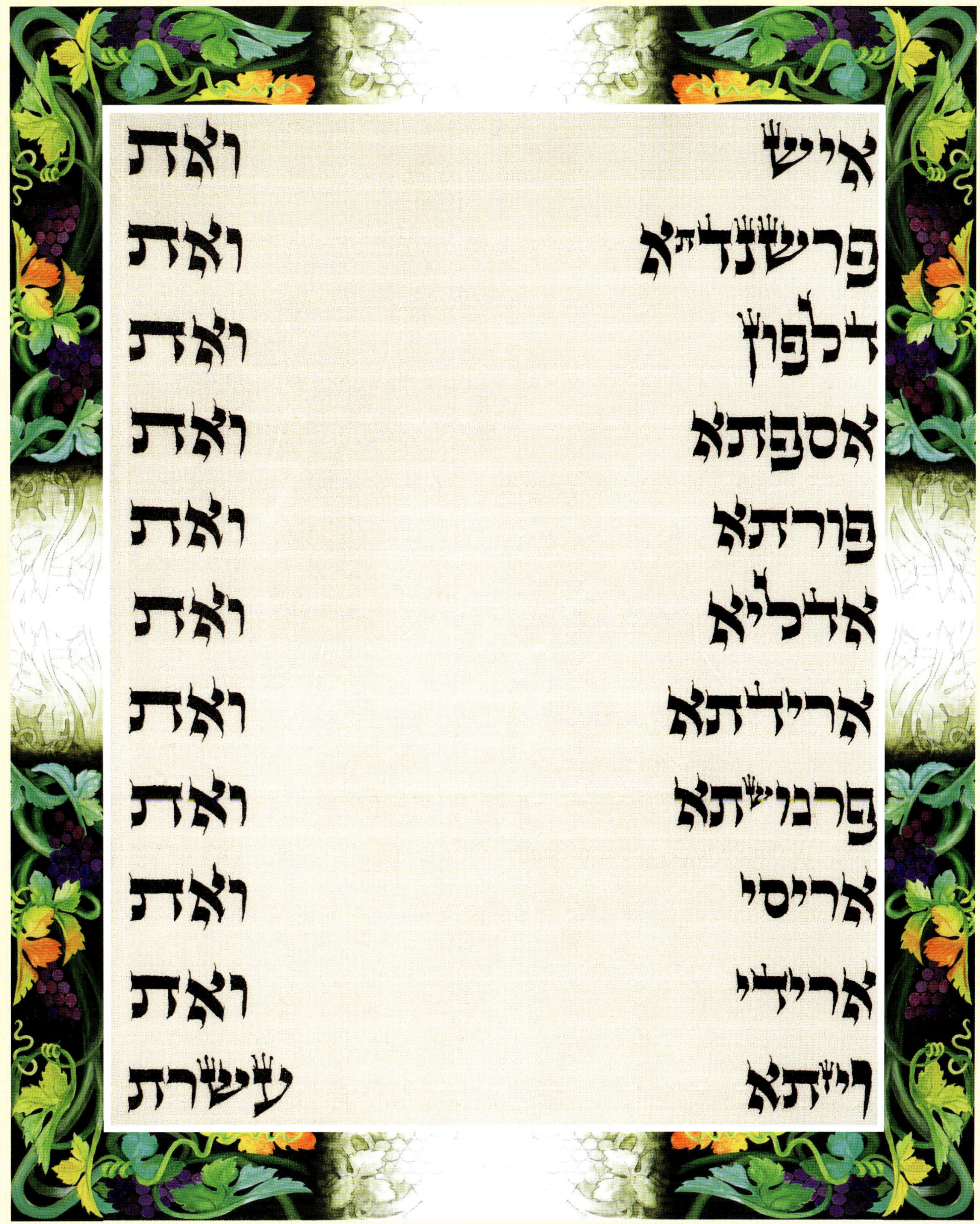

איש ואת
פרשנדתא ואת
דלפון ואת
אספתא ואת
פורתא ואת
אדליא ואת
ארידתא ואת
פרמשתא ואת
אריסי ואת
ארידי ואת
ויזתא עשרת

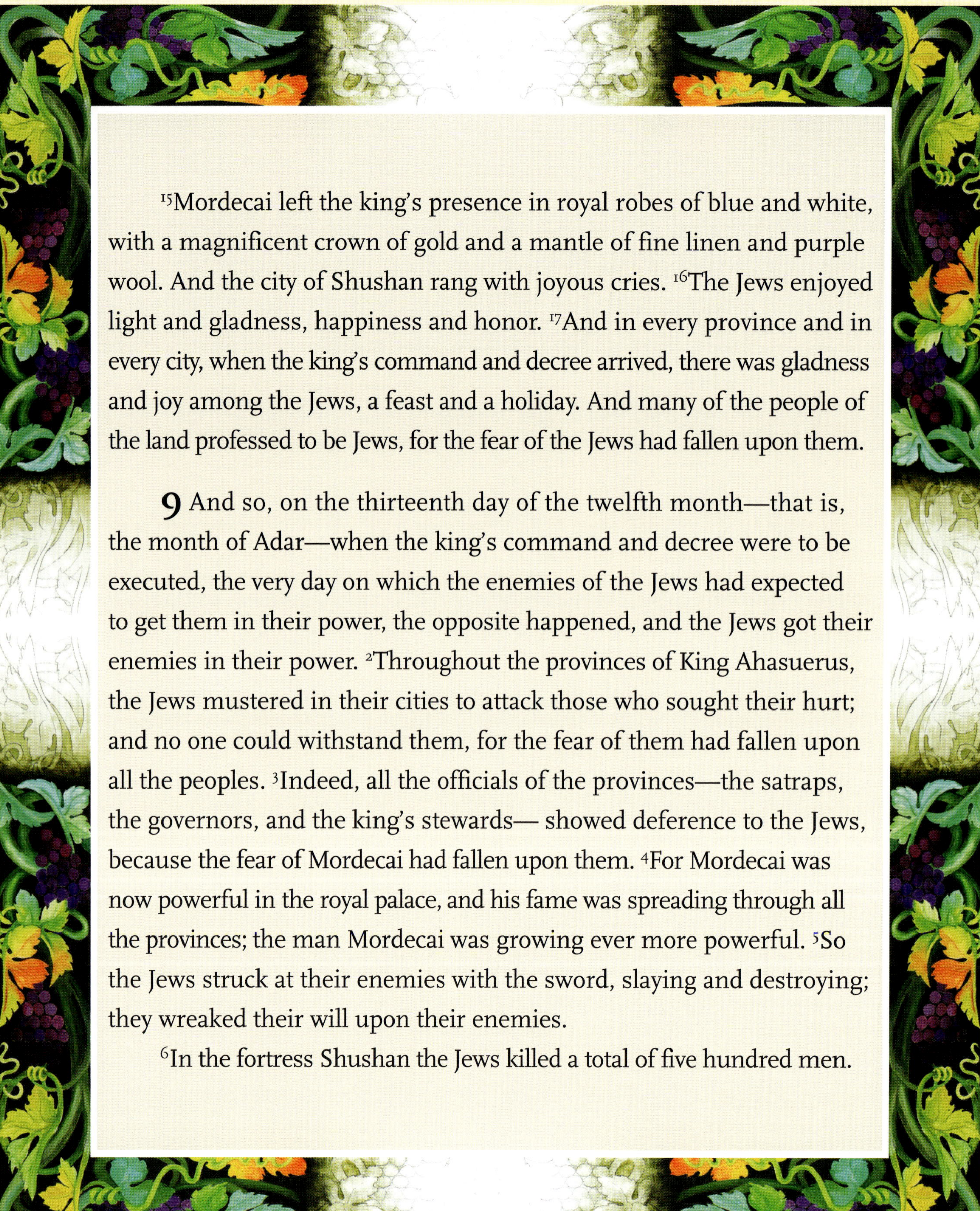

15 Mordecai left the king's presence in royal robes of blue and white,
with a magnificent crown of gold and a mantle of fine linen and purple
wool. And the city of Shushan rang with joyous cries. 16 The Jews enjoyed
light and gladness, happiness and honor. 17 And in every province and in
every city, when the king's command and decree arrived, there was gladness
and joy among the Jews, a feast and a holiday. And many of the people of
the land professed to be Jews, for the fear of the Jews had fallen upon them.

9 And so, on the thirteenth day of the twelfth month—that is,
the month of Adar—when the king's command and decree were to be
executed, the very day on which the enemies of the Jews had expected
to get them in their power, the opposite happened, and the Jews got their
enemies in their power. 2 Throughout the provinces of King Ahasuerus,
the Jews mustered in their cities to attack those who sought their hurt;
and no one could withstand them, for the fear of them had fallen upon
all the peoples. 3 Indeed, all the officials of the provinces—the satraps,
the governors, and the king's stewards— showed deference to the Jews,
because the fear of Mordecai had fallen upon them. 4 For Mordecai was
now powerful in the royal palace, and his fame was spreading through all
the provinces; the man Mordecai was growing ever more powerful. 5 So
the Jews struck at their enemies with the sword, slaying and destroying;
they wreaked their will upon their enemies.

6 In the fortress Shushan the Jews killed a total of five hundred men.

המלך בלבוש מלכות תכלת וחור ועטרת זהב
גדולה ותכריך בוץ וארגמן והעיר שושן צהלה
ושמחה ליהודים היתה אורה ושמחה וששן
ויקר ובכל מדינה ומדינה ובכל עיר ועיר מקום
אשר דבר המלך ודתו מגיע שמחה וששון
ליהודים משתה ויום טוב ורבים מעמי הארץ
מתיהדים כי נפל פחד היהודים עליהם ובשנים
עשר חדש הוא חדש אדר בשלושה עשר יום
בו אשר הגיע דבר המלך ודתו להעשות ביום
אשר שברו איבי היהודים לשלוט בהם ונהפוך
הוא אשר ישלטו היהודים המה בשנאיהם
נקהלו היהודים בעריהם בכל מדינות המלך
אחשורוש לשלח יד במבקשי רעתם ואיש
לא עמד בפניהם כי נפל פחדם על כל העמים
וכל שרי המדינות והאחשדרפנים והפחות ועשי
המלאכה אשר למלך מנשאים את היהודים כי
נפל פחד מרדכי עליהם כי גדול מרדכי בבית
המלך ושמעו הולך בכל המדינות כי האיש
מרדכי הולך וגדול ויכו היהודים בכל איביהם
מכת חרב והרג ואבדן ויעשו בשנאיהם כרצונם
ובשושן הבירה הרגו היהודים ואבד חמש מאות

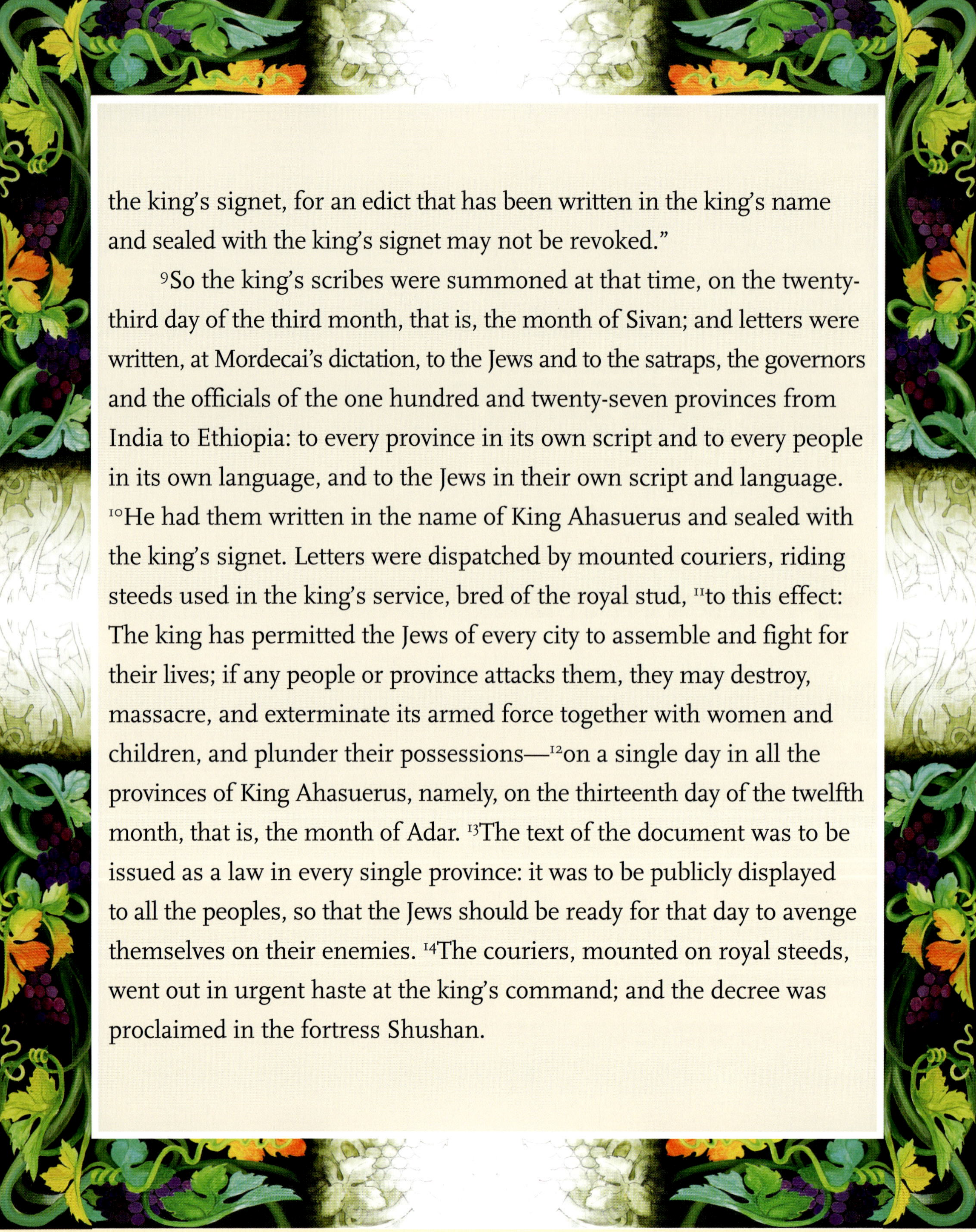

the king's signet, for an edict that has been written in the king's name
and sealed with the king's signet may not be revoked."
9So the king's scribes were summoned at that time, on the twenty-
third day of the third month, that is, the month of Sivan; and letters were
written, at Mordecai's dictation, to the Jews and to the satraps, the governors
and the officials of the one hundred and twenty-seven provinces from
India to Ethiopia: to every province in its own script and to every people
in its own language, and to the Jews in their own script and language.
10He had them written in the name of King Ahasuerus and sealed with
the king's signet. Letters were dispatched by mounted couriers, riding
steeds used in the king's service, bred of the royal stud, 11to this effect:
The king has permitted the Jews of every city to assemble and fight for
their lives; if any people or province attacks them, they may destroy,
massacre, and exterminate its armed force together with women and
children, and plunder their possessions—12on a single day in all the
provinces of King Ahasuerus, namely, on the thirteenth day of the twelfth
month, that is, the month of Adar. 13The text of the document was to be
issued as a law in every single province: it was to be publicly displayed
to all the peoples, so that the Jews should be ready for that day to avenge
themselves on their enemies. 14The couriers, mounted on royal steeds,
went out in urgent haste at the king's command; and the decree was
proclaimed in the fortress Shushan.

המלך כי כתב אשר נכתב בשם המלך ונחתום
בטבעת המלך אין להשיב ויקראו ספרי המלך
בעת ההיא בחדש השלישי הוא חדש סיון
בשלושה ועשרים בו ויכתב ככל אשר צוה
מרדכי אל היהודים ואל האחשדרפנים והפחות
ושרי המדינות אשר מהדו ועד כוש שבע
ועשרים ומאה מדינה מדינה ומדינה ככתבה ועם
ועם כלשנו ואל היהודים ככתבם וכלשונם ויכתב
בשם המלך אחשורש ויחתם בטבעת המלך
וישלח ספרים ביד הרצים בסוסים רכבי הרכש
האחשתרנים בני הרמכים אשר נתן המלך
ליהודים אשר בכל עיר ועיר להקהל ולעמד
על נפשם להשמיד להרג ולאבד את כל חיל עם
ומדינה הצרים אתם טף ונשים ושללם לבוז ביום
אחד בכל מדינות המלך אחשורוש בשלושה
עשר לחדש שנים עשר הוא חדש אדר פתשגן
הכתב להנתן דת בכל מדינה ומדינה גלוי לכל
העמים ולהיות היהודיים עתודים ליום הזה להנקם
מאיביהם הרצים רכבי הרכש האחשתרנים יצאו
מבהלים ודחופים בדבר המלך והדת נתנה בשושן
הבירה ומרדכי יצא מלפני

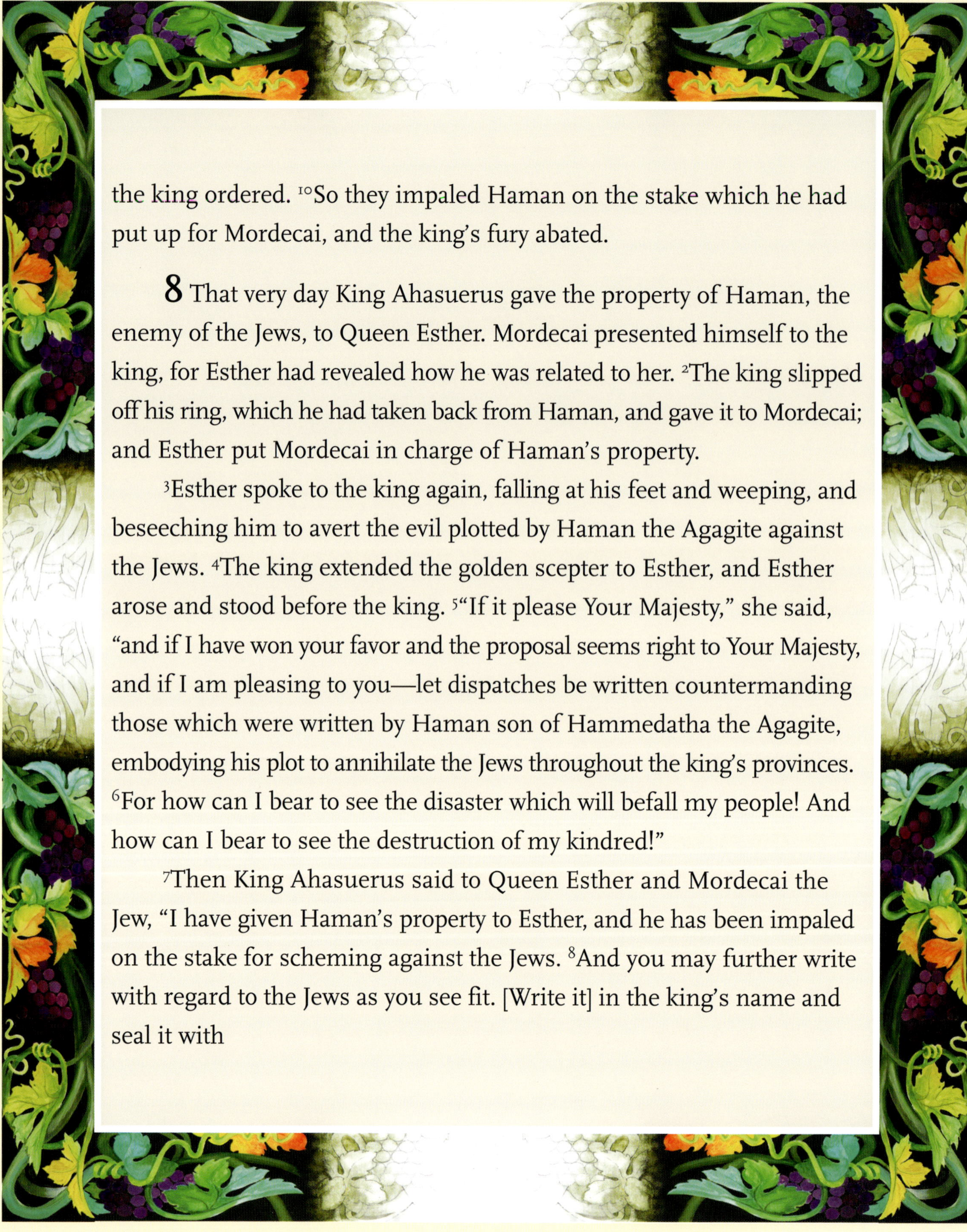

the king ordered. 10So they impaled Haman on the stake which he had
put up for Mordecai, and the king's fury abated.

8 That very day King Ahasuerus gave the property of Haman, the
enemy of the Jews, to Queen Esther. Mordecai presented himself to the
king, for Esther had revealed how he was related to her. 2The king slipped
off his ring, which he had taken back from Haman, and gave it to Mordecai;
and Esther put Mordecai in charge of Haman's property.

3Esther spoke to the king again, falling at his feet and weeping, and
beseeching him to avert the evil plotted by Haman the Agagite against
the Jews. 4The king extended the golden scepter to Esther, and Esther
arose and stood before the king. 5"If it please Your Majesty," she said,
"and if I have won your favor and the proposal seems right to Your Majesty,
and if I am pleasing to you—let dispatches be written countermanding
those which were written by Haman son of Hammedatha the Agagite,
embodying his plot to annihilate the Jews throughout the king's provinces.
6For how can I bear to see the disaster which will befall my people! And
how can I bear to see the destruction of my kindred!"

7Then King Ahasuerus said to Queen Esther and Mordecai the
Jew, "I have given Haman's property to Esther, and he has been impaled
on the stake for scheming against the Jews. 8And you may further write
with regard to the Jews as you see fit. [Write it] in the king's name and
seal it with

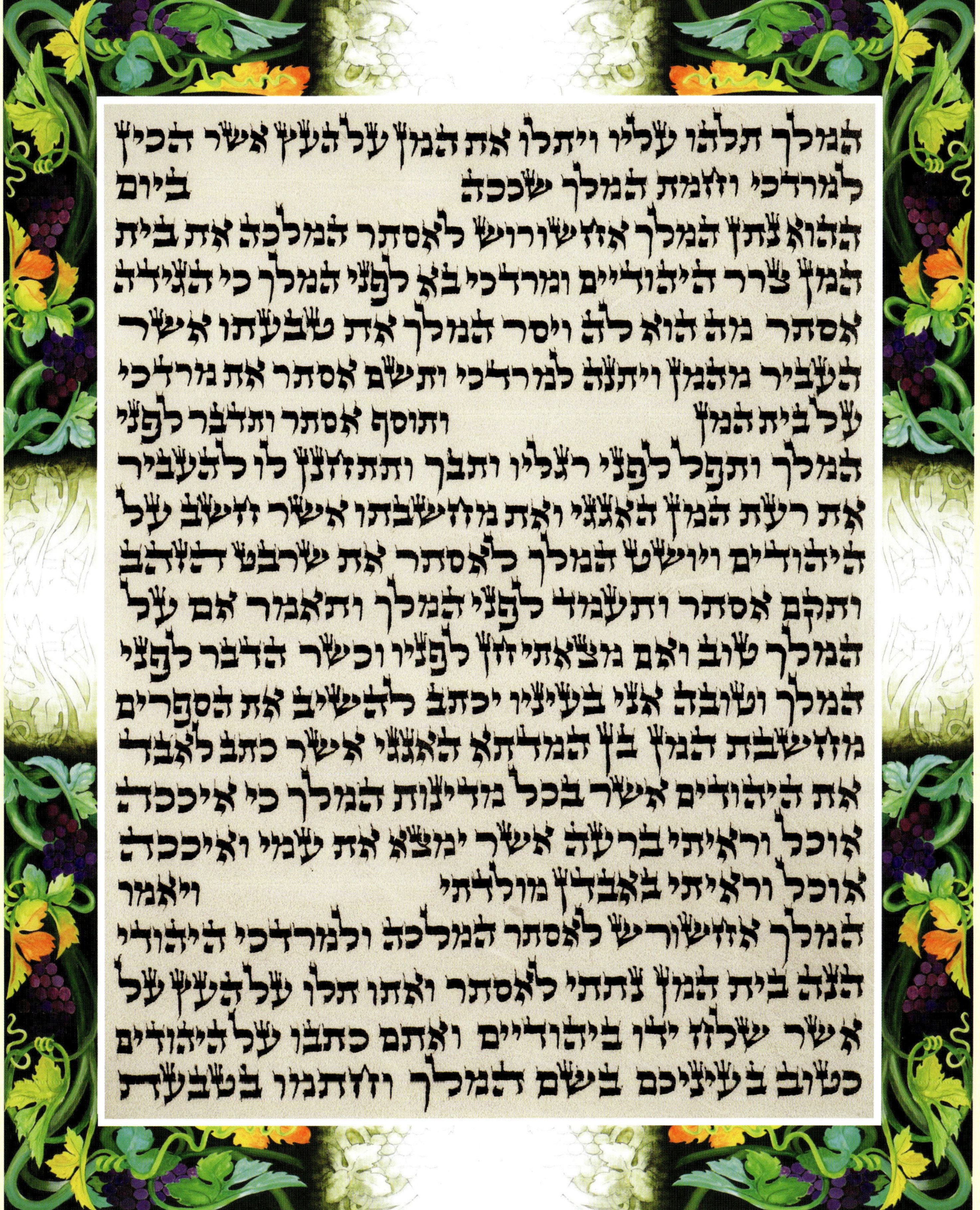
המלך תלהו עליו ויתלו את המן על העץ אשר הכין
למרדכי וחמת המלך שככה ביום
ההוא נתן המלך אחשורוש לאסתר המלכה את בית
המן צרר היהודיים ומרדכי בא לפני המלך כי הגידה
אסתר מה הוא לה ויסר המלך את טבעתו אשר
העביר מהמן ויתנה למרדכי ותשם אסתר את מרדכי
על בית המן ותוסף אסתר ותדבר לפני
המלך ותפל לפני רגליו ותבך ותתחנן לו להעביר
את רעת המן האגגי ואת מחשבתו אשר חשב על
היהודים ויושט המלך לאסתר את שרבט הזהב
ותקם אסתר ותעמד לפני המלך ותאמר אם על
המלך טוב ואם מצאתי חן לפניו וכשר הדבר לפני
המלך וטובה אני בעיניו יכתב להשיב את הספרים
מחשבת המן בן המדתא האגגי אשר כתב לאבד
את היהודים אשר בכל מדינות המלך כי איככה
אוכל וראיתי ברעה אשר ימצא את עמי ואיככה
אוכל וראיתי באבדן מולדתי ויאמר
המלך אחשורש לאסתר המלכה ולמרדכי היהודי
הנה בית המן נתתי לאסתר ואתו תלו על העץ על
אשר שלח ידו ביהודיים ואתם כתבו על היהודים
כטוב בעיניכם בשם המלך וחתמו בטבעת

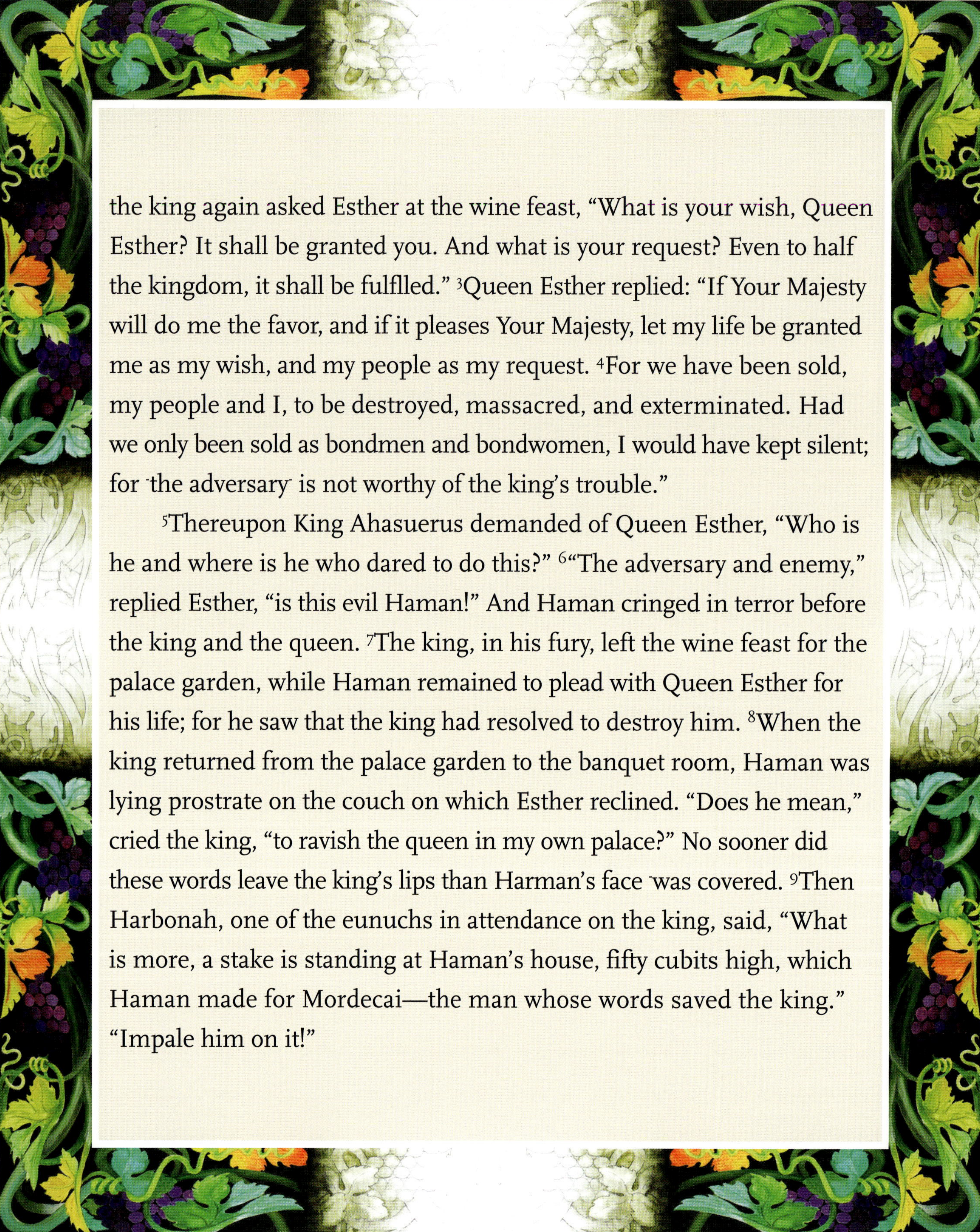

the king again asked Esther at the wine feast, “What is your wish, Queen
Esther? It shall be granted you. And what is your request? Even to half
the kingdom, it shall be fulfilled.” 3Queen Esther replied: “If Your Majesty
will do me the favor, and if it pleases Your Majesty, let my life be granted
me as my wish, and my people as my request. 4For we have been sold,
my people and I, to be destroyed, massacred, and exterminated. Had
we only been sold as bondmen and bondwomen, I would have kept silent;
for the adversary is not worthy of the king’s trouble.”

5Thereupon King Ahasuerus demanded of Queen Esther, “Who is
he and where is he who dared to do this?” 6“The adversary and enemy,”
replied Esther, “is this evil Haman!” And Haman cringed in terror before
the king and the queen. 7The king, in his fury, left the wine feast for the
palace garden, while Haman remained to plead with Queen Esther for
his life; for he saw that the king had resolved to destroy him. 8When the
king returned from the palace garden to the banquet room, Haman was
lying prostrate on the couch on which Esther reclined. “Does he mean,”
cried the king, “to ravish the queen in my own palace?” No sooner did
these words leave the king’s lips than Harman’s face was covered. 9Then
Harbonah, one of the eunuchs in attendance on the king, said, “What
is more, a stake is standing at Haman’s house, fifty cubits high, which
Haman made for Mordecai—the man whose words saved the king.”
“Impale him on it!”

המלך לאסתר גם ביום השני במשתה היין מה
שאלתך אסתר המלכה ותנתן לך ומה בקשתך
עד חצי המלכות ותעש ותען אסתר המלכה ותאמר
אם מצאתי חן בעיניך המלך ואם על המלך טוב
תנתן לי נפשי בשאלתי ועמי בבקשתי כי נמכרנו
אני ועמי להשמיד להרוג ולאבד ואלו לעבדים
ולשפחות נמכרנו החרשתי כי אין הצר שוה בנזק
המלך ויאמר המלך
אחשורוש ויאמר לאסתר המלכה מי הוא זה ואי
זה הוא אשר מלאו לבו לעשות כן ותאמר אסתר
איש צר ואויב המן הרע הזה והמן נבעת מלפני
המלך והמלכה והמלך קם בחמתו ממשתה היין
אל גנת הביתן והמן עמד לבקש על נפשו מאסתר
המלכה כי ראה כי כלתה אליו הרעה מאת המלך
והמלך שב מגנת הביתן אל בית משתה היין
והמן נפל על המטה אשר אסתר עליה ויאמר
המלך הגם לכבוש את המלכה עמי בבית
הדבר יצא מפי המלך ופני המן חפו ויאמר
חרבונה אחד מן הסריסים לפני המלך גם הנה
העץ אשר עשה המן למרדכי אשר דבר טוב על
המלך עמד בבית המן גבה חמשים אמה ויאמר

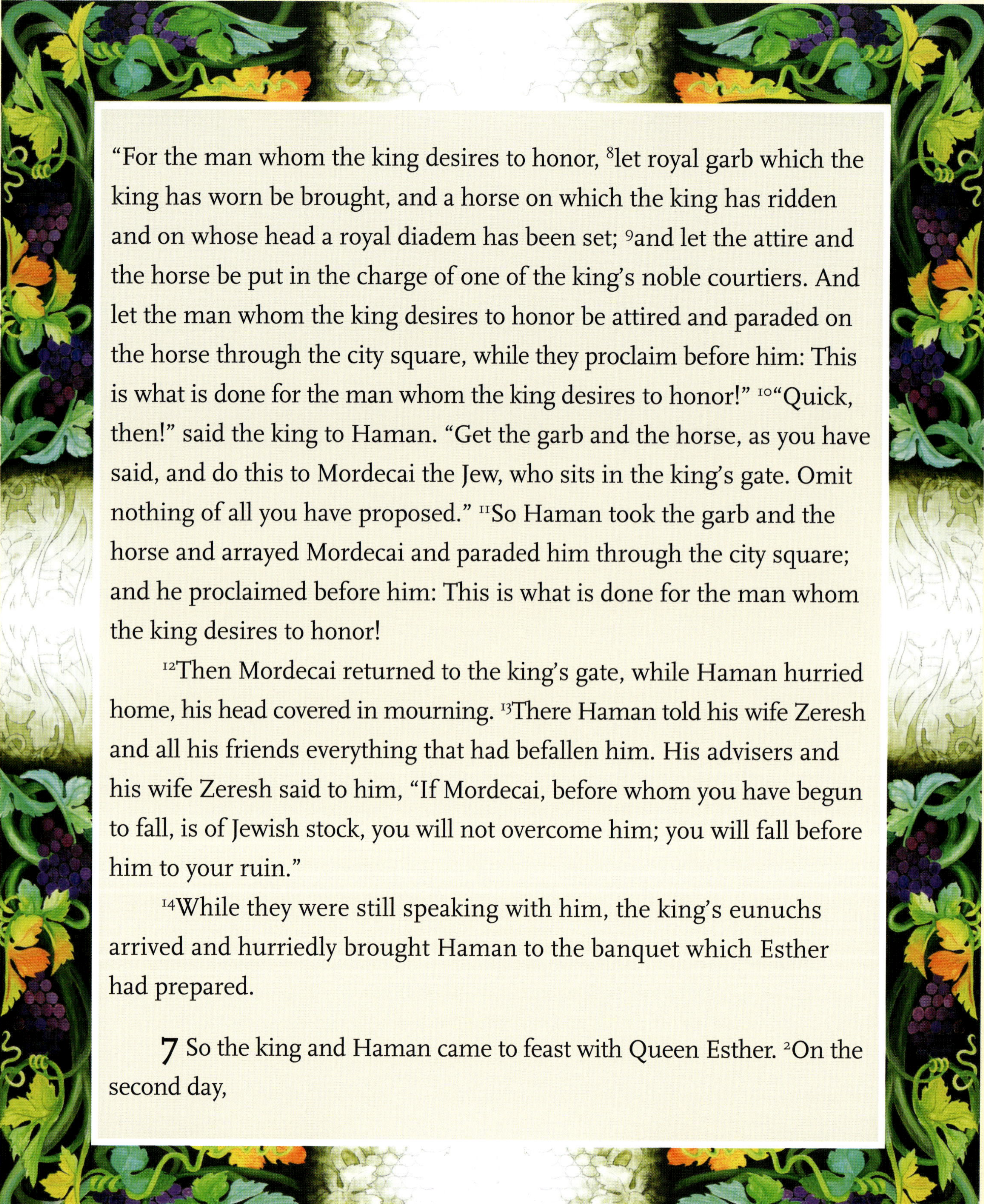

“For the man whom the king desires to honor, 8let royal garb which the
king has worn be brought, and a horse on which the king has ridden
and on whose head a royal diadem has been set; 9and let the attire and
the horse be put in the charge of one of the king’s noble courtiers. And
let the man whom the king desires to honor be attired and paraded on
the horse through the city square, while they proclaim before him: This
is what is done for the man whom the king desires to honor!” 10“Quick,
then!” said the king to Haman. “Get the garb and the horse, as you have
said, and do this to Mordecai the Jew, who sits in the king’s gate. Omit
nothing of all you have proposed.” 11So Haman took the garb and the
horse and arrayed Mordecai and paraded him through the city square;
and he proclaimed before him: This is what is done for the man whom
the king desires to honor!

12Then Mordecai returned to the king’s gate, while Haman hurried
home, his head covered in mourning. 13There Haman told his wife Zeresh
and all his friends everything that had befallen him. His advisers and
his wife Zeresh said to him, “If Mordecai, before whom you have begun
to fall, is of Jewish stock, you will not overcome him; you will fall before
him to your ruin.”

14While they were still speaking with him, the king’s eunuchs
arrived and hurriedly brought Haman to the banquet which Esther
had prepared.

7 So the king and Haman came to feast with Queen Esther. 2On the
second day,

המלך חפץ ביקרו יביאו לבוש מלכות אשר
לבש בו המלך וסוס אשר רכב עליו המלך
ואשר נתן כתר מלכות בראשו ונתון הלבוש
והסוס על יד איש משרי המלך הפרתמים
והלבשו את האיש אשר המלך חפץ ביקרו
והרכיבהו על הסוס ברחוב העיר וקראו לפניו
ככה יעשה לאיש אשר המלך חפץ ביקרו
ויאמר המלך להמן מהר קח את הלבוש ואת
הסוס כאשר דברת ועשה כן למרדכי היהודי
היושב בשער המלך אל תפל דבר מכל אשר
דברת ויקח המן את הלבוש ואת הסוס וילבש
את מרדכי וירכיבהו ברחוב העיר ויקרא לפניו
ככה יעשה לאיש אשר המלך חפץ ביקרו וישב
מרדכי אל שער המלך והמן נדחף אל ביתו
אבל וחפוי ראש ויספר המן לזרש אשתו ולכל
אהביו את כל אשר קרהו ויאמרו לו חכמיו וזרש
אשתו אם מזרע היהודים מרדכי אשר החלות
לנפל לפניו לא תוכל לו כי נפול תפול לפניו
עודם מדברים עמו וסריסי המלך הגיעו ויבהלו
להביא את המן אל המשתה אשר עשתה אסתר
ויבא המלך והמן לשתות עם אסתר המלכה ויאמר

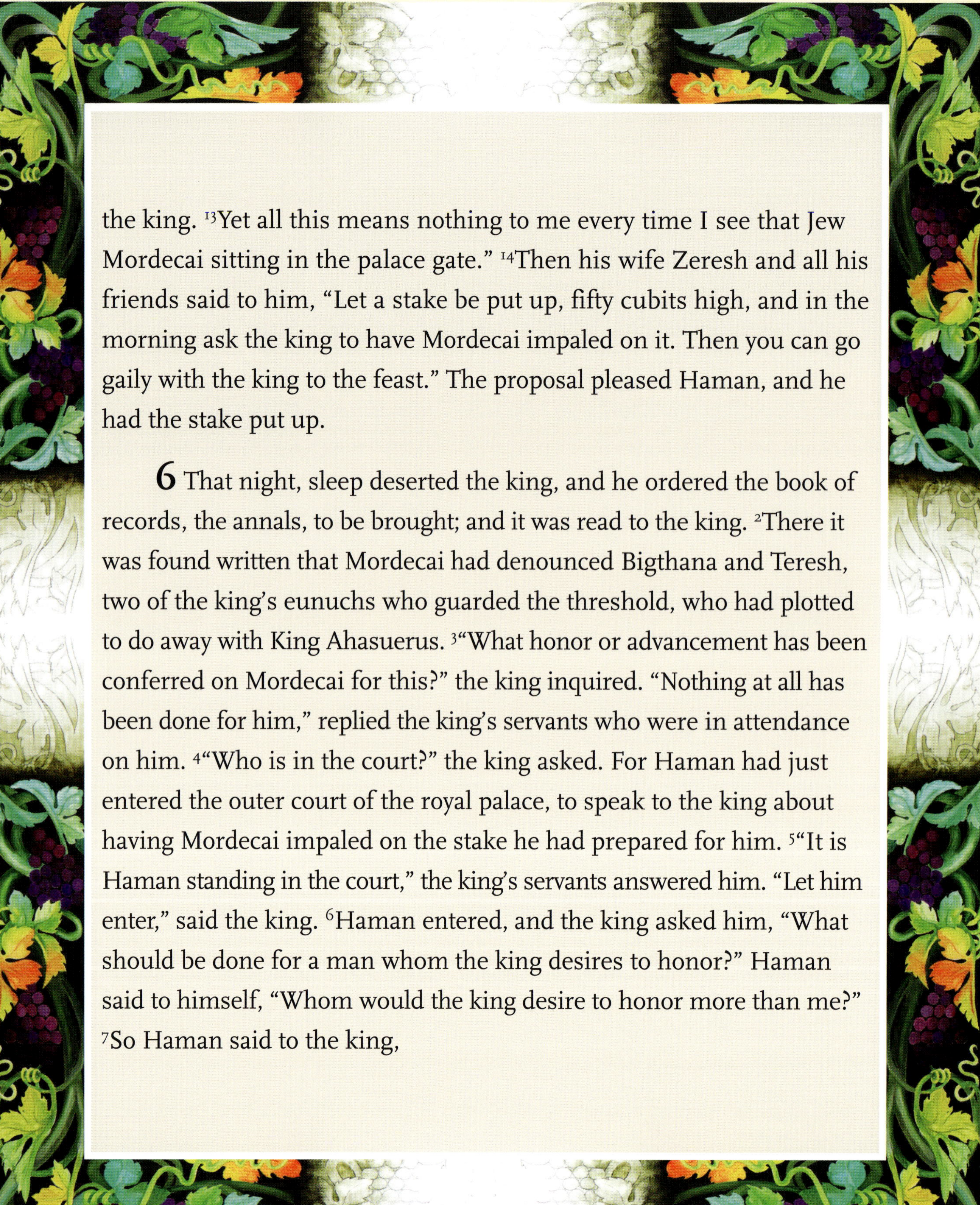

the king. [13]Yet all this means nothing to me every time I see that Jew
Mordecai sitting in the palace gate." [14]Then his wife Zeresh and all his
friends said to him, "Let a stake be put up, fifty cubits high, and in the
morning ask the king to have Mordecai impaled on it. Then you can go
gaily with the king to the feast." The proposal pleased Haman, and he
had the stake put up.

6 That night, sleep deserted the king, and he ordered the book of
records, the annals, to be brought; and it was read to the king. [2]There it
was found written that Mordecai had denounced Bigthana and Teresh,
two of the king's eunuchs who guarded the threshold, who had plotted
to do away with King Ahasuerus. [3]"What honor or advancement has been
conferred on Mordecai for this?" the king inquired. "Nothing at all has
been done for him," replied the king's servants who were in attendance
on him. [4]"Who is in the court?" the king asked. For Haman had just
entered the outer court of the royal palace, to speak to the king about
having Mordecai impaled on the stake he had prepared for him. [5]"It is
Haman standing in the court," the king's servants answered him. "Let him
enter," said the king. [6]Haman entered, and the king asked him, "What
should be done for a man whom the king desires to honor?" Haman
said to himself, "Whom would the king desire to honor more than me?"
[7]So Haman said to the king,

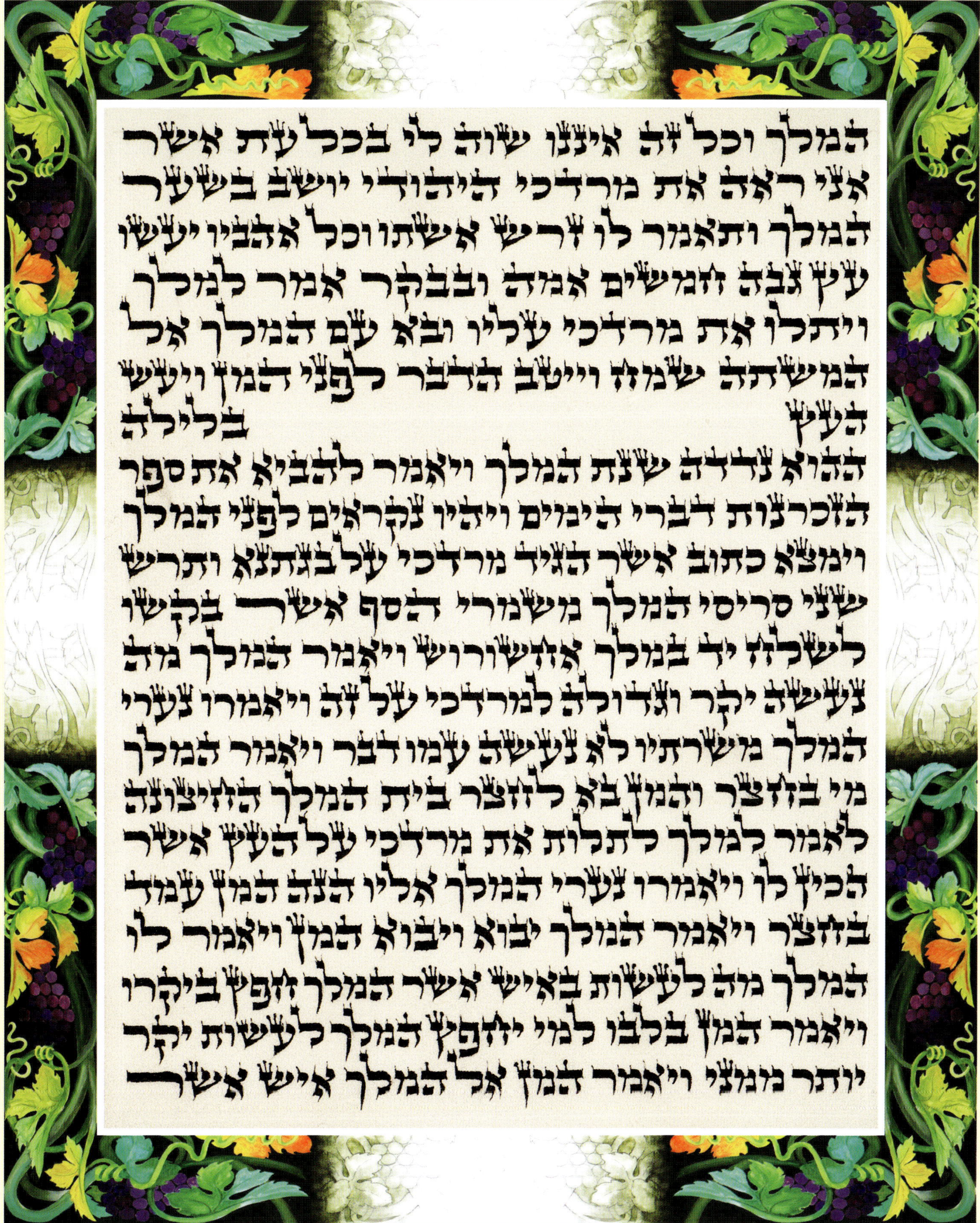

המלך וכל זה איננו שוה לי בכל עת אשר
אני ראה את מרדכי היהודי יושב בשער
המלך ותאמר לו זרש אשתו וכל אהביו יעשו
עץ גבה חמשים אמה ובבקר אמר למלך
ויתלו את מרדכי עליו ובא עם המלך אל
המשתה שמח וייטב הדבר לפני המן ויעש
העץ   בלילה
ההוא נדדה שנת המלך ויאמר להביא את ספר
הזכרנות דברי הימים ויהיו נקראים לפני המלך
וימצא כתוב אשר הגיד מרדכי על בגתנא ותרש
שני סריסי המלך משמרי הסף אשר בקשו
לשלח יד במלך אחשורוש ויאמר המלך מה
נעשה יקר וגדולה למרדכי על זה ויאמרו נערי
המלך משרתיו לא נעשה עמו דבר ויאמר המלך
מי בחצר והמן בא לחצר בית המלך החיצונה
לאמר למלך לתלות את מרדכי על העץ אשר
הכין לו ויאמרו נערי המלך אליו הנה המן עמד
בחצר ויאמר המלך יבוא ויבוא המן ויאמר לו
המלך מה לעשות באיש אשר המלך חפץ ביקרו
ויאמר המן בלבו למי יחפץ המלך לעשות יקר
יותר ממני ויאמר המן אל המלך איש אשר

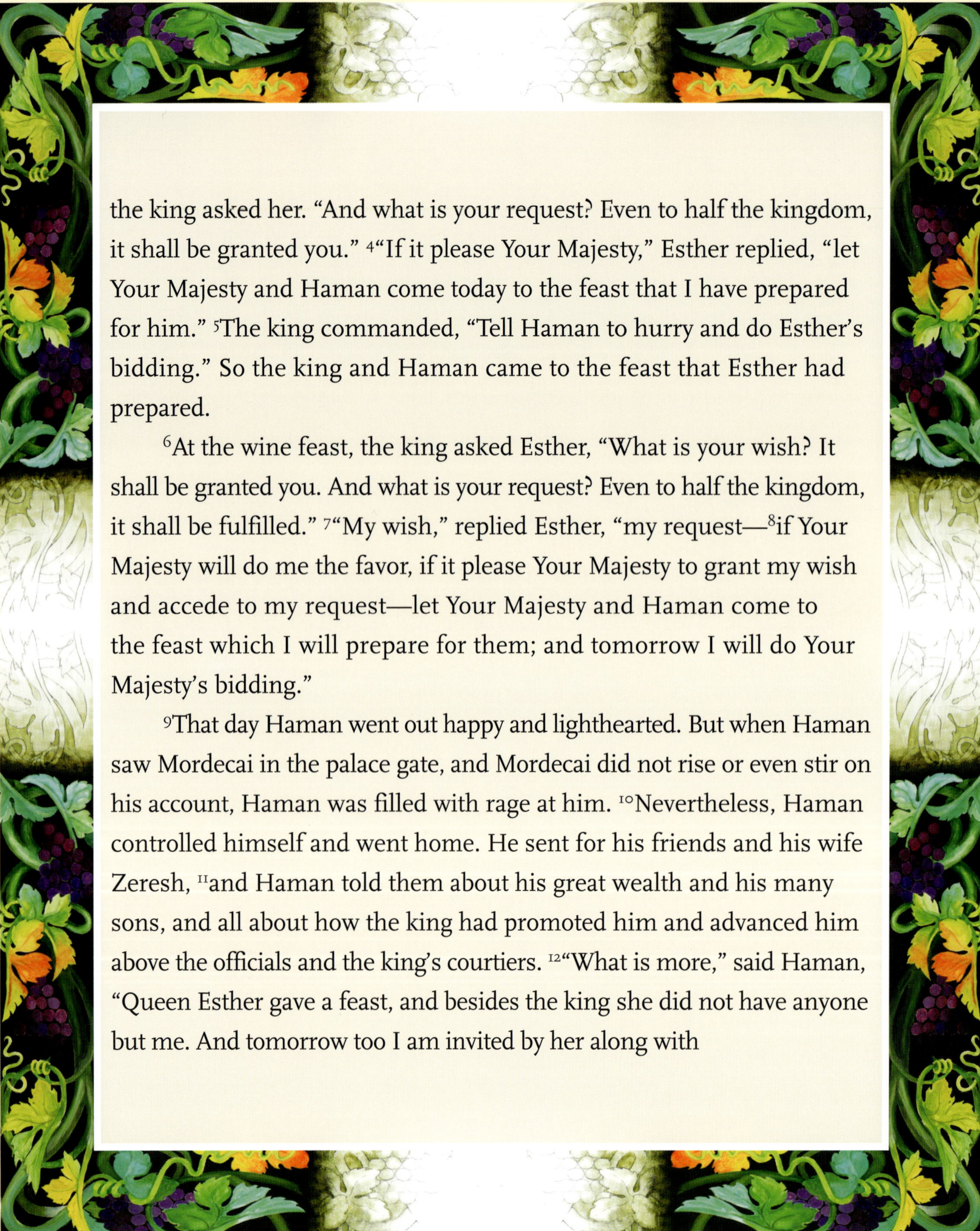

the king asked her. “And what is your request? Even to half the kingdom,
it shall be granted you.” 4“If it please Your Majesty,” Esther replied, “let
Your Majesty and Haman come today to the feast that I have prepared
for him.” 5The king commanded, “Tell Haman to hurry and do Esther’s
bidding.” So the king and Haman came to the feast that Esther had
prepared.

6At the wine feast, the king asked Esther, “What is your wish? It
shall be granted you. And what is your request? Even to half the kingdom,
it shall be fulfilled.” 7“My wish,” replied Esther, “my request—8if Your
Majesty will do me the favor, if it please Your Majesty to grant my wish
and accede to my request—let Your Majesty and Haman come to
the feast which I will prepare for them; and tomorrow I will do Your
Majesty’s bidding.”

9That day Haman went out happy and lighthearted. But when Haman
saw Mordecai in the palace gate, and Mordecai did not rise or even stir on
his account, Haman was filled with rage at him. 10Nevertheless, Haman
controlled himself and went home. He sent for his friends and his wife
Zeresh, 11and Haman told them about his great wealth and his many
sons, and all about how the king had promoted him and advanced him
above the officials and the king’s courtiers. 12“What is more,” said Haman,
“Queen Esther gave a feast, and besides the king she did not have anyone
but me. And tomorrow too I am invited by her along with

המלך מה לך אסתר המלכה ומה בקשתך עד
חצי המלכות וינתן לך ותאמר אסתר אם על
המלך טוב יבוא המלך והמן היום אל המשתה
אשר עשיתי לו ויאמר המלך מהרו את המן
לעשות את דבר אסתר ויבא המלך והמן אל
המשתה אשר עשתה אסתר ויאמר המלך לאסתר
במשתה היין מה שאלתך וינתן לך ומה בקשתך
עד חצי המלכות ותעש ותען אסתר ותאמר
שאלתי ובקשתי אם מצאתי חן בעיני המלך
ואם על המלך טוב לתת את שאלתי ולעשות את
בקשתי יבוא המלך והמן אל המשתה אשר
אעשה להם ומחר אעשה כדבר המלך ויצא
המן ביום ההוא שמח וטוב לב וכראות המן את
מרדכי בשער המלך ולא קם ולא זע ממנו וימלא
המן על מרדכי חמה ויתאפק המן ויבוא אל ביתו
וישלח ויבא את אהביו ואת זרש אשתו ויספר
להם המן את כבוד עשרו ורב בניו ואת כל
אשר גדלו המלך ואת אשר נשאו על השרים
ועבדי המלך ויאמר המן אף לא הביאה
אסתר המלכה עם המלך אל המשתה אשר
עשתה כי אם אותי וגם למחר אני קרוא לה עם

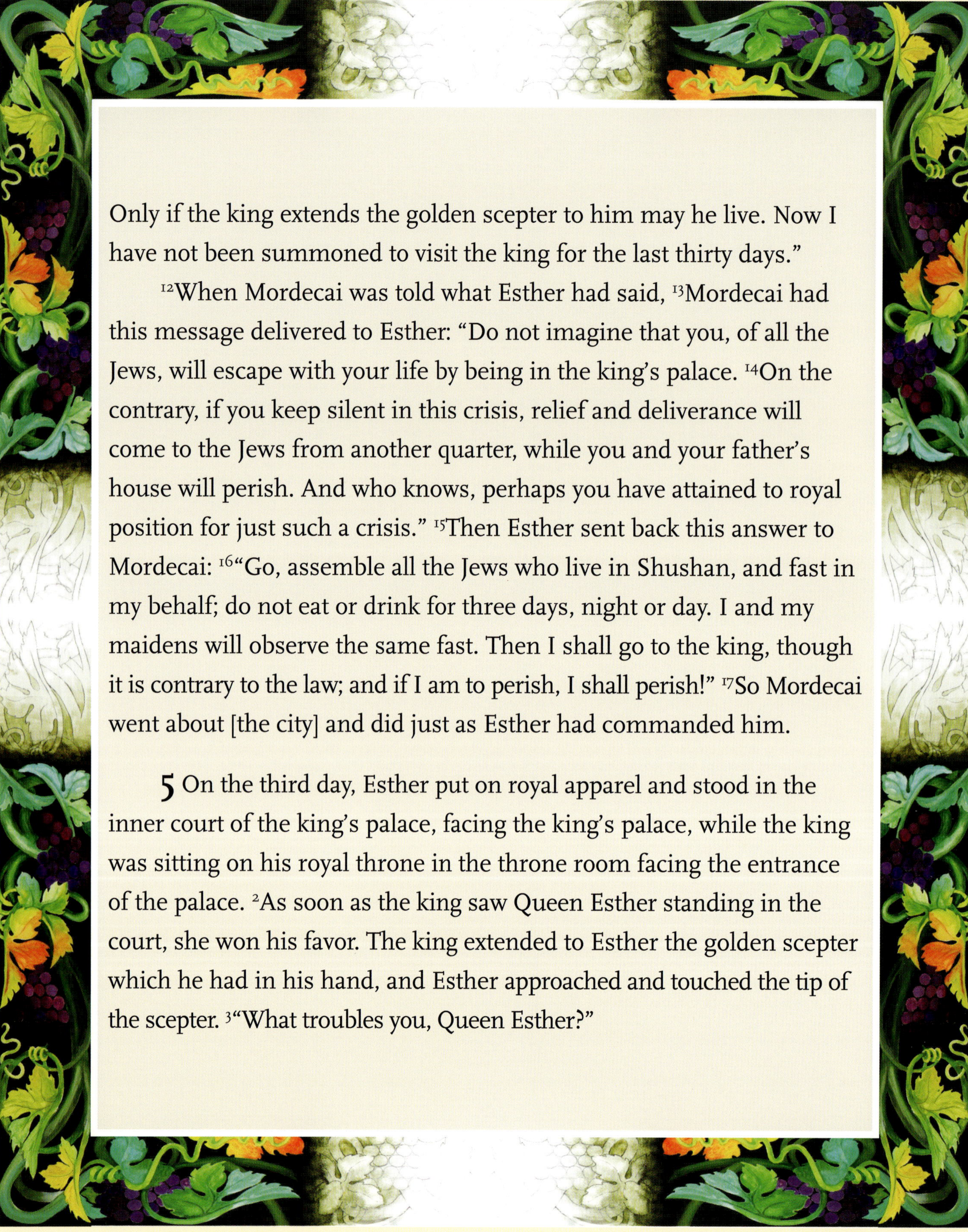

Only if the king extends the golden scepter to him may he live. Now I have not been summoned to visit the king for the last thirty days."

[12]When Mordecai was told what Esther had said, [13]Mordecai had this message delivered to Esther: "Do not imagine that you, of all the Jews, will escape with your life by being in the king's palace. [14]On the contrary, if you keep silent in this crisis, relief and deliverance will come to the Jews from another quarter, while you and your father's house will perish. And who knows, perhaps you have attained to royal position for just such a crisis." [15]Then Esther sent back this answer to Mordecai: [16]"Go, assemble all the Jews who live in Shushan, and fast in my behalf; do not eat or drink for three days, night or day. I and my maidens will observe the same fast. Then I shall go to the king, though it is contrary to the law; and if I am to perish, I shall perish!" [17]So Mordecai went about [the city] and did just as Esther had commanded him.

5 On the third day, Esther put on royal apparel and stood in the inner court of the king's palace, facing the king's palace, while the king was sitting on his royal throne in the throne room facing the entrance of the palace. [2]As soon as the king saw Queen Esther standing in the court, she won his favor. The king extended to Esther the golden scepter which he had in his hand, and Esther approached and touched the tip of the scepter. [3]"What troubles you, Queen Esther?"

המלך את שרביט הזהב וחיה ואני לא
נקראתי לבוא אל המלך זה שלושים יום
ויגידו למרדכי את דברי אסתר ויאמר מרדכי
להשיב אל אסתר אל תדמי בנפשך להמלט
בית המלך מכל היהודים כי אם החרש תחרישי
בעת הזאת רוח והצלה יעמוד ליהודים
ממקום אחר ואת ובית אביך תאבדו ומי יודע
אם לעת כזאת הגעת למלכות ותאמר אסתר
להשיב אל מרדכי לך כנוס את כל היהודים
הנמצאים בשושן וצומו עלי ואל תאכלו ואל
תשתו שלשת ימים לילה ויום גם אני ונערתי
אצום כן ובכן אבוא אל המלך אשר לא כדת
וכאשר אבדתי אבדתי ויעבר מרדכי ויעש
ככל אשר צותה עליו אסתר ויהי ביום השלישי
ותלבש אסתר מלכות ותעמד בחצר בית
המלך הפנימית נכח בית המלך והמלך
יושב על כסא מלכותו בבית המלכות נכח
פתח הבית ויהי כראות המלך את אסתר
המלכה עמדת בחצר נשאה חן בעיניו ויושט
המלך לאסתר את שרביט הזהב אשר בידו
ותקרב אסתר ותגע בראש השרביט ויאמר לה

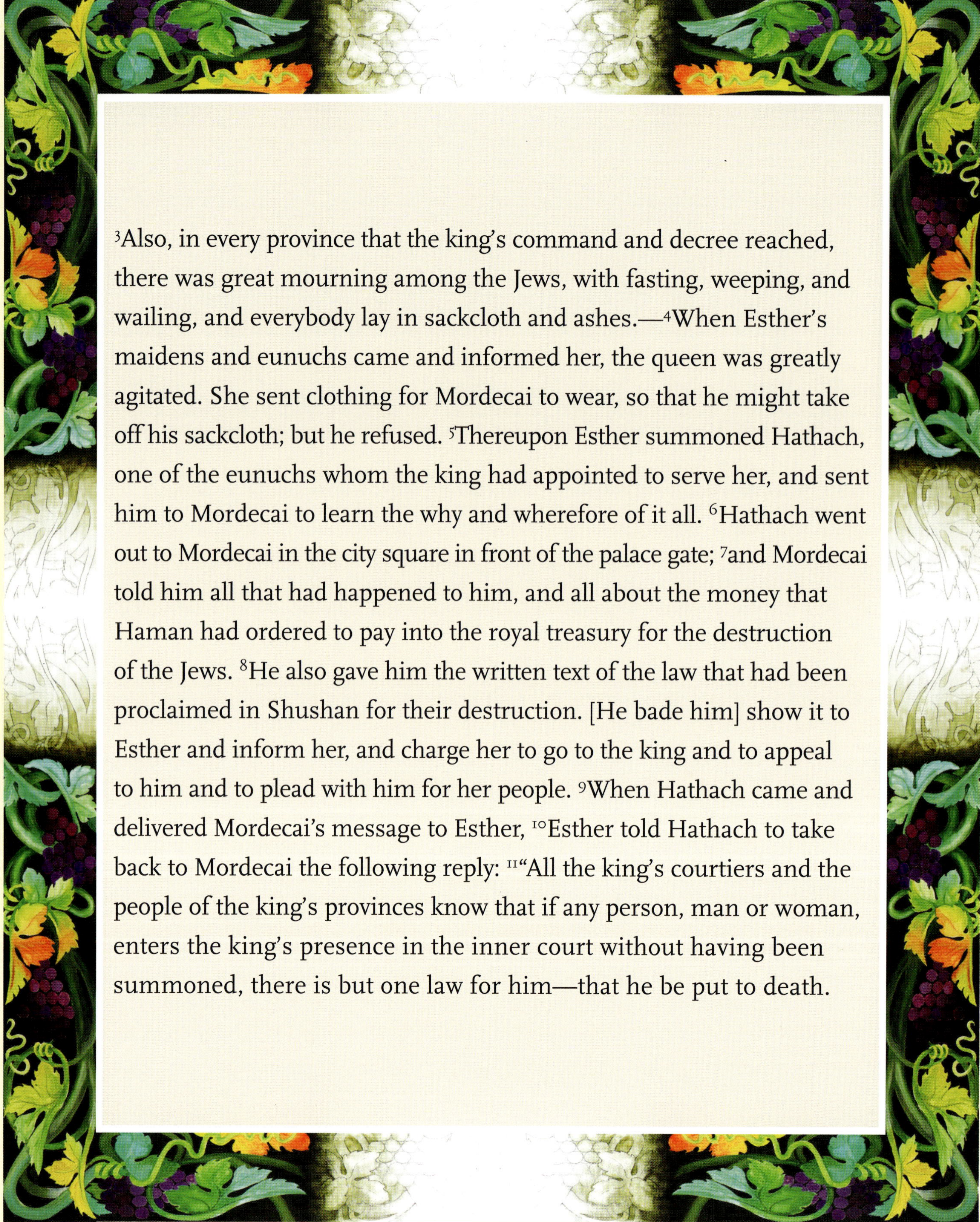

3Also, in every province that the king's command and decree reached,
there was great mourning among the Jews, with fasting, weeping, and
wailing, and everybody lay in sackcloth and ashes.—4When Esther's
maidens and eunuchs came and informed her, the queen was greatly
agitated. She sent clothing for Mordecai to wear, so that he might take
off his sackcloth; but he refused. 5Thereupon Esther summoned Hathach,
one of the eunuchs whom the king had appointed to serve her, and sent
him to Mordecai to learn the why and wherefore of it all. 6Hathach went
out to Mordecai in the city square in front of the palace gate; 7and Mordecai
told him all that had happened to him, and all about the money that
Haman had ordered to pay into the royal treasury for the destruction
of the Jews. 8He also gave him the written text of the law that had been
proclaimed in Shushan for their destruction. [He bade him] show it to
Esther and inform her, and charge her to go to the king and to appeal
to him and to plead with him for her people. 9When Hathach came and
delivered Mordecai's message to Esther, 10Esther told Hathach to take
back to Mordecai the following reply: 11"All the king's courtiers and the
people of the king's provinces know that if any person, man or woman,
enters the king's presence in the inner court without having been
summoned, there is but one law for him—that he be put to death.

המלך כי אין לבוא אל שער המלך בלבוש
שק ובכל מדינה ומדינה מקום אשר דבר
המלך ודתו מגיע אבל גדול ליהודים וצום ובכי
ומספד שק ואפר יצע לרבים ותבואינה נערות
אסתר וסריסיה ויגידו לה ותתחלחל המלכה
מאד ותשלח בגדים להלביש את מרדכי
ולהסיר שקו מעליו ולא קבל ותקרא אסתר
להתך מסריסי המלך אשר העמיד לפניה
ותצוהו על מרדכי לדעת מה זה ועל מה זה ויצא
התך אל מרדכי אל רחוב העיר אשר לפני שער
המלך ויגד לו מרדכי את כל אשר קרהו ואת
פרשת הכסף אשר אמר המן לשקול על גנזי
המלך ביהודיים לאבדם ואת פתשגן כתב הדת
אשר נתן בשושן להשמידם נתן לו להראות את
אסתר ולהגיד לה ולצוות עליה לבוא אל המלך
להתחנן לו ולבקש מלפניו על עמה ויבוא
התך ויגד לאסתר את דברי מרדכי ותאמר אסתר
להתך ותצוהו אל מרדכי כל עבדי המלך ועם
מדינות המלך ידעים אשר כל איש ואשה אשר
יבוא אל המלך אל החצר הפנימית אשר לא
יקרא אחת דתו להמית לבד מאשר יושיט לו

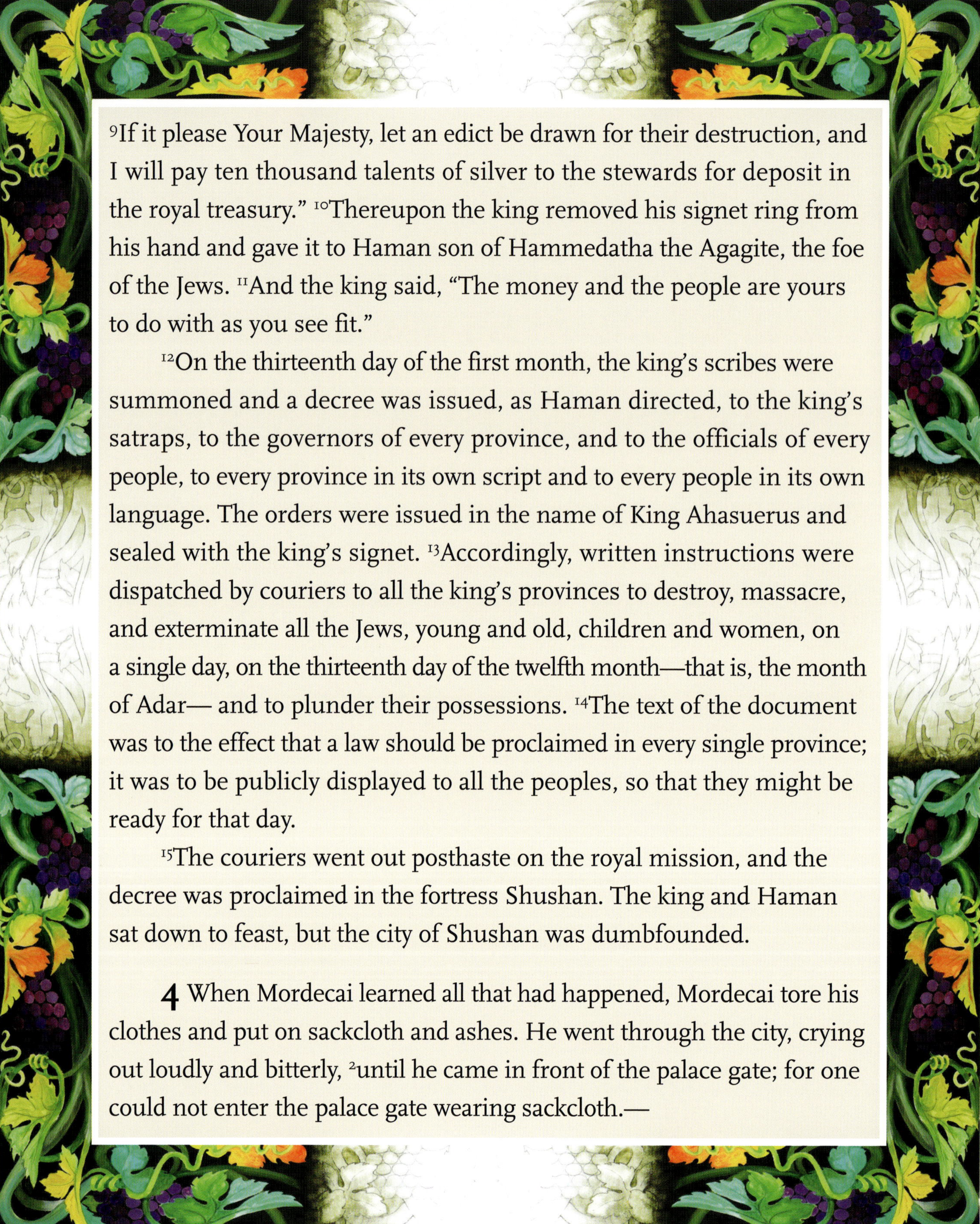

9If it please Your Majesty, let an edict be drawn for their destruction, and
I will pay ten thousand talents of silver to the stewards for deposit in
the royal treasury." 10Thereupon the king removed his signet ring from
his hand and gave it to Haman son of Hammedatha the Agagite, the foe
of the Jews. 11And the king said, "The money and the people are yours
to do with as you see fit."

12On the thirteenth day of the first month, the king's scribes were
summoned and a decree was issued, as Haman directed, to the king's
satraps, to the governors of every province, and to the officials of every
people, to every province in its own script and to every people in its own
language. The orders were issued in the name of King Ahasuerus and
sealed with the king's signet. 13Accordingly, written instructions were
dispatched by couriers to all the king's provinces to destroy, massacre,
and exterminate all the Jews, young and old, children and women, on
a single day, on the thirteenth day of the twelfth month—that is, the month
of Adar— and to plunder their possessions. 14The text of the document
was to the effect that a law should be proclaimed in every single province;
it was to be publicly displayed to all the peoples, so that they might be
ready for that day.

15The couriers went out posthaste on the royal mission, and the
decree was proclaimed in the fortress Shushan. The king and Haman
sat down to feast, but the city of Shushan was dumbfounded.

4 When Mordecai learned all that had happened, Mordecai tore his
clothes and put on sackcloth and ashes. He went through the city, crying
out loudly and bitterly, 2until he came in front of the palace gate; for one
could not enter the palace gate wearing sackcloth.—

המלך טוב יכתב לאבדם ועשרת אלפים ככר כסף
אשקול על ידי עשי המלאכה להביא אל גנזי המלך
ויסר המלך את טבעתו מעל ידו ויתנה להמן בן
המדתא האגגי צרר היהודים ויאמר המלך להמן
הכסף נתון לך והעם לעשות בו כטוב בעיניך ויקראו
ספרי המלך בחדש הראשון בשלושה עשר יום בו
ויכתב ככל אשר צוה המן אל אחשדרפני המלך
ואל הפחות אשר על מדינה ומדינה ואל שרי עם
ועם מדינה ומדינה ככתבה ועם ועם כלשונו בשם
המלך אחשורש נכתב ונחתם בטבעת המלך
ונשלוח ספרים ביד הרצים אל כל מדינות המלך
להשמיד להרג ולאבד את כל היהודים מנער ועד
זקן טף ונשים ביום אחד בשלושה עשר לחדש
שנים עשר הוא חדש אדר ושללם לבוז פתשגן
הכתב להנתן דת בכל מדינה ומדינה גלוי לכל העמים
להיות עתדים ליום הזה הרצים יצאו דחופים בדבר
המלך והדת נתנה בשושן הבירה והמלך והמן ישבו
לשתות והעיר שושן נבוכה ומרדכי
ידע את כל אשר נעשה ויקרע מרדכי את
בגדיו וילבש שק ואפר ויצא בתוך העיר
ויזעק זעקה גדולה ומרה ויבוא עד לפני שער

3 Some time afterward, King Ahasuerus promoted Haman son of Hammedatha the Agagite; he advanced him and seated him higher than any of his fellow officials. 2All the king's courtiers in the palace gate knelt and bowed low to Haman, for such was the king's order concerning him; but Mordecai would not kneel or bow low. 3Then the king's courtiers who were in the palace gate said to Mordecai, "Why do you disobey the king's order?" 4When they spoke to him day after day and he would not listen to them, they told Haman, in order to see whether Mordecai's resolve would prevail; for he had explained to them that he was a Jew. 5When Haman saw that Mordecai would not kneel or bow low to him, Haman was filled with rage. 6But he disdained to lay hands on Mordecai alone; having been told who Mordecai's people were, Haman plotted to do away with all the Jews, Mordecai's people, throughout the kingdom of Ahasuerus.

7In the first month, that is, the month of Nisan, in the twelfth year of King Ahasuerus, pur —which means "the lot"—was cast before Haman concerning every day and every month, [until it fell on] the twelfth month, that is, the month of Adar. 8Haman then said to King Ahasuerus, "There is a certain people, scattered and dispersed among the other peoples in all the provinces of your realm, whose laws are different from those of any other people and who do not obey the king's laws; and it is not in Your Majesty's interest to tolerate them.

המלך אחר הדברים האלה
גדל המלך אחשורוש את המן בן המדתא האגגי
וינשאהו וישם את כסאו מעל כל השרים אשר
אתו וכל עבדי המלך אשר בשער המלך כרעים
ומשתחוים להמן כי כן צוה לו המלך ומרדכי לא
יכרע ולא ישתחוה ויאמרו עבדי המלך אשר
בשער המלך למרדכי מדוע אתה עובר את
מצות המלך ויהי באמרם אליו יום ויום ולא שמע
אליהם ויגידו להמן לראות היעמדו דברי מרדכי
כי הגיד להם אשר הוא יהודי וירא המן כי אין
מרדכי כרע ומשתחוה לו וימלא המן חמה ויבז
בעיניו לשלח יד במרדכי לבדו כי הגידו לו את
עם מרדכי ויבקש המן להשמיד את כל היהודים
אשר בכל מלכות אחשורוש עם מרדכי בחדש
הראשון הוא חדש ניסן בשנת שתים עשרה
למלך אחשורוש הפיל פור הוא הגורל לפני המן
מיום ליום ומחדש לחדש שנים עשר הוא חדש
אדר ויאמר המן למלך אחשורוש
ישנו עם אחד מפזר ומפרד בין העמים בכל
מדינות מלכותך ודתיהם שנות מכל עם ואת דתי
המלך אינם עשים ולמלך אין שוה להניחם אם על

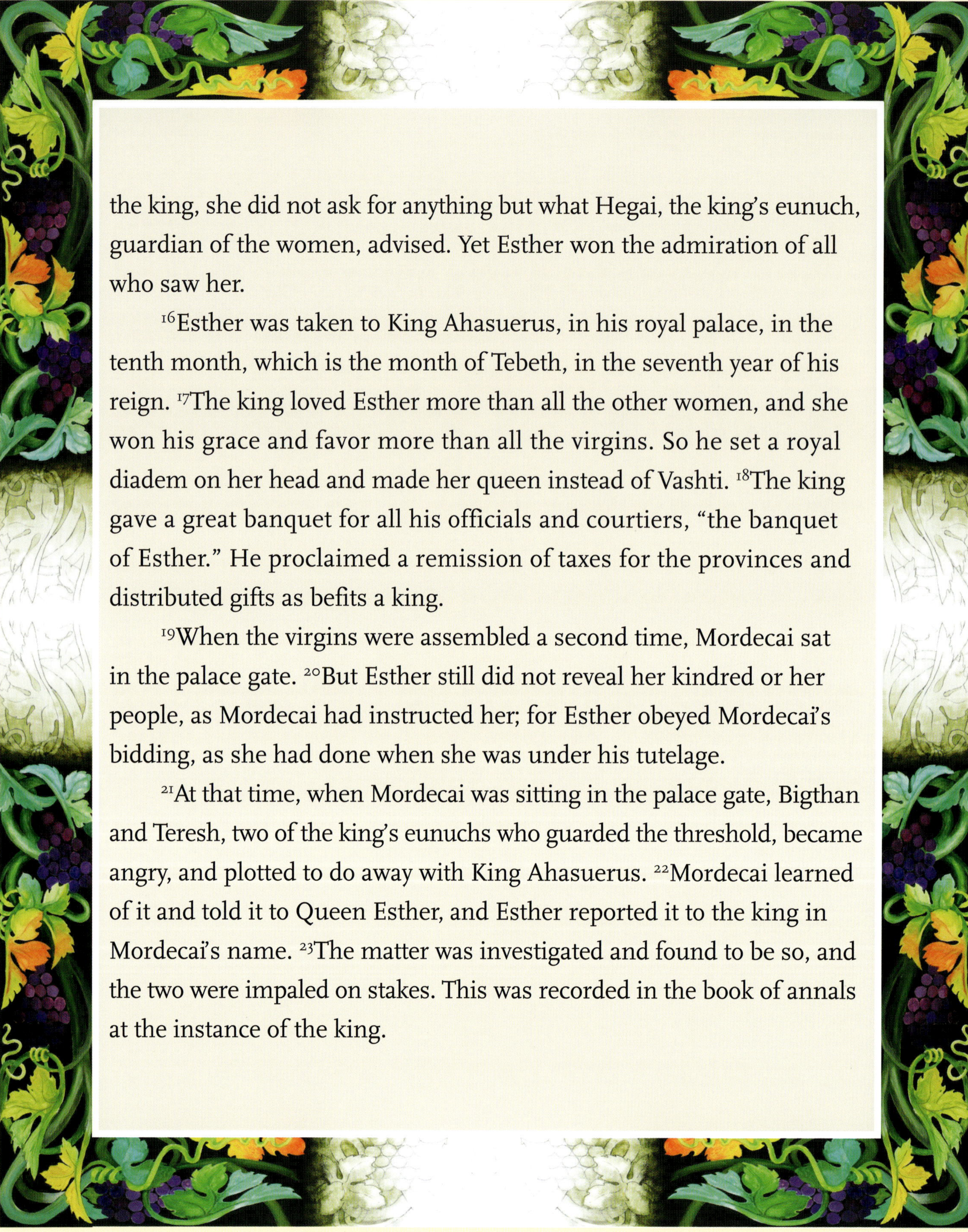

the king, she did not ask for anything but what Hegai, the king's eunuch,
guardian of the women, advised. Yet Esther won the admiration of all
who saw her.

16Esther was taken to King Ahasuerus, in his royal palace, in the
tenth month, which is the month of Tebeth, in the seventh year of his
reign. 17The king loved Esther more than all the other women, and she
won his grace and favor more than all the virgins. So he set a royal
diadem on her head and made her queen instead of Vashti. 18The king
gave a great banquet for all his officials and courtiers, "the banquet
of Esther." He proclaimed a remission of taxes for the provinces and
distributed gifts as befits a king.

19When the virgins were assembled a second time, Mordecai sat
in the palace gate. 20But Esther still did not reveal her kindred or her
people, as Mordecai had instructed her; for Esther obeyed Mordecai's
bidding, as she had done when she was under his tutelage.

21At that time, when Mordecai was sitting in the palace gate, Bigthan
and Teresh, two of the king's eunuchs who guarded the threshold, became
angry, and plotted to do away with King Ahasuerus. 22Mordecai learned
of it and told it to Queen Esther, and Esther reported it to the king in
Mordecai's name. 23The matter was investigated and found to be so, and
the two were impaled on stakes. This was recorded in the book of annals
at the instance of the king.

המלך לא בקשה דבר כי אם את אשר יאמר
הגי סריס המלך שמר הנשים ותהי אסתר
נשאת חן בעיני כל ראיה ותלקח אסתר אל
המלך אחשורוש אל בית מלכותו בחדש
העשירי הוא חדש טבת בשנת שבע למלכותו
ויאהב המלך את אסתר מכל הנשים ותשא חן
וחסד לפניו מכל הבתולות וישם כתר מלכות
בראשה וימליכה תחת ושתי ויעש המלך
משתה גדול לכל שריו ועבדיו את משתה
אסתר והנחה למדינות עשה ויתן משאת
כיד המלך ובהקבץ בתולות שנית ומרדכי
ישב בשער המלך אין אסתר מגדת מולדתה
ואת עמה כאשר צוה עליה מרדכי ואת מאמר
מרדכי אסתר עשה כאשר היתה באמנה
אתו   בימים
ההם ומרדכי ישב בשער המלך קצף בגתן
ותרש שני סריסי המלך משמרי הסף ויבקשו
לשלח יד במלך אחשורש ויודע הדבר
למרדכי ויגד לאסתר המלכה ותאמר אסתר
למלך בשם מרדכי ויבקש הדבר וימצא ויתלו
שניהם על עץ ויכתב בספר דברי הימים לפני

8 When the king's order and edict was proclaimed, and when many
girls were assembled in the fortress Shushan under the supervision of
Hegai, Esther too was taken into the king's palace under the supervision
of Hegai, guardian of the women. 9 The girl pleased him and won his
favor, and he hastened to furnish her with her cosmetics and her rations,
as well as with the seven maids who were her due from the king's palace;
and he treated her and her maids with special kindness in the harem.
10 Esther did not reveal her people or her kindred, for Mordecai had told
her not to reveal it. 11 Every single day Mordecai would walk about in front
of the court of the harem, to learn how Esther was faring and what was
happening to her.

12 When each girl's turn came to go to King Ahasuerus at the end
of the twelve months' treatment prescribed for women (for that was the
period spent on beautifying them: six months with oil of myrrh and six
months with perfumes and women's cosmetics, 13 and it was after that
that the girl would go to the king), whatever she asked for would be given
her to take with her from the harem to the king's palace. 14 She would go
in the evening and leave in the morning for a second harem in charge
of Shaashgaz, the king's eunuch, guardian of the concubines. She would
not go again to the king unless the king wanted her, when she would
be summoned by name. 15 When the turn came for Esther daughter
of Abihail—the uncle of Mordecai, who had adopted her as his own
daughter—to go to

המלך ודתו ובהקבץ נערות רבות אל שושן
הבירה אל יד הגי ותלקח אסתר אל בית המלך
אל יד הגי שמר הנשים ותיטב הנערה בעיניו
ותשא חסד לפניו ויבהל את תמרוקיה ואת
מנותה לתת לה ואת שבע הנערות הראיות
לתת לה מבית המלך וישנה ואת נערותיה לטוב
בית הנשים לא הגידה אסתר את עמה ואת מולדתה
כי מרדכי צוה עליה אשר לא תגיד ובכל יום
ויום מרדכי מתהלך לפני חצר בית הנשים
לדעת את שלום אסתר ומה יעשה בה ובהגיע
תר נערה ונערה לבוא אל המלך אחשורוש מקץ
היות לה כדת הנשים שנים עשר חדש כי כן
ימלאו ימי מרוקיהן ששה חדשים בשמן המר
וששה חדשים בבשמים ובתמרוקי הנשים ובזה
הנערה באה אל המלך את כל אשר תאמר
ינתן לה לבוא עמה מבית הנשים עד בית המלך
בערב היא באה ובבקר היא שבה אל בית
הנשים שני אל יד שעשגז סריס המלך שמר
הפילגשים לא תבוא עוד אל המלך כי אם חפץ
בה המלך ונקראה בשם ובהגיע תר אסתר בת
אביחיל דד מרדכי אשר לקח לו לבת לבוא אל

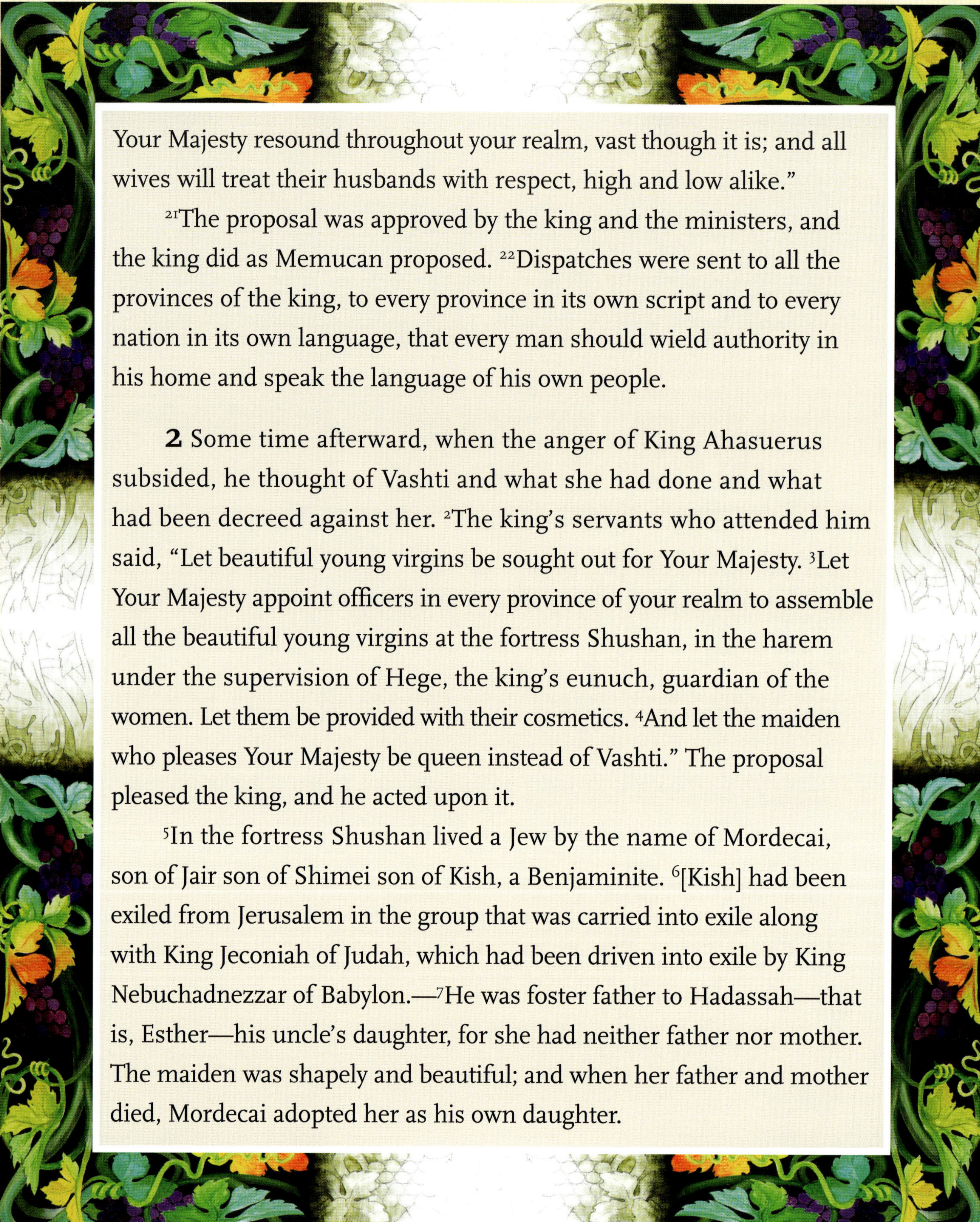

Your Majesty resound throughout your realm, vast though it is; and all
wives will treat their husbands with respect, high and low alike."

21 The proposal was approved by the king and the ministers, and
the king did as Memucan proposed. 22 Dispatches were sent to all the
provinces of the king, to every province in its own script and to every
nation in its own language, that every man should wield authority in
his home and speak the language of his own people.

2 Some time afterward, when the anger of King Ahasuerus
subsided, he thought of Vashti and what she had done and what
had been decreed against her. 2 The king's servants who attended him
said, "Let beautiful young virgins be sought out for Your Majesty. 3 Let
Your Majesty appoint officers in every province of your realm to assemble
all the beautiful young virgins at the fortress Shushan, in the harem
under the supervision of Hege, the king's eunuch, guardian of the
women. Let them be provided with their cosmetics. 4 And let the maiden
who pleases Your Majesty be queen instead of Vashti." The proposal
pleased the king, and he acted upon it.

5 In the fortress Shushan lived a Jew by the name of Mordecai,
son of Jair son of Shimei son of Kish, a Benjaminite. 6 [Kish] had been
exiled from Jerusalem in the group that was carried into exile along
with King Jeconiah of Judah, which had been driven into exile by King
Nebuchadnezzar of Babylon.—7 He was foster father to Hadassah—that
is, Esther—his uncle's daughter, for she had neither father nor mother.
The maiden was shapely and beautiful; and when her father and mother
died, Mordecai adopted her as his own daughter.

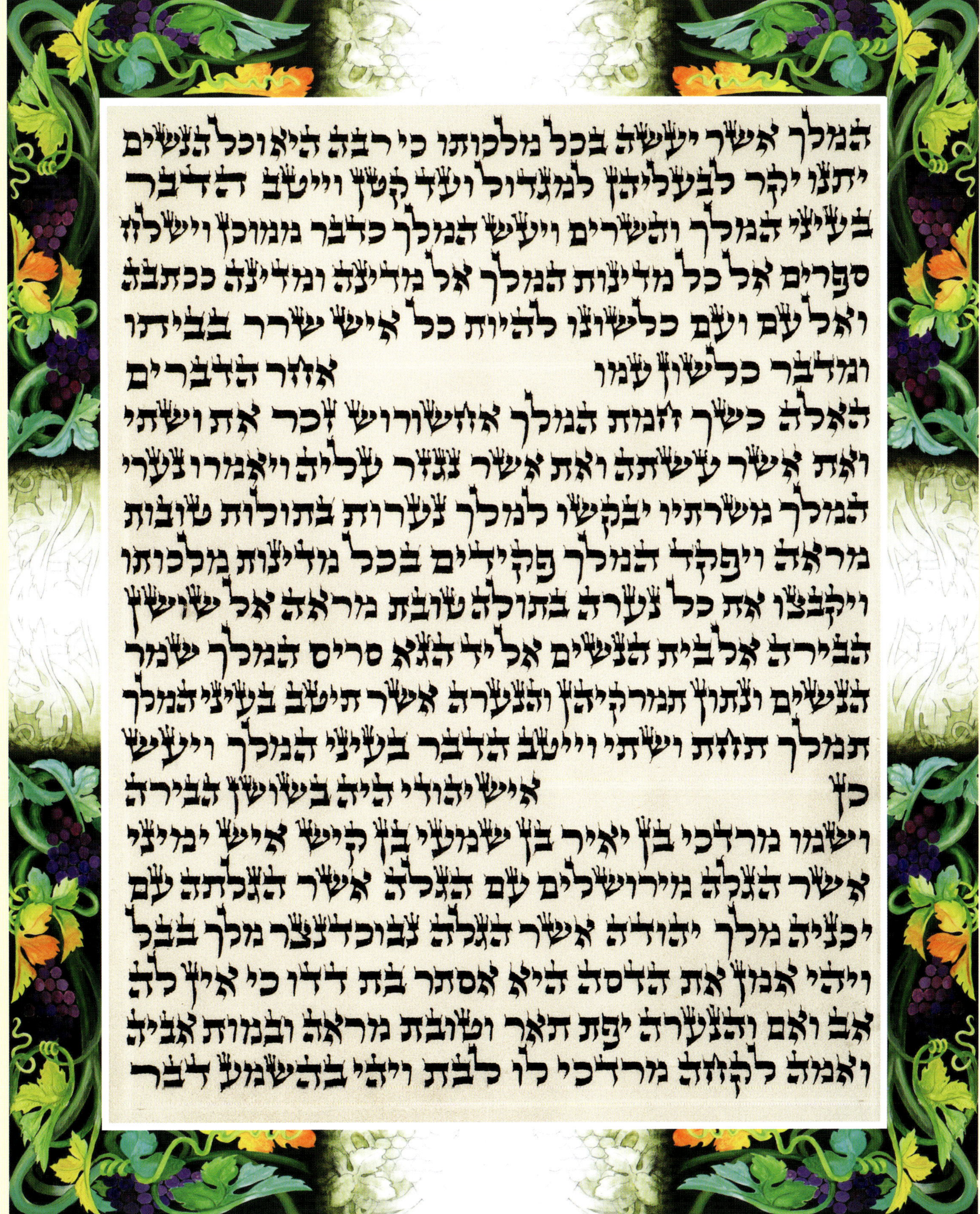

המלך אשר יעשה בכל מלכותו כי רבה היא וכל הנשים
יתנו יקר לבעליהן למגדול ועד קטן וייטב הדבר
בעיני המלך והשרים ויעש המלך כדבר ממוכן וישלח
ספרים אל כל מדינות המלך אל מדינה ומדינה ככתבה
ואל עם ועם כלשונו להיות כל איש שרר בביתו
ומדבר כלשון עמו אחר הדברים
האלה כשך חמת המלך אחשורוש זכר את ושתי
ואת אשר עשתה ואת אשר נגזר עליה ויאמרו נערי
המלך משרתיו יבקשו למלך נערות בתולות טובות
מראה ויפקד המלך פקידים בכל מדינות מלכותו
ויקבצו את כל נערה בתולה טובת מראה אל שושן
הבירה אל בית הנשים אל יד הגא סריס המלך שמר
הנשים ונתון תמרוקיהן והנערה אשר תיטב בעיני המלך
תמלך תחת ושתי וייטב הדבר בעיני המלך ויעש
כן איש יהודי היה בשושן הבירה
ושמו מרדכי בן יאיר בן שמעי בן קיש איש ימיני
אשר הגלה מירושלים עם הגלה אשר הגלתה עם
יכניה מלך יהודה אשר הגלה נבוכדנצר מלך בבל
ויהי אמן את הדסה היא אסתר בת דדו כי אין לה
אב ואם והנערה יפת תאר וטובת מראה ובמות אביה
ואמה לקחה מרדכי לו לבת ויהי בהשמע דבר

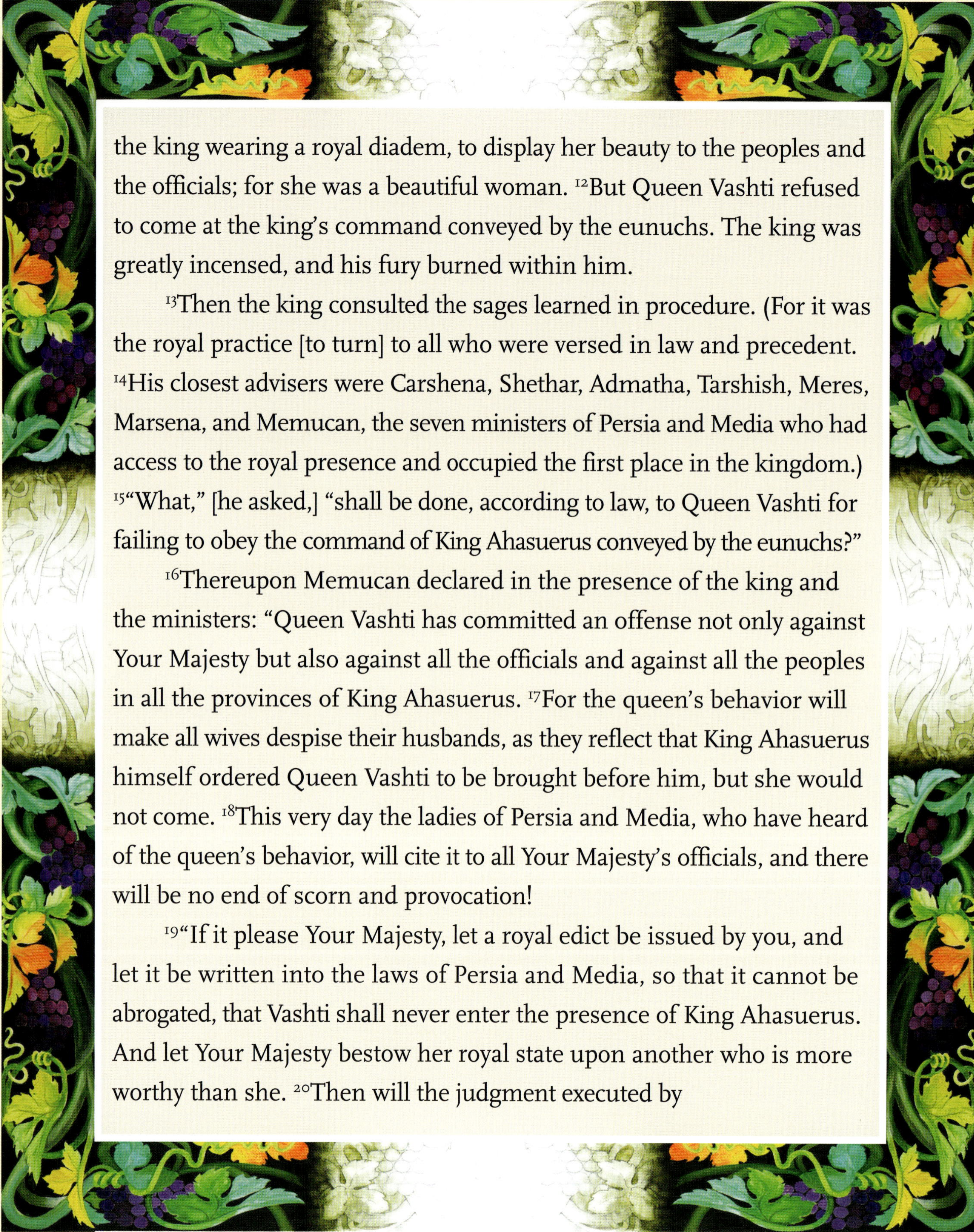

the king wearing a royal diadem, to display her beauty to the peoples and
the officials; for she was a beautiful woman. 12But Queen Vashti refused
to come at the king's command conveyed by the eunuchs. The king was
greatly incensed, and his fury burned within him.

13Then the king consulted the sages learned in procedure. (For it was
the royal practice [to turn] to all who were versed in law and precedent.
14His closest advisers were Carshena, Shethar, Admatha, Tarshish, Meres,
Marsena, and Memucan, the seven ministers of Persia and Media who had
access to the royal presence and occupied the first place in the kingdom.)
15"What," [he asked,] "shall be done, according to law, to Queen Vashti for
failing to obey the command of King Ahasuerus conveyed by the eunuchs?"

16Thereupon Memucan declared in the presence of the king and
the ministers: "Queen Vashti has committed an offense not only against
Your Majesty but also against all the officials and against all the peoples
in all the provinces of King Ahasuerus. 17For the queen's behavior will
make all wives despise their husbands, as they reflect that King Ahasuerus
himself ordered Queen Vashti to be brought before him, but she would
not come. 18This very day the ladies of Persia and Media, who have heard
of the queen's behavior, will cite it to all Your Majesty's officials, and there
will be no end of scorn and provocation!

19"If it please Your Majesty, let a royal edict be issued by you, and
let it be written into the laws of Persia and Media, so that it cannot be
abrogated, that Vashti shall never enter the presence of King Ahasuerus.
And let Your Majesty bestow her royal state upon another who is more
worthy than she. 20Then will the judgment executed by

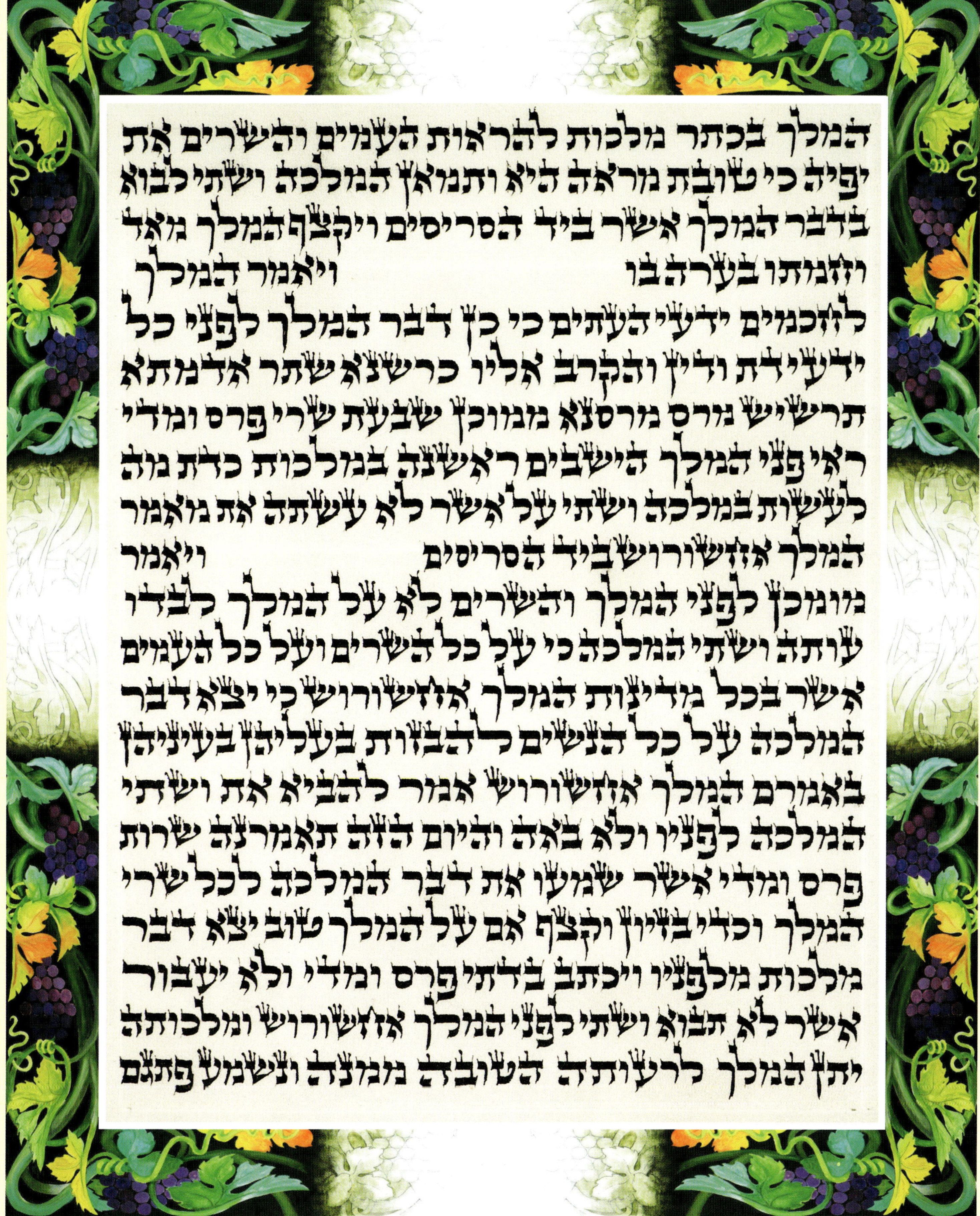
המלך בכתר מלכות להראות העמים והשרים את
יפיה כי טובת מראה היא ותמאן המלכה ושתי לבוא
בדבר המלך אשר ביד הסריסים ויקצף המלך מאד
וחמתו בערה בו ויאמר המלך
לחכמים ידעי העתים כי כן דבר המלך לפני כל
ידעי דת ודין והקרב אליו כרשנא שתר אדמתא
תרשיש מרס מרסנא ממוכן שבעת שרי פרס ומדי
ראי פני המלך הישבים ראשנה במלכות כדת מה
לעשות במלכה ושתי על אשר לא עשתה את מאמר
המלך אחשורוש ביד הסריסים ויאמר
מומכן לפני המלך והשרים לא על המלך לבדו
עותה ושתי המלכה כי על כל השרים ועל כל העמים
אשר בכל מדינות המלך אחשורוש כי יצא דבר
המלכה על כל הנשים להבזות בעליהן בעיניהן
באמרם המלך אחשורוש אמר להביא את ושתי
המלכה לפניו ולא באה והיום הזה תאמרנה שרות
פרס ומדי אשר שמעו את דבר המלכה לכל שרי
המלך וכדי בזיון וקצף אם על המלך טוב יצא דבר
מלכות מלפניו ויכתב בדתי פרס ומדי ולא יעבור
אשר לא תבוא ושתי לפני המלך אחשורוש ומלכותה
יתן המלך לרעותה הטובה ממנה ונשמע פתגם

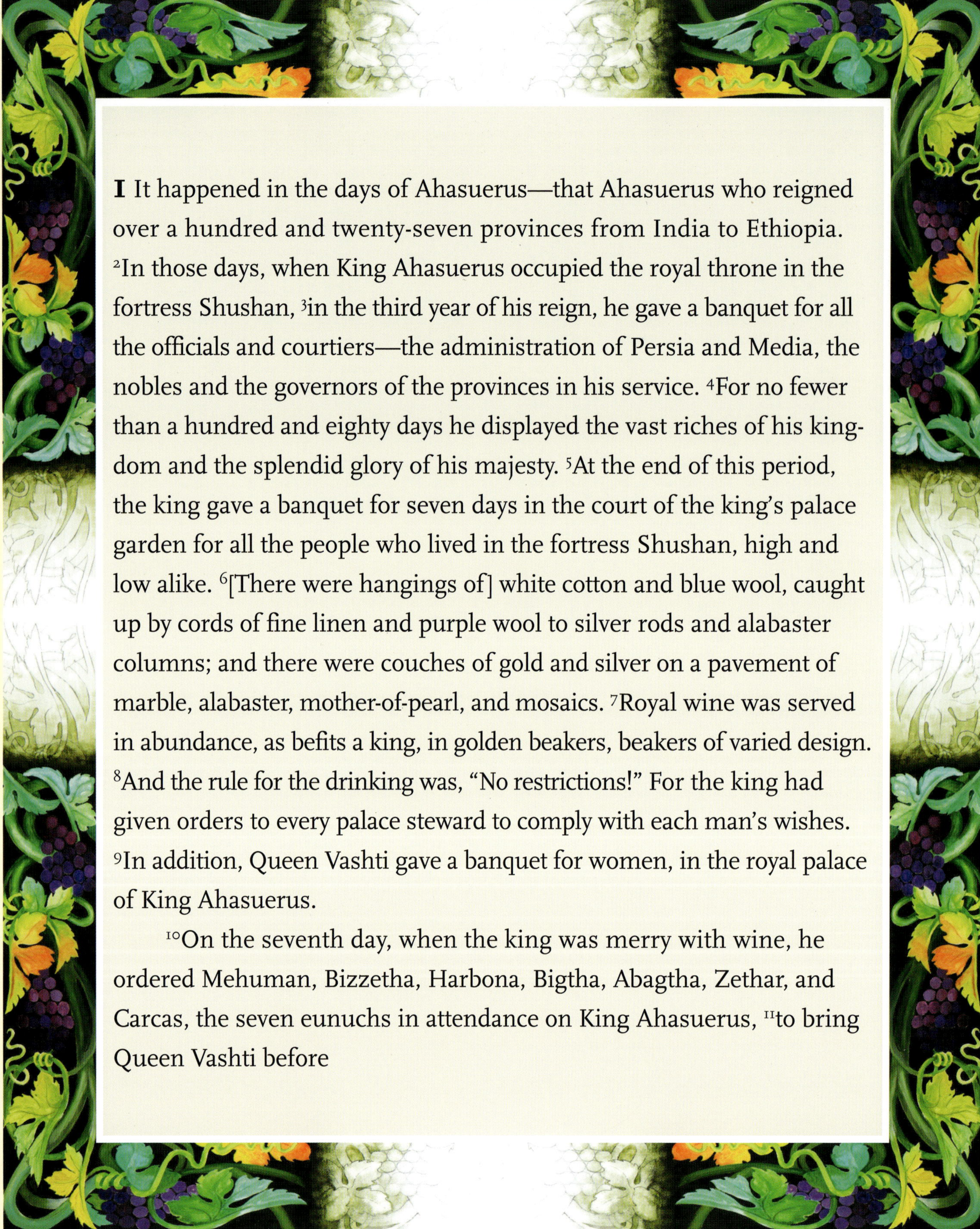

1 It happened in the days of Ahasuerus—that Ahasuerus who reigned
over a hundred and twenty-seven provinces from India to Ethiopia.
2In those days, when King Ahasuerus occupied the royal throne in the
fortress Shushan, 3in the third year of his reign, he gave a banquet for all
the officials and courtiers—the administration of Persia and Media, the
nobles and the governors of the provinces in his service. 4For no fewer
than a hundred and eighty days he displayed the vast riches of his kingdom and the splendid glory of his majesty. 5At the end of this period,
the king gave a banquet for seven days in the court of the king's palace
garden for all the people who lived in the fortress Shushan, high and
low alike. 6[There were hangings of] white cotton and blue wool, caught
up by cords of fine linen and purple wool to silver rods and alabaster
columns; and there were couches of gold and silver on a pavement of
marble, alabaster, mother-of-pearl, and mosaics. 7Royal wine was served
in abundance, as befits a king, in golden beakers, beakers of varied design.
8And the rule for the drinking was, "No restrictions!" For the king had
given orders to every palace steward to comply with each man's wishes.
9In addition, Queen Vashti gave a banquet for women, in the royal palace
of King Ahasuerus.

10On the seventh day, when the king was merry with wine, he
ordered Mehuman, Bizzetha, Harbona, Bigtha, Abagtha, Zethar, and
Carcas, the seven eunuchs in attendance on King Ahasuerus, 11to bring
Queen Vashti before

ויהי בימי אחשורוש הוא אחשורוש המלך מהדו
ועד כוש שבע ועשרים ומאה מדינה בימים ההם
כשבת המלך אחשורוש על כסא מלכותו אשר
בשושן הבירה בשנת שלוש למלכו עשה משתה
לכל שריו ועבדיו חיל פרס ומדי הפרתמים ושרי
המדינות לפניו בהראתו את עשר כבוד מלכותו
ואת יקר תפארת גדולתו ימים רבים שמונים ומאת
יום ובמלואת הימים האלה עשה המלך לכל העם
הנמצאים בשושן הבירה למגדול ועד קטן משתה
שבעת ימים בחצר גנת ביתן המלך חור כרפס
ותכלת אחוז בחבלי בוץ וארגמן על גלילי כסף
ועמודי שש מטות זהב וכסף על רצפת בהט ושש
ודר וסחרת והשקות בכלי זהב וכלים מכלים שונים
ויין מלכות רב כיד המלך והשתיה כדת אין אנס כי
כן יסד המלך על כל רב ביתו לעשות כרצון איש
ואיש גם ושתי המלכה
עשתה משתה נשים בית המלכות אשר למלך
אחשורוש ביום השביעי כטוב לב המלך ביין
אמר למהומן בזתא חרבונא בגתא ואבגתא זתר
וכרכס שבעת הסריסים המשרתים את פני
המלך אחשורוש להביא את ושתי המלכה לפני

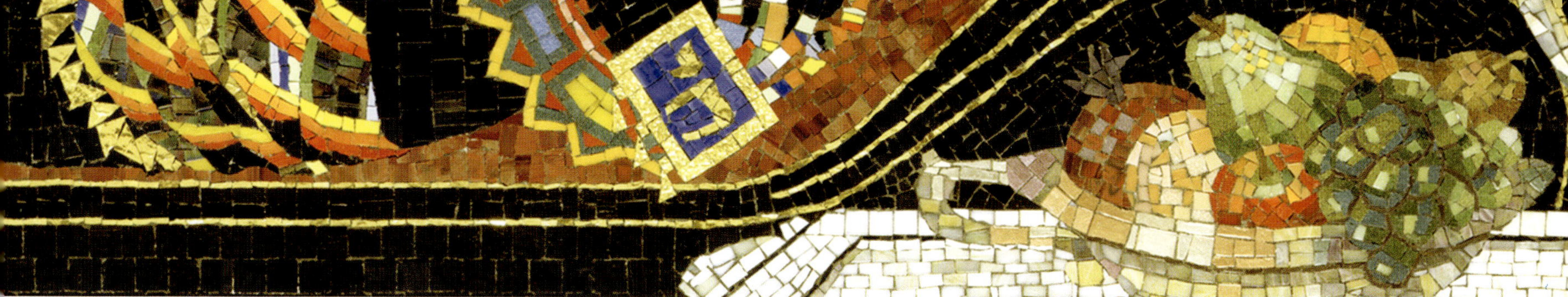

Contributors

Lilian Broca Vancouver artist Lilian Broca received a BFA from Concordia University in Montreal and an MFA from the Pratt Institute in New York. In a career spanning over thirty years, including thirteen teaching painting and drawing at Kwantlen Polytechnic University in the Greater Vancouver area, her work has been featured in sixty-five exhibitions in Canada, the United States, and Europe. Celebrated for her spirited exploration of contemporary societal issues in a variety of media, Broca draws on historical iconography, legends, and popular myths. *The Queen Esther Mosaic Series* addresses women's sacrifices and self-empowerment. An earlier series of paintings and drawings on the theme of Lilith also led to a book, *The Song of Lilith*, produced collaboratively with the acclaimed Canadian writer Joy Kogawa. Among many distinctions, Broca was the subject of a retrospective exhibition at the Frye Art Museum in Seattle in 2001 and was invited to exhibit at the 2003 Florence Biennale International Exhibition, where her mosaics won the coveted Lorenzo il Magnifico Gold Medal in the mixed media category. Broca's mosaics also received First Prize in the two-dimensional category at the international juried exhibition at the Italian-American Museum in San Francisco in 2004 and at the High Risk Gallery in Chicago in 2006. A documentary on Broca's art and life is currently in production.

Sheila Campbell An archaeologist, art historian, and curator, Campbell has worked at Roman and Early Byzantine sites in Turkey, and directed the excavation of a thirteenth-century Cistercian monastery in Greece, from the time of the fourth Crusade. She holds a doctorate degree in Byzantine Art History and Archaeology, specializing in Roman and Early Byzantine mosaics. She is a past president of the Canadian Institute in Greece. As a curator, she has worked at the University of Toronto Art Centre and produced exhibitions at a variety of institutions in Toronto and elsewhere, including an exhibit at the Royal Ontario

Museum showcasing the work of the Scuola Mosaicisti del Friuli, Italy. Her publications include eight books and numerous articles covering such topics as ancient and contemporary mosaics, medieval medicine, post-Byzantine icons, and medieval monasticism. For many years, she taught medieval art history and archaeology at the Pontifical Institute of Mediaeval Studies, Toronto, and upon retirement was named Professor Emerita.

Yosef Wosk Former Director of Interdisciplinary Programs in Continuing Studies and Adjunct Professor of Humanities, Wosk developed several seminal programs at British Columbia's Simon Fraser University, including the Philosophers' Café and the Canadian Academy of Independent Scholars. In addition to receiving an honorary doctorate of letters, he holds doctorates in Psychology and Religion & Literature, and master's degrees in Education and Theology. An ordained rabbi, he has lectured at a number of universities and institutes of higher learning throughout the world. Identified as one of the top ten thinkers and most thoughtful citizens in the province, he is an appointed member of the Order of British Columbia and a recipient of the Queen Elizabeth II Golden Jubilee Medal. Active in communal affairs in the areas of education, libraries, museums, the arts, social services, heritage conservation, philanthropy, and religion, Wosk is a media commentator, public speaker, and published author.

Judy Chicago Artist, author, feminist, educator, and an intellectual whose career spans over four decades, Judy Chicago's work has been featured in numerous solo and group exhibitions worldwide, and her art and writing have been included in hundreds of publications. Already a leading pioneer in feminist art and art education, Chicago was widely acclaimed in the 1970s for her monumental multimedia series *The Dinner Party.* She went on to produce other groundbreaking series, including the *Birth Project*, the *Holocaust Project*, and *Resolutions: A Stitch in Time*. Chicago received her master of arts degree from the University of California, Los Angeles, and has been awarded five honorary doctorates. In addition to a life of prodigious art making, she is the author of twelve books, has taught at a many colleges and universities, and has received numerous awards. Chicago's life and work are a model of the power of art as a vehicle for intellectual transformation and social change.

Gareth Sirotnik A graduate of Reed College in Portland, Oregon, Sirotnik has worked as a freelance writer, editor, and consultant for nearly forty years. Previous published works include *Running Tough,* the biography of Canadian industrialist and philanthropist Jack Diamond, and a motivational book, *Words Become You.* He also founded and for a number of years edited an international journal on injury and healing, and is an ordained Zen Buddhist monk.

Linda Coe A graduate of the Vancouver School of Art (now Emily Carr University of Art+Design), Coe has worked as a professional graphic designer for over thirty years and has taught design courses at Emily Carr University, the University of British Columbia, and at various workshops. She is a Fellow of the Society of Graphic Designers of Canada, a former President and Charter member of the British Columbia Chapter.

Colophon

This book was typeset in Scala and Scala Sans, designed in the Netherlands by Martin Majoor and issued in digital form by FontShop International, Berlin, in 1991.

The paper is McCoy Silk Dull by Sappi Fine Paper and is of archival quality and acid free.

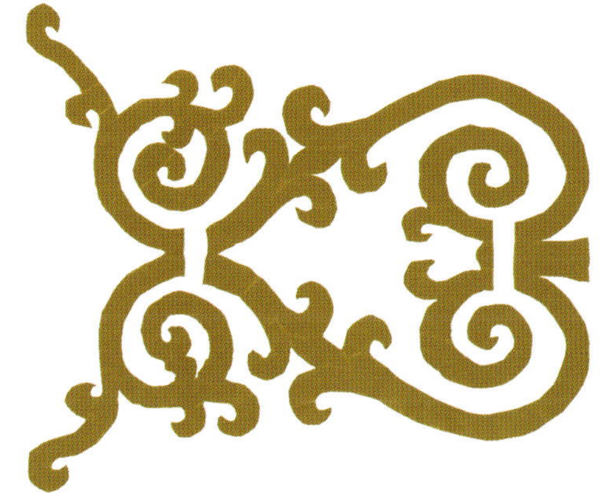

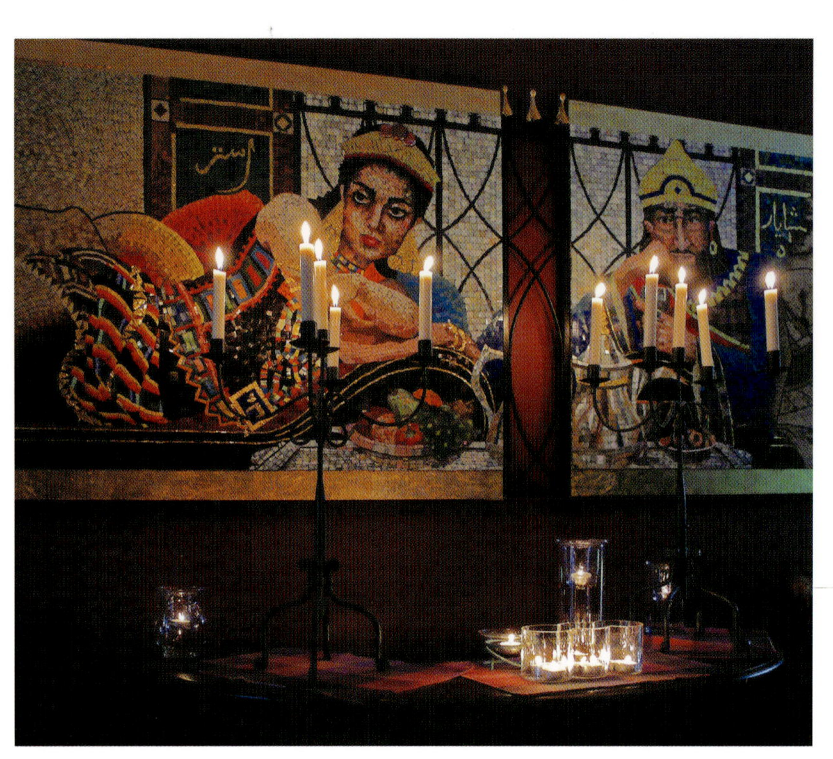